"Simon and Taylor present a useful and grounding book on discerning multiple opportunities in solution-building conversations with clients, as well as multiple possibilities and rationale for solution-building responses to those opportunities. I especially appreciated the ample examples of microanalysis in action that can inform and improve one's own work in solution-building."

Dr. Thorana Nelson, PhD, *Professor Emerita Utah State University*

"One big question is, 'From all the things that people say in therapy, how do therapists select what to build on?' Another important question, at least for someone who wants to get better at what they do, is 'What other opportunities were there?' If you have the slightest interest in any of these questions, read this book."

Harry Korman MD, SIKT, *Malmö, Sweden*

"What a brilliant elaboration of Solution-Focused Therapy in our current pedagogical context where it is indeed our ethical imperative to be reflective of our own work! As an educator in this field, I have found their original exercise 'opportunities' to be particularly useful in class, and have observed a tangible difference in learner progress as a result. The 'opportunities' exercise is just one example of the practical techniques presented in this book, which highlight the authors' expertise in bridging the gap between theory and practice, history and current elaborations, and practice and pedagogy. The ability to provide real-world examples of how these techniques can be incorporated into one's practice and supervision is highly useful, and allows learners to see how these concepts can be applied in a range of settings and contexts. I believe the book would be valuable for learners at all levels, as it provides a useful tool regardless of their experience level. The emphasis on reflection, dialogue, and ongoing learning and growth is crucial for developing one's craft and perhaps increasing the likelihood of having more useful conversations with our clients."

Haesun Moon, PhD, Executive Director, *Canadian Centre for Brief Coaching*

Opportunities in Solution-Focused Interviewing

Written by the developers of the microanalysis of opportunities approach, this book describes how clinicians can use this model when listening and responding to clients in solution-focused therapy, training, coaching, and supervision.

Joel K. Simon and Lance Taylor begin by reviewing the evolution, philosophical foundations, and intervention tools of solution-focused brief therapy, sharing how their practice has evolved over time from their clinical experience with clients, trainees, supervisees, and colleagues. Moving from theory to practice, the book then explores microanalysis of opportunities, beginning with how the authors developed the approach and created the process. Replete with actual examples of conversations between clients and therapists, and between trainer and trainee, the book demonstrates how the model can be applied in practice with analyses and discussions about analyzed material throughout. It displays the application of the approach to coaching, supervision, and training.

This valuable book will not only be useful to therapists new to solution-focused brief therapy, but also to those who are experienced solution-focused practitioners. Psychotherapists, clinical social workers, counselors, and other mental health professionals will find this an illuminating read.

Joel K. Simon has been in clinical social work practice for over 40 years in a variety of both inpatient and outpatient settings. He has been a solution-focused practitioner, trainer, presenter, and consultant since 1992. He is a founding member of the Solution Focused Brief Therapy Association.

Lance Taylor, MSc, RPsych, in a career spanning 53 years, has worked as a therapist, clinical supervisor, trainer, manager and mentor in community mental health and private psychology practice. He trained with the originators of the model, was a founding member and served as president of the Solution Focused Brief Therapy Association in North America.

Opportunities in Solution-Focused Interviewing

Clients' Key Words and Therapists' Responses

Joel K. Simon and Lance Taylor

Routledge
Taylor & Francis Group

NEW YORK AND LONDON

Designed cover image: Photo by Joel K. Simon

First published 2024
by Routledge
605 Third Avenue, New York, NY 10158

and by Routledge
4 Park Square, Milton Park, Abingdon, Oxon, OX14 4RN

Routledge is an imprint of the Taylor & Francis Group, an informa business

Library of Congress Cataloging-in-Publication Data
Names: Simon, Joel K., author. | Taylor, Lance (Psychotherapist), author.
Title: Opportunities in solution-focused interviewing : clients' key words
and therapists' responses / Joel K. Simon, Lance Taylor.
Description: New York, NY : Routledge, 2024. |
Includes bibliographical references and index. |
Identifiers: LCCN 2023010098 (print) | LCCN 2023010099 (ebook) |
ISBN 9781032500522 (hardback) | ISBN 9781032500539 (paperback) |
ISBN 9781003396703 (ebook)
Subjects: LCSH: Solution-focused therapy. | Interviewing in psychiatry–Technique. |
Behavioral assessment.
Classification: LCC RC489.S65 S56 2024 (print) | LCC RC489.S65 (ebook) |
DDC 616.89/147–dc23/eng/20230508
LC record available at https://lccn.loc.gov/2023010098
LC ebook record available at https://lccn.loc.gov/2023010099

ISBN: 9781032500522 (hbk)
ISBN: 9781032500539 (pbk)
ISBN: 9781003396703 (ebk)

DOI: 10.4324/9781003396703

Typeset in Times New Roman
by Newgen Publishing UK

To my wife and companion of over 50 years, Joanna. You give my life meaning. To my children, Mike and Alicia, and their spouses, Stacy and Gabe. And to my granddaughters, Lily and Eleanor. To my colleagues in the solution-focused community who inspire me. Finally, to my colleague, friend, and co-author, Lance Taylor – thanks for this journey!

Joel

To my partner Catherine. Thank you for all our precious moments and the trails we travel together. Thank you for your generous contribution of artwork. To my daughter, Deanne, her husband, Ron, and their fine young men, Christian, Parker, and Aiden: I admire you. To Joel for a once-in-a-lifetime conversation that has allowed us to delight in both our predominant similarities and our minor differences in solution-focused practice.

Lance

Tribute: Janet Beavin Bavelas (February 1940–December 12, 2022)

As we were preparing the final draft of this book, we learned of the passing of Janet Bavelas. We were fortunate to have trained in microanalysis with Janet and her team from the University of Victoria after the Solution-Focused Brief Therapy Association conference in 2009. Our original article published in the *Journal of Systemic Therapies* and this current book are a direct result of her influence. Especially in the preparation of the journal article, Janet was generous with her time and ideas, often meeting with us as we mulled over different options. We hope that in some small part this book will signify not only how she has influenced us and the practice of solution-focused brief therapy in general, but also her legacy.

Joel Simon and Lance Taylor

Contents

Foreword

There is a maxim in solution-focused brief therapy (SFBT) circles: "Simple but not easy." That is to say, it is much easier to understand the concepts and principles of SFBT than to effectively put these ideas into practice with clients. Instructive in this regard is a story in the lore of the SFBT community that comes from Harry Korman (personal communication). He tells of a walk and conversation he had with Insoo Kim Berg in 2006 after the two of them had attended a research day with Janet Bavelas and her microanalysis team and, soon thereafter, a teaching event with several prominent SFBT trainers. In their discussion of what they had learned from these recent events, Korman was wondering how long one would have to observe a therapy session before being able to tell whether it was a SFBT conversation or not. He thought about three to five minutes and asked Berg what she thought. She said, "Less than a minute." That led to a long and interesting conversation about: "What is IT?" – that is, what is the essence of doing a SFBT conversation and how can one tell when "IT" is happening? Various answers to this question have been presented in writing and at conferences both before and since Korman and Berg shared their thoughts on the matter.

Steve de Shazer (one of the inventors of SFBT along with Berg and their colleagues at the Brief Family Therapy Center (BFTC) in Milwaukee) was fond of saying that he clearly knew SFBT worked because clients told him these conversations were helpful; however, he admitted that he knew much less about how or why this way of interacting with clients worked. So, while he had his own version of the essence of doing SFBT, he said it was only one version and all SFBT practitioners should continue to pay attention to what was working with their clients, and thereby continue to develop their own views of what IT or the essence of doing SFBT is.

Just a few years before they passed away, both de Shazer and Berg had become interested in the microanalysis of face-to-face dialogue as a research approach that could shed further light on the perplexing question of the essence of doing SFBT. Microanalysis offers a rigorous research analysis of face-to-face dialogue, utterance by utterance as the dialogue unfolds. The method complements SFBT because it stays "at the surface" of face-to-face conversations such as therapy sessions. It does so by counting as admissible data only verbal and non-verbal actions that are directly observable. In the 15 years since the deaths of de Shazer and Berg, Janet Bavelas, her microanalysis team at the University of Victoria, and several therapists with solution-focused (SF) leanings have conducted a number of primary research projects about how therapy conversations work. This research, among other findings, has shown that: (1) therapy questions are not merely information gathering devices but directly influence the direction of a therapy conversation through their embedded presuppositions; (2) therapist formulations (i.e., therapist paraphrases and summaries) are not neutral, but transform what clients say by preserving only some client words, editing out the rest, and sometimes adding their own content; and (3) therapy conversations are built by therapist and client together, interactionally, utterance by utterance, co-constructing one mutual understanding after another that both draws on previously built understandings in the conversation and accumulates in an identifiable direction influenced by the presuppositions of the therapist's questions and the transformations of the therapist's formulations. In several of these projects, SFBT has been compared with other modalities which is telling us more and more about what is different about SFBT and the "IT" or essence of doing SFBT.

As the body of microanalysis research about therapy conversations has grown, several SFBT therapists, supervisors, and trainers have begun experimenting with how the findings of this research may be applied in their work. Joel Simon and Lance Taylor are two of these innovators. After giving us a promising and useful article in 2014 about examining client utterances for multiple "opportunities" for SF response by the therapist, they now present us with a more detailed, book-length version of the same subject-matter.

Their book is based on the conviction that an effective SFBT conversation proceeds utterance by utterance, and that it is the therapist's responsibility to lead or influence the conversation in SF directions. The therapist leads by selecting out from the client's utterances those words, phrases, and ideas that have the best chance of inviting clients to build clearer visions of what they want to be different in their lives and how to make these changes happen. This process of listening for and selecting out SF opportunities from client utterances and then developing an effective therapist response is guided by the principle of the therapist offering a response that is most likely to elicit a SF utterance from the client. Herein lies the "IT," or the essence of doing SFBT according to the authors.

The value of this book lies in the authors' step-by-step methodology and detailed illustrations of doing an applied microanalysis of opportunities for constructing SF therapist responses. The process involves two or more therapists independently studying a limited number of preselected client utterances from a SF therapy conversation. Each therapist enumerates the various SF opportunities they see for a possible SF therapist response in each of the client utterances. For each opportunity, the therapist constructs at least one and usually multiple SF responses. Then the therapist chooses a preferred response to the client utterance from all the possibilities generated and records a rationale for that choice. Once the therapists have completed their individual work on the preselected client utterances, they combine their respective microanalyses on a chart and make comparisons. The comparisons are instructive, both in their analyses of what opportunities exist in the client utterances, the possible therapist responses to the opportunities, the final choice of a preferred therapist response and the rationale for the preferred response.

The authors lay out and illustrate how SF practitioners can employ the microanalysis of opportunities in therapy, coaching, supervision, and training situations. I would encourage anyone who wants to sharpen their SF skills and thinking to not only read this valuable book but also to find at least one partner and conduct their own "microanalysis of opportunities" in their professional context. Another of Berg and de Shazer's favorite sayings was "Doing is Knowing." One will learn the most by putting in the effort to do their own microanalyses of opportunities and continue to pay attention to what becomes different and more useful in their practice. This suggestion probably comes as no surprise, as SFBT originally was invented in the same way at BFTC.

Peter De Jong
International Microanalysis Associates
Co-author with Insoo Kim Berg, *Interviewing for Solutions*

Introduction

A professor of Eastern philosophy considered himself an expert on Zen. Seeking further knowledge, he went to see a Zen master. The master graciously welcomed him, invited him in, and offered the professor tea. As the master prepared the tea, first boiling the water, then steeping the tea leaves, the professor regaled the master with his vast knowledge of Zen philosophy. Soon the tea was ready. The master placed a cup in front of the professor and began pouring the tea as the professor continued to speak. As he spoke, the master slowly filled the cup to the brim with the hot liquid and then continued to pour as the cup overflowed and the tea spilled onto the table. It was then that the professor stopped talking and looked at the master in surprise and shock. The master finally spoke: "You are like that cup. Return when you have emptied yourself."

Solution-focused therapists approach therapeutic conversations with the "emptiness" recommended by the Zen master. That is, we guard against being over-filled with our own ideas about people, their troubles, and their hopes, in order to have space available to first absorb the clients' own ideas about what brings us together and their hopes for what may come of our work. We believe that in order to be an effective therapist, one must listen closely to the narratives clients present and build our therapeutic responses upon that foundation.

As solution-focused practitioners, we maintain a non-expert stance, preferring instead to recognize and utilize the expertise that clients have accumulated about themselves. That doesn't mean we discount the training, experiences, and knowledge that we may bring to bear in helping clients to co-construct useful possibilities. After all, clients engage with therapists because they expect the encounter to offer additional resources that will make a difference. We just want to make sure client expertise is privileged so we do our "leading from behind", a mantra that is fondly embraced by solution-focused practitioners. In a presentation in Albany, New York several years ago, Insoo Kim Berg (personal communication) stated that, as solution-focused practitioners, we have expertise in asking questions that help clients to usefully change perspectives, feelings, and behaviors.

DOI: 10.4324/9781003396703-1

Experienced solution-focused practitioners develop what we have come to call "listening with solution-focused ears". We construct our next questions based on key information provided by the client. In their responses to our questions, clients provide us with additional solution-building clues. Continually building upon these clues, we gradually move conversations in the direction of possibilities, hope, and the expectation of a different and more positive future.

This book is as a result of the question we asked: "How exactly do we navigate therapeutic conversations and develop these positive solution-focused feedback loops that build possibilities? What choices do clients present to us as options for intervention? How do we minimize interference from our own assumptions and theories so that we may listen very carefully to clients to hear the choices offered?" This is important for us not only in our own work as solution-focused therapists, but also as solution-focused trainers. How do we teach those new to the model how to achieve requisite emptiness of mind in order to listen with solution-building ears?

Both authors had the great fortune of learning about microanalysis from Janet Bavelas and her colleagues at the University of Victoria. The collaboration between the authors arose out of our shared interest in the application of microanalysis to solution-focused practice. As a result of that collaboration, we authored an article, "Opportunities: Organizing the Solution-Focused Interview", published in the *Journal of Systemic Therapies* (2014).

At first glance, it seemed to us to be a pretty simple concept: listen to clients, note possibilities, make choices, and respond in a solution-focusing fashion to their key ideas. We were struck by the encouraging feedback we both independently received after the article had been published. We heard from colleagues that they not only found it useful for themselves but were incorporating the ideas into their trainings. We noticed how readily practitioners adopted the language of "opportunities" in practice, supervision, and training. In their written evaluations of the trainings, trainees wrote statements such as, "I was surprised about how many possibilities you have in one utterance"; "I was amazed at how much could be learned from the client in the first five minutes of the session"; "I'm fascinated with both the commonalities and differences in therapists' choices for intervention".

While we made every attempt to describe the process of opportunities, journals must limit the length of their articles for practical reasons. Given the positive responses we received, Joel suggested it might be time to expand on the concepts and develop a book as a more detailed and comprehensive guide to applying the notion of opportunities in practice.

We believe the concepts may be applicable to many models of clinical practice. However, it should be noted that both authors are solution-focused practitioners and trainers, so we are interested specifically in the applicability of the opportunities' framework to that particular model.

We cannot assume that everyone who will use this book is cognizant of solution-focused brief therapy (SFBT). Accordingly, the first chapters describe the principles and practice of SFBT: its assumptions, a view of how language co-constructs meanings and reality, and the tools of practice. Those who are already familiar with the model are welcome to forgo the introductory chapters, although it might be interesting and useful for them to review the basics.

The next chapters describe the basic principles of microanalysis, the evolution of opportunities as a concept and practice, and the application of opportunities in clinical practice and training. We have included ample examples and opportunities for readers to practice the concepts. Most of all, we have written this book in the hope that it will offer an organized way to listen and respond to clients that will present a useful addition to practice.

1 Solution-Focused Brief Therapy
Foundations

SFBT: Its Origins and Development

The authors believe it is important to write about the early foundations of the solution-focused brief therapy (SFBT) model and how it has evolved over time. This is especially relevant for those who may be new to SFBT, for it helps to place the model in context – in time and place. For those who are practicing SFBT already, it is often useful to return to the basics. Accordingly, this chapter details the following topics: the development of the SFBT model from the Mental Research Institute (MRI) to the present; solution-focused assumptions; elements of goal-setting; the brief in SFBT; and problem-solving vs. solution-building.

Solution-focused practice has always highlighted the practical intervention techniques that help keep the practice brief and effective. Since the beginnings of the model – a decade before it was even called SFBT – the major thrust of the model's evolution has been, and continues to be, learning from clients about what works. Because of this focus, various intervention tools have evolved and been strengthened: the "best hopes" question, future-oriented questions, the Miracle Question, exception questions, scaling questions, coping questions, and the "thinking break".

In discussing the format of this book, the authors came to realize that the topic of solution-focused interventions is quite extensive. We thought it best to address the details of interventive tools and maps separately in Chapter 3.

Since its origins over 40 years ago, there has been much written about the historical foundations of SFBT. Almost every book and article published on the subject contains some version of this topic. This is the authors' version of the evolution of SFBT. There is a general agreement that any discussion of the origins of SFBT begins with Steve de Shazer. De Shazer identifies himself as one of the "inventors" of solution-focused therapy (Miller & de Shazer, 1998). Many of those who practice and teach SFBT would add that de Shazer can be identified as the "father of SFBT" – although he likely would have protested. However, his early work in Palo Alto, California certainly laid the groundwork for what would eventually be called solution-focused brief therapy.

DOI: 10.4324/9781003396703-2

De Shazer earned a Bachelor of Fine Arts degree at the University of Wisconsin in Milwaukee (UWM) in 1964 (www.solution-focusedbrieftherapy.com/BFTC/Steve&Insoo_PDFs/deshazer-vita.pdf). In addition, he was a professional jazz saxophonist. Every indication was that de Shazer was not destined for a career in psychotherapy.

Several articles (e.g., Cade, 2007; Simon & Berg, 2004) point to *Strategies of Psychotherapy* by Jay Haley (1990) as a pivotal influence on de Shazer's decision to pursue social work as a career. Cade (2007, p. 42) cites de Shazer:

> Until I read this book, as far as I can remember, I had never even heard the term, "psychotherapy." Certainly, this was the first book on the topic that I read. I enjoyed it perhaps more than any other "professional" book.

Haley's book resulted in two major decisions for de Shazer: he returned to study for his Master's of Science in Social Work (MSSW) at the University of Wisconsin in Milwaukee (UWM) and he was introduced to the practice of Dr. Milton Erickson.

Milton Erickson

Milton Erickson was a psychiatrist, best known for reintroducing hypnosis as a clinical tool. He had a major influence on moving psychotherapy practice away from psychoanalysis and the related psychodynamic psychotherapy, prevalent during the early to mid-twentieth century. So, while Erickson might be best known for his study and practice of hypnotherapy, Haley (1973, p. 3) reflects on how Erickson's practice of psychotherapy in general moved beyond hypnosis:

> Out of hypnotic training comes skill in observing people and the complex ways they communicate, skill in motivating people to follow directives, and skill in using one's own words, intonations, and body movements to influence other people. Also, out of hypnosis come a conception of people as changeable, an appreciation of the malleability of space and time, and specific ideas about how to direct another person to become more autonomous.

A central Ericksonian concept is utilization. Whatever the client brings to the therapeutic engagement needs to be seen as useful and the job of the therapist is to mobilize its usefulness. Erickson proposed that problems are actually obsolete solutions. Problems were adopted because of a lack of experience and/or information and may even have served a useful purpose at one time. However, they no longer serve that purpose and may lock the client into less than useful thoughts, behaviors, and feelings. From an Ericksonian perspective, the therapist's task is to help the client develop more useful solutions that result in better ways of thinking, acting, and feeling.

The Ericksonian technique of pattern disruption has also been adopted by many of the therapies that have been influenced by him. Erickson would study a client's patterns and prescribe a change. One of his cases was a woman who came to him because she complained that she kept losing and then gaining weight (Rosen, 1982).

After making her promise to follow his directive, he told her that she needed to gain 20 pounds before she could begin losing weight: "She literally begged me [Erickson], on her knees, to be released from her promise" (Rosen, 1982, p. 124). Once she had gained the 20 pounds, she lost 70 pounds and stated that she would never gain weight again. The woman's usual pattern was to lose and gain. Erickson's directive was to disrupt the pattern and have her gain and then lose.

Pattern disruption technique is found in other therapies influenced by Erickson. For example, in the video *Coming Through the Ceiling*, a woman complains that the man living upstairs has built a machine that emits shockwaves that keep her awake at night. After consulting with the team, de Shazer suggests that she sleep on the floor in another room.

The woman returns, reporting that she has been able to sleep well for several nights. She reasons that since the bedframe is made of metal, it conducts the electrical shocks. She removed the bedframe but, just to be sure, she also removed the mattress and slept on the floor next to the bed to confirm her logical conclusion. This allowed her to have a good night's sleep, something she had not been able to do in quite a while. In turn, she appeared more rested and, while she hadn't given up her thinking about the upstairs neighbor, her ability to think logically was remarkably improved.

There is no doubt that Erickson had a profound influence on de Shazer and the development of SFBT. De Shazer (1982, p. 28) states:

> Brief family therapy owes a large debt to Milton Erickson's methods of therapy and the world view that these imply. His procedures involve a "process of evoking and utilizing a patient's own mental process in ways that are outside his usual range of intentional or voluntary control".

References to Erickson can also be found in *Keys to Solutions* (de Shazer, 1985b, p. 5): "The published history of brief therapy as presented here can be traced from Milton Erickson's "Special Techniques of Brief Hypnotherapy", and *Clues* (de Shazer, 1988, p. 49): "Our work at BFTC, since 1982, has been built on solving the puzzle posed in Erickson's paper, "Pseudo-Orientation in Time as a Hypnotic Procedure (1954)".

De Shazer (1978) in fact wrote a paper in 1978 entitled "Brief Hypnotherapy of Two Sexual Dysfunctions: The Crystal Ball Technique, '(which was built on Erickson's paper)'" (p. 49). Solution-focused practice emphasizes a respect for the client, acceptance of the client's frame of reference, an emphasis on the client's social and personal resources, and the assumption that clients are capable of discovering their own solutions. These elements can be traced directly to the practice and teachings of Dr. Erickson.

Mental Research Institute (MRI)

In 1952, the anthropologist Gregory Bateson was awarded a research grant. He convinced his colleague, John Weakland, to relocate to the West Coast of the United States and:

> Joined the following year by Jay Haley and William Fry, they formed the highly creative, prolific, and influential research group, producing many of the early seminal papers in the family therapy field.
>
> (Cade, 2007, p. 31)

Essentially, they formed a think tank, which was interested in the application of systems theory to a number of different contexts. Systems theory suggests that in human social systems where there are independent but connected individuals, a change in any part of the system results in a concomitant change in all parts of the system – in this case, other individuals within that system.

The psychiatrist Don Jackson formed the Mental Research Institute in Palo Alto, California in 1958 as "a centre [sic] for both developing and researching the clinical applications of the interactional view" (Cade, 2007, p. 31).

In 1966, the Brief Therapy Center (BTC) was formed and included Dick Fisch, John Weakland, and Paul Watzlawick. BTC is a family therapy program that diverged from the psychoanalytic theory that was much more prevalent at the time. In turn, BTC was also influenced by Milton Erickson's work, especially the orientation toward pattern disruption.

A word or two about the impact of BTC on the field, and especially the divergence from psychodynamic theory, is appropriate here. Psychoanalysis views problems as symptoms of underlying intrapsychic conflicts (Brenner, 1974). As such, practitioners are advised not to address problems directly because such an action does not resolve the underlying structural issues and may result in redirecting the symptoms elsewhere.

In contrast, MRI saw problems as the ways in which systems form and maintain dysfunction. Symptoms are useful in that they serve to maintain a homeostasis, albeit at the expense of one or more individuals in the system. De Shazer (1985a, p. 42), citing Simon et al. (1985) states:

> In these and other self-organizing, cybernetic systems in which all the elements are linked to one another, and the presenting problem of the family fulfills a specific function for the family system.

Thus, problems were not viewed as a deeper structure within an individual but as part of their social systems. Watzlawick et al. (1974, p. 10) outline four steps toward problem-resolution:

1. a clear definition of the problem in concrete terms.
2. an investigation of the solutions attempted so far.
3. a clear definition of the concrete change to be achieved.
4. the formulation and implementation of a plan to produce this change.

As opposed to the psychoanalytic orientation toward symptoms and treatment, clearly MRI not only viewed problems as externally caused, but the treatment involved addressing the problem directly.

While de Shazer and his colleagues diverged from the problem-focused reso- lution model of MRI, its influence on the development of BFTC is evident:

> Outside of the Brief Family Therapy Center world, a special thanks is due to John H. Weakland for his interest and support. His yearly visits help us remain connected to the tradition of which he, his team at the Brief Family Center at the Mental Research Institute, and the BFTC team are a part. Over the years we have known each other, he has helped me to clarify what I think is worthwhile in both his model and mine.
>
> (de Shazer (1985a), pp. xix–xx)

Insoo Kim Berg (personal communication) once stated that the original intention was to develop the MRI of the Midwest. It was the recognition of exceptions, which we will discuss later in this chapter, that moved the model from the problem- focused resolution model of MRI to the solution-focused model of BFTC.

Ludwig Wittgenstein

Much has been written about Wittgenstein and much has also been written attempting to interpret Wittgenstein. De Shazer (personal communication) once said that we read Wittgenstein not to find out what he thinks, but to find out what we think.

It is not our intention to provide an exhaustive introduction to Wittgenstein's philosophy in this book. Rather, we want to demonstrate how his philosophy has influenced de Shazer and the development of SFBT. De Shazer coined the phrase "post-structural" as a way to describe how some therapies, such as SFBT, view the way language functions very differently from other therapies, most notably psychodynamic orientations.

We distinguish between structuralism and post-structuralism or construct- ivism. Simon and Nelson (2007, p. 157, referencing de Shazer (1994), describe structuralism:

A structuralist philosophy is positivistic in that it is based on a view of the world wherein language represents reality; that is, a "true" correspondence exists between a word and what the word represents ... We can understand what the word means by looking behind or beneath it for what it represents. Meaning thus is fixed by consensus among those using the language.

For example, if a client seeks out a structurally oriented therapist because they are phobic about dogs, the theoretical assumption would most likely be that there is a "deeper" meaning to the concept "dog". The goal of therapy, therefore, would be to help the client develop insight into the underlying, "real" meaning of "dog".

In contrast, a post-structural orientation to language suggests we create meanings through conversations. Meanings are dependent upon context – when, where, and with whom – and therefore are not fixed, but fluid. The words we use have meaning only within a given conversation – or, as Wittgenstein (1958, p. 20) writes:

For a *large* class of cases – though not for all – in which we employ the word "meaning" it can be defined thus: the meaning of a word is its use in the language.

Returning to the dog example, a solution-focused therapist would be curious about how the client might want to think, feel, or act differently. While this might relate to dogs – if that is what the client wants to be different –it does not necessarily follow that it has to be. This may become more evident as we review the solution-focused assumptions later in this chapter.

If, from a constructivism point of view, meanings are negotiated through usage, it would logically follow that so is our sense of what is real. De Shazer (1991, p. 44) addresses this:

As such, constructivism involves a philosophical point of view, not a theory or model of therapy. If it is to be useful as a frame for looking at therapy, then it needs to be more than a simple slogan: *reality is invented rather than discovered.* Broadly speaking, therapy looked at from within a constructivist frame only suggests a shared principle: *Reality arises from consensual linguistic processes* (italics in original).

This essentially means that conversations between therapists and clients co-construct together a shared reality that is bounded by language and dependent upon context – or, as Wittgenstein (1958, p. 74) states, *"The limits of my language* mean the limits of my world."

Essential to understanding – or, as de Shazer (personal communication) stated, "more or less usefully misunderstanding" – Wittgenstein (1958) is his concept "language-game:"

We can also think of the whole process of using words as one of those games by means of which children learn their native language. I will call these games "language-games" and will sometime speak of primitive language as a language-game.

... I shall call the whole consisting of language, and the actions into which it is woven, the "language-game."

(Wittgenstein, 1958, p. 5)

A conversation about problems is one type of language-game; a conversation about how clients want their lives to be different, better, and more satisfying is a very different language-game. The importance of this concept to solution-focused conversations is encapsulated in Wittgenstein's statement above, and his assertion that "words are also deeds" (Wittgenstein, 1958, p. 146) – that language and actions are intertwined in language-games. Co-constructive conversations result in actions: they determine how we feel, think, and act.

Conversations that center on problems co-create realities around problems. They result in clients and therapists thinking, feeling, and acting in problem-focused ways. They create realities around purely theoretical concepts such as resistance, denial, transference, and counter-transference. The contradiction here is that if we are co-constructing problems, how then do they eventually become resolved? They get resolved when the client and therapist begin to move beyond the details of the problem to the details of intervention.

Alternatively, what possibilities lie in language-games that are centered on goals, personal and social resources, and more satisfying and fulfilling futures? This is why solution-focused conversations result in clients doing something different that not only changes their lives for the better but can have a positive effect on others within their social systems. De Shazer (1991, p.151) states:

When therapist and clients focus the conversation on a solution-developing language-game during the sessions, then the clients will frequently report on the construction and development of satisfactory solutions.

The Development of SFBT: From Problem-Resolution to Solution Focus

In the early 1970s, De Shazer was living and practicing in Palo Alto, California. At that time, he was seeing clients using a one-way mirror. On the other side was a professor of sociology from Stanford University, Joseph Berger. De Shazer and Berger together were researching therapy from a sociological perspective. This is reflective of Erickson's description of his therapy as "observe and utilize" or the anthropological orientation of MRI. which designed interventions based not on theory but rather on observation and description.

De Shazer was a fan of mystery novels, and especially enjoyed quoting Arthur Conan Doyle's character Sherlock Holmes. Apropos of the concept of observation and description is one of de Shazer's favorite Holmes' quotes: "It is a capital mistake to theorize before one has data. Insensibly one begins to twist facts to suit theories, instead of theories to suit facts."

Together, de Shazer and Berg designed several research projects (Simon & Berg, 2004). One of those was initially asking the question "What do therapists do that is helpful to clients?" That question was later changed to "What do therapists and clients do together that is helpful to clients?" Many therapies begin with a meta-theory and that theory dictates how the therapist co-constructs realities with clients. As such, this is a deductive approach to treatment: begin with the theory and the treatment intervention follows.

Fiske (2007, p. 319), a solution-focused practitioner, states that "many students (and teachers) view an understanding of theory as necessary in defining a therapeutic approach".

Simon and Nelson (2007, pp. 94–95) address this point:

> In fact, when a practitioner holds to one theory, it more likely dampens possibilities than creates new ones or identifies existing potentially usefully ones for the client. The therapist stays focused within that theory rather than the client's theory or context. Behaviors that exist outside of the theoretical explanations are viewed as irrelevant, mere static to be ignored.

Essentially de Shazer and Berg were developing an inductive approach to therapy – a practice that continues to this day. As we learn from clients what they and we do together that is helpful, this is applied to other clients and in turn enlarges our repertoire of useful interventions. This motivates us to remain descriptive rather than seek explanations of client behavior or intrapsychic motivations. As Wittgenstein (1958, p. 47) states, "We must do away with all *explanation,* and description alone must take its place."

Another project that de Shazer undertook (Simon, 2010) was researching short-term therapy. He randomly assigned clients to two different sets: one group was told they were limited to 20 sessions and the other to ten. What he found was that little happened in therapy for the 20 session clients until about sessions 17 or 18. A similar result occurred for the ten-session clients. Accordingly, he abandoned short-term therapy for brief therapy.

Short-term therapy is usually limited by two factors: time and the number of sessions allowed. The major issue for short-term therapy is the inherent meaning for the client. Essentially, the message is that given the limited number of sessions, the client needs to lower their expectation for outcome; in-depth therapy is not possible given a short-term stance. This was reinforced when managed care came on the scene in the mid-1990s. Therapists who practiced in accordance with long-term theories were now forced to work in the short term. The danger here is that managed care conveys to clients the disparity between what the therapist believes is necessary for effective treatment versus the limitations that managed care imposes. Edmunds et al. (1997, p. 51) state:

Given the pressures on health plans to reduce costs, consumers who need behavioral health care may thus be especially vulnerable to cost control strategies that unselectively affect the quality and accessibility of appropriate services.

In addition, Joyce and Piper (1998, p. 247) point out:

The findings clearly argue for the preparation of patients for short-term, time-limited individual psychotherapy. Referring therapists, or the treating therapist at the time of a treatment contract, *should seek to reinforce moderate patient expectancies*. Overly high expectancies are likely to be painfully disconfirmed and perhaps increase the likelihood of a treatment dropout. (italics added)

In contrast to short-term treatment, we define brief therapy as the number of sessions required to develop a satisfactory solution to the question "What does the client want to be different and better in his or her life" and not one session more or less than that (Dolan, 1991).[1] The client determines that their situation is good enough to decide that therapy is no longer necessary and that they can continue making progress on their own.

The main determinant of short-term therapy is time (the limited number of sessions within a specified period of time). Brief therapy emphasizes the goal of a better and more satisfactory future. From our perspective, the former limits possibilities; the latter enhances them.

Insoo Kim Berg and Steve de Shazer

Insoo Kim Berg is also credited with the development of the SFBT model. Berg was a first-generation immigrant who arrived in the United States from Korea with her family. She had studied pharmacy in Korea and had arrived in the United States with the expectation of continuing her medical training. When she arrived, she became interested in social work and graduated from the University of Wisconsin at Milwaukee with her MSSW in 1969.

Berg became interested in the MRI model, and while training there she was introduced to de Shazer by John Weakland. This began a collaboration as both business and life partners that spanned over 30 years, which has had (and continues to have) a major impact on psychotherapy practice.

De Shazer returned to Milwaukee in 1978. Initially he and Berg worked together in a family therapy agency. They began experimenting using a one-way mirror; however, other staff began to complain that this was a violation of client confidentiality and de Shazer left the agency to begin a private practice.

A custom of training at BFTC was the pizza party at de Shazer's and Berg's home. Joel recalls Berg relating how they began to see clients from their home. The client and therapist would meet in the living room while someone stood on the stairway to the second floor with a video camera connected to a tape machine and television/monitor in the bedroom upstairs.

In the chapter "Solution-Focused Brief Therapy with Adolescents", Simon and Berg (2004, p. 134) described the formation of the first BFTC: "De Shazer returned to Milwaukee in 1978, when he and Berg invested their limited financial resources in a training center, they named the Brief Family Therapy Center." Joel recalls Berg (personal communication) stating financially, "It was make it or break it."

Exceptions

As stated previously, their intention was to develop a therapy and training center patterned after the MRI problem-focused, resolution model. However, as they listened carefully, they began to hear clients detailing problem exceptions: circumstances when the problem was either absent or of less consequence. In turn, they began to deliberately ask clients about these problem exceptions. "It was this shift that moved the therapy from problem resolution to solution development" (Simon & Berg, 1999, p. 117).

In 1982, de Shazer, Berg and their colleagues began to call the model that was being developed at BFTC "solution-focused brief therapy". The placement of the descriptor "brief" was deliberate. In the early 1990s, managed care was becoming widespread in the United States. At that time, it was often speculated that SFBT was developed because of managed care. In fact, many managed care organizations began to require that practitioners at least state that they practiced SFBT. Of course, several of them named it "brief solution-focused therapy".

In response, it should be noted that SFBT had been in development in the 1970s and was finally called SFBT at least ten years prior to managed care. De Shazer insisted on the placement of "brief" after "solution-focused" because the intention was to develop an effective therapy practice. Brief happens because of the focus on solutions.

Lance recalls de Shazer acknowledging that there were other "brief" therapies – indeed, at BTC – that were not solution focused. "He told me he wanted to be clear that the adjective 'brief' modified the word therapy not the words solution-focused therapy." Otherwise, it might imply that there is some solution-focused therapy that is not brief. The adjective solution-focused modifies the words "brief therapy", not the other way around.

Assumptions

There has been an ongoing debate within the solution-focused community whether there is a Theory of the model. Note that here we have adopted Steve de Shazer's practice of capitalizing the term "Theory" to denote a mega-theory. By "Theory", we mean a primary set of beliefs that are required in order to adhere to a particular model. For example, one could not practice psycho-analysis without knowing the Theory of the model. It is not our intention to enter the debate about theory and SFBT. There is a general consensus among solution-focused practitioners that a set of approximately 11 assumptions guides our practice:

1. Solutions can be constructed without attention to the details of the problem.
2. Change is inevitable.
3. Small changes lead to bigger ones.
4. One area of control leads to other areas of control.
5. People have the necessary resources.
6. People are experts on their own lives.
7. We are all part of social systems.
8. Every problem has at least one exception.
9. Every one of the client's responses has the potential to be useful.
10. People are invested in solutions that they create.
11. Everyone does the best they can.

Solutions Can Be Constructed Without Attention to the Details of the Problem

Many theories and models of therapy practice begin with the assumption that in order to solve the problem that motivated a client to seek out therapy, clinicians need to know more about the problem. The analogy to solving a jigsaw puzzle is often applied to this way of thinking. The more pieces of the problem puzzle that are connected, the better the chance of getting a clearer picture. Applied to problem-solving, the clearer the picture, the better the chance of arriving at the problem solution.

We view problem-solving and solution-building as two separate processes that have little relationship with each other. Conversations about how people want their lives to be different and more satisfying co-construct different realties than conversations about problems. Conversations about exceptions reinforce solutions that have already happened, and may also be happening in the present, and could continue in the future. Building on these exceptions and how they make a difference to the client and to others in the client's life co-constructs possibilities. We often hear clients leaving a solution-building conversation speaking about their renewed hope and possibilities for the future.

Change is Inevitable

The Greek Philosopher Heraclitus wrote, "No one can bathe twice in the same river; the river endures, but the water is no longer the same. Reality is changing, unstable" (Marías, 1967, p. 27). Heraclitus speaks to the inevitability of change. In our experience, most clients agree with that statement, yet they talk about problems as if they are constant and immutable. Once the perceived *status quo* is challenged and deconstructed, possibilities and hope for change become the alternative. Here again we see the importance of the discovery of exceptions that moved the SFBT model development from problem-resolution to solution-building; exceptions are about difference and change arising inevitably within problems.

Small Changes Lead to Bigger Ones

We often use the analogy of a snowball rolling down a hill. Once you give the snowball an initial push, it begins to build up momentum, grows larger, and has a momentum of its own. The same is true of change: once it is given a push, it tends to grow, and gain momentum. Talk of possibilities, no matter how small, leads to more possibilities: change begets change.

There are three corollaries to this assumption. The first is that it doesn't matter how complex the problem is: just start somewhere. We often say complex problems don't necessarily require complicated solutions. The second is that the solution does not necessarily need to be related to the problem. Solutions and problems are separate and not necessarily logically or causally connected.

The following conversation will serve to illustrate the first two points. Joel is the therapist working with John:

JOEL: You said something about getting to where you want to be.

JOHN: Yeah [nods his head].

JOEL: Where's that?

JOHN: So, I feel that some of the … it's been a very frustrating 11 months for me. Just because I feel in some ways almost that … so, I guess it's kind of a long story, sorry, I'm kind of …

JOEL: [Interrupting] take your time.

JOHN: So, last summer, my dad died. And then I feel like I put pressure on myself to get through it and I haven't resolved my grief. As a result of that, I've now have had some adverse effects in terms of in my performance at work. It's almost turned into a crisis for me because I'm used to performing very well at work. In the first company I was at, I set the company record in sales. I'm used to going in and being successful, and no matter what else is going on, being a consistent performer. This is something – the grief – I haven't been able to manage correctly. I feel it's now affecting me in other areas. It has been very frustrating for me. I know that getting frustrated with it is continuing to almost make things worse. It's been frustrating for me not to be able to work through something. It's impacting on something that I identify myself with. I could always be counted on. I feel that I'm not that person.

JOEL: So, what would you be doing, or thinking, or feeling that would tell you that things were just starting to turn around?

JOHN: If I was excited to get started in the morning.

At first blush, it may seem counterintuitive – what really is the connection between the problem of grief and being excited about getting started in the morning? Practitioners working from a more problem-focused framework would likely suggest that grief would need to be resolved as the first agenda of therapy. The essential difference with solution-focused practice is that the therapist and client co-construct a meaning of excitement "to get started in the morning" without any further need to co-construct, deconstruct, or resolve "grief".

Joel's question, "So, what would you be doing, or thinking, or feeling that would tell you that things were just starting to turn around?", begins the co-construction by bringing forth client language for difference. Continuing in a solution-focused interview puts this difference to work in multiple ways, which are presented in the next chapters. In all likelihood, later in this conversation or subsequent sessions, John will speak of some exceptions where he actually experiences a little more "excitement" in the morning or some other related change.

Solution-focused interviewing is structured first to notice and then to increase the frequency of the emergence of such exceptions, which are in turn amplified and put to work toward more satisfying successes. John's final statement begins a conversation about change and allows the therapist and client together to build on the future possibilities that "being excited to get started in the morning" will create.

The third corollary is that change comes from many different directions. Most of a client's life is not spent inside a therapist's office. Therapy conversations are just one possible way in which clients are helped to think, feel, and act differently. Outside of the therapy office, clients have multiple conversations with others and many of them have the same capacity for both positive and negative impacts on a client's life. If a therapist's focus is only on the traditional 50 minutes in their office, they will miss the myriad possibilities that exist for co-constructing change in clients' lives.

One Area of Control Leads to Other Areas of Control

Most people try several problem-solving strategies before contacting a therapist. The fact that they've taken the step to see a therapist suggests that those strategies have not been successful to the extent they wished. It's not unusual for them to perceive that their situation is hopeless and out of control.

One frequent result of solution-focused conversations is the co-construction of future possibilities – not necessarily directly pursuant to the perceived problem. When clients leave the therapy session with the thought that change is possible and have some idea of where to begin, they start to believe they have control over their situation.

The previous dialogue is a good example of this. John lists a number of issues that he is facing and even says, "It's impacting on something that I identify myself with. I could always be counted on. I feel that I'm not that person." The next session about two weeks later illustrates how a solution-focused conversation often results in clients taking control.

JOEL: So, uh, what's better?

JOHN: Yeah, um, I think overall my mood, my energy, my thoughts, my … I feel more confident; especially how I react to things. I've been enjoying my days a lot more. And it's been tested. The day I left I was actually let go from my job.

JOEL: Oh, my goodness, oh my goodness!

JOHN: So, obviously that's pretty stressful, but I've been approaching it well. I mean, you know, even with that, I feel better than I did when I walked in here last time. My situation is a little tougher now, but in terms of myself, I'm personally in a better place right now.

Joel received an email from John six months after their last session together:

> When I came to see you, I was in a bad place – personally and professionally. I was dealing with unresolved grief and that was impacting my habits and behaviors. After a few short sessions, I started the road back to being the person who I believe myself to be. It has been about six months since my first session – I am now working a good job, I have returned to a hobby that I love, and I just completed my first semester of a degree program towards a more rewarding profession.

People Have the Necessary Resources

Joel is reminded of a case of one of his solution-focused colleagues. She was working with a woman who vowed she didn't have any social supports. Together they had a conversation about how having friends would make a difference in the client's life. The client returned a couple of weeks later with this narrative. She lives in an apartment building. One day she was getting on the elevator returning from work when she crossed paths with a neighbor also taking the elevator. The client said that, in the past, she and this neighbor often greeted each other in passing. As they rode on the elevator, they had enough time to have a brief conversation. The client decided spontaneously to invite her neighbor for a cup of coffee. This one encounter began a friendship and, more importantly, a mutual support system. While we cannot say for sure, we can at least speculate that having a solution-focused conversation helped the client to become more aware of her own life contexts, her hopes, and possibilities that brought already existing resources into the client's awareness.

People are Experts on Their Own Lives

What is most helpful and most important is not what therapists know, but what clients know about themselves and their own life situations. Solution-focused practitioners take a "not-knowing" stance. Anderson and Goolishian (1992, pp. 28–29) expand on this concept:

> Not-knowing requires that our understandings, explanations, and interpret-ations in therapy not be limited by prior experiences or theoretically formed truths, and knowledge ... The not-knowing position entails a general attitude or stance in which the therapist's actions communicate an abundant, genuine curiosity. That is, the therapist's actions and attitudes express a need to know more about what has been said rather than convey preconceived opinions and expectations about the client, the problem, or what must be changed. The ther-apist, therefore, positions himself or herself in such a way as always to be in a state of "being informed" by the client.

Insoo Kim Berg (personal communication) once said that clients are experts on themselves; therapists need to be experts on asking useful questions. The sociolo-gist Gale Miller has spent many years studying solution-focused conversations. One of his insights was that in order to be an effective solution-focused ther-apist, one has to "appreciate the extraordinary acts that ordinary people do in their ordinary lives" (Blundo & Simon, 2016, p. 18). Therapists can do that by allowing clients to be their own experts.

We are All Part of Social Systems

People live and work in many different social configurations: families, work, and various social contexts. These all comprise systems. We can think of human social systems as a group of individuals who are connected in such a way that changes in one result in changes in others within the system. Waltzlawick, Beavin, and Jackson (1967, p. 123) state that "every part of a system is so related to its fellow parts that changes in one part will cause a change in all of them and in the total system".

When individuals, couples, or families come to see a therapist, the therapist enters into and becomes part of that system at that moment in time. Through the therapist's actions, they can either help the family to co-construct a more satisfying way of being for its system's members, or they can end up unwittingly reinforcing the family's less-than-useful patterns of behaviors.

It has long been a prevalent edict of family therapy that in order to treat the family, the therapist must demand that all members of the family be present. Since all it takes is one member of a family to do something different that makes a difference, their actions will affect the other members of the family. This is why therapists can do family therapy with only one member of the system. De Shazer (1985b, p. 108) states:

> The idea that the whole family needs to be involved in the therapy stems from the view held by some therapists that the family is the patient and, therefore, it is not therapeutic to see only some members of the family. However, Szapocznic et al. [1986] show the assumption behind this perspective is questionable.

Many solution-focused practitioners contend that all therapy is about relationships to the extent that changes with one person will inevitably impact others in their social context.

Every Problem Has at Least One Exception

When Joel first began working with his local hospice as the director of social work, he was asked to present at the annual mandatory staff training. As part of that presentation, he talked about this assumption. One of the therapists asked, "What if the problem is death?" Joel's response was that death is not a problem but a fact of life. He went on to explain individuals with terminal conditions might want to consider how they wish to spend whatever time they might have, or they might want to make meaning of their lives, or they might want to resolve issues with others in their lives. Even when a terminal illness is involved, there are still possibilities.

De Shazer and Dolan (2007, p. 4) define exceptions:

> An exception is thought of as a time when a problem could occur but does not. The difference between a previous solution and an exception is small but significant. A previous solution is something that the family has tried on their own that has worked, but for some reason they have not continued this successful solution, and probably forgot about it. An exception is something that happens instead of the problem, usually without the client's intervention or maybe even understanding.

Problems are defined by their exceptions. When a client presents a problem narrative, the solution-focused therapist can assume that there is going to be at least one exception to the problem. In reality, the practice of SFBT is about exceptions: exceptions in the past, exceptions in the present, and exceptions in the future. The questions we ask don't just serve to highlight these exceptions, but also enable us to co-construct useful meanings around them – collaborating with the client about how exceptions might make a difference if they continue to happen and then happen even more.

Initially, exceptions may be viewed by the client as random and of little significance. The solution-focused therapist's task is to co-construct with the client how exceptions might have useful meanings about change and possibilities. Further, the identification of exceptions serves to deconstruct the idea that problems are constant and fixed. As we will see in Chapter 3, the solution-focused tools serve the purpose of highlighting and co-constructing exceptions.

Every One of the Client's Responses Has the Potential to Be Useful

The pathway to developing a collaborative relationship with clients is by careful listening, accepting, and (most importantly) utilizing their worldview. De Shazer uses the term "radical acceptance" (Durrant, 2004) to connote that we accept the client's point of view without question and that, by accepting that point of view, we can help the client to co-construct something useful.

Earlier in this chapter, we referenced the video *Coming Through the Ceiling* (de Shazer, 1985a). This is a good example of radical acceptance. De Shazer was able to develop a collaborative conversation by accepting the woman's reality. The result was that the woman was able to think beyond the problem, which enabled her to have a good night's sleep.

Microanalysis of opportunities, the subject of this book, is a tool for listening to and responding to clients. As we expand on identifying and capitalizing on opportunities, this concept of responding usefully to clients will become more evident.

People are Invested in Opportunities They Create

Recently, Joel was consulted by a master's student in a counseling program. The student expressed the opinion that he saw nothing wrong with giving advice to clients. Joel explained that clients are more likely to do something different if it is their own idea. It certainly makes the therapist's job much simpler if they elicit strategies for change from the client and then suggest that the client try them. The posture of advice-giving also contradicts two of the other assumptions. The first is that people have the necessary resources. Giving advice may confuse clients about whether to look within their own experience or to others for the seeds of change. The second is that clients are experts in their own lives. When therapists give clients advice, they are speaking from the expert position. Advice is always part of the advice-giver's context and not necessarily the client's.

Everyone Does the Best They Can

We all have limited resources and knowledge. We make decisions based upon what is available to us and what we know. Simon (2010, p. 67) reflects the importance of accepting these limitations:

> When we acknowledge our trust that the client is doing the best he or she can and then help him or her do what is working (or find alternatives to that which is not), we help the client take the first meaningful steps toward greater control over his or her own life.

Goals

As stated previously in this chapter, the client's goal of a more satisfying life determines when therapy is no longer necessary. There are eight characteristics of a well-defined goal:

1. The goal is important to the client.
2. The goal is possible within the client's life context (i.e., it is realistic and achievable).
3. The goal is the presence of a difference (not the absence).
4. The goal involves a second-order change.
5. The goal is a good enough beginning.
6. The goal is concrete and measurable.
7. The goal is meaningful for the client and others in the client's life (including the therapist).
8. The goal is perceived by the client as involving hard work.

The Goal is Important to the Client and the Goal is the Presence of a Difference

Harry Korman is the therapist in the following dialogue taken from a video of an actual solution-focused session. Cary has just returned with her 14-month-old daughter to live with her parents following a divorce.

HARRY: I'm Harry. So, is it okay if we start like what will have to happen as a result of you coming here today – this afternoon, tomorrow, the day after tomorrow –to feel that it's been somewhat useful to be here?

CARY: I don't know, I guess maybe to sort together everything I'm feeling. I don't exactly know what that is yet. I don't exactly know what's bothering me. I'm in the process of going through a divorce. I'm sure that's the majority of it. Just recently I haven't been able to sleep too well. So I thought maybe this might help me sort out whatever I need to get my life back together.

HARRY: Help you sort something out to get your life together. What would be a feeling, a thought, an action – something you would do, or think or feel – that would tell you that you were sort of getting your life together – this afternoon, tomorrow?

CARY: I guess just relaxing.

Discussion

The client begins by stating that she is not sure about what she wants to be different and continues detailing the problems that she is facing: what she wants *not* to be happening. As the conversation continues, and the therapist repeats his question about change, adding her phrase "getting your life together," Cary is able to simply state "I guess just relaxing."

This is the presence of change, and the therapist can now help Cary to co-construct a useful meaning from "I guess just relaxing." As the conversation around that simple phrase continues, it not only co-creates possibilities and hope, but it also creates a goal that becomes important for the client.

Taken a step further, from a constructivist point of view, we would say that by bringing forth the language "relaxing" we begin to co-create with Cary her unique experience of relaxation. Chapter 3 on tools for SF interviewing will show how an experience like "relaxing" is brought into the foreground and built into a stronger presence in the client's daily experience.

As in Cary's case, when clients are initially asked what they want to be different and better, they often respond with the details of their problems. Helping clients to think about what will be happening when the problem is gone begins the process of transforming from what they don't want to what they do – the presence of a meaningful change.

The Goal is Realistic and Achievable in the Client's Context

It is not enough for a client to state a goal; it needs to make sense given the client's capabilities, social, and personal resources. When challenged about the practicalities, the client needs to clearly state why he or she believes that the goal can happen. Solution-focused questioning includes options for gracefully shifting from what might initially be expressed as an unrealistic goal to one described in terms of more grounded details of daily experience.

The Goal Represents a Second-Order Change

Watzlawick et al. (1974, p. 10) distinguish between first and second order changes: "There are two different types of change: one that occurs within a given system which itself remains unchanged, and one whose occurrence changes the system itself." First-order change is a change that results in no difference to the client and the client's social system – for example, the couple who seek out a therapist because they want to learn to communicate better. They complain that they often argue about a variety of issues. While they certainly change what they argue about and might even change how they argue, it doesn't alter the fact that they argue.

"Second-order change is thus *change of change*" (Watzlawick et al., 1974, p. 11). Second-order change makes a difference to the client and to their social system. The authors go on to describe:

> While first-order change always appears to be based on common sense (for instance, the "more of the more" recipe). Second-order change usually appears weird, unexpected, and uncommonsensicle: there is a puzzling element in the process of change.
>
> (Watzlawick et al., 1974, p. 83)

Joel recalls James, who came to him because of a strange concern. He said that when he was in elementary school, he learned that the Earth rotates. Since then, every time he thinks about this (and there are times when he can't help but think about this), he wonders why we don't fall off of the Earth and he begins to feel disoriented and dizzy.

James was very bright, college educated with a good job, and he knew that these thoughts were irrational. Even so, he found that that he thought about this so often that it intruded on his life in general. He had been to other therapists who had suggested ways of helping him not think about this issue – for example, breathing exercises, and cognitive shifts away from his thoughts, but these were no help.

Joel suggested that, rather than a strategy of avoidance, perhaps something different could be tried. He suggested that James spend 15 minutes a day in a place where he felt secure and enjoy the sensations that came from thinking about a rotating Earth. Rather than doing more of the strategy of ignoring the problem (first-order change), Joel suggested a way of reframing the thoughts. In addition, by restricting James to just 15 minutes, Joel was helping James take control of his thoughts. This is also consistent with the assumption that one area of control leads to other areas of control.

James returned two weeks later, reporting that he had tried the suggestion and was worrying much less about falling off the Earth when he did think about it. He reported that the thoughts were fleeting, and he experienced little of the dizziness he had encountered previously.

The Goal is a Good Enough Beginning

John Weakland is reported to have said that people seek out therapy because life becomes the same damned thing over and over again. Once therapy is over, life goes back to being one damned thing after another. Life is about transitions and changes. There is every indication that therapy needs to end when the clients believe they have the tools that help them stay on track, and that they have the confidence that they can continue making progress on their own.

The Goal is Concrete and Behavioral

The goal needs to be stated in ways that enable both the therapist and the client to know it is being accomplished. A good rule of thumb is the ABCD of treatment planning:

- *Audience:* in addition to the client, who else will be noticing the difference?
- *Behavior:* what will the client and others be doing that will make a difference?
- *Context:* where and when will the change take place?
- *Degree:* how much of the behavior (either in terms of time or activity) will be sufficient?

The Goal is Meaningful for the Client and Others in the Client's Life (Including the Therapist)

This element is heart and soul of social constructionism. When we use goal for-mulation as the motivation for change, we co-construct with clients their visions of a more satisfying future and co-create future possibilities that become real as clients detail how the goal will make a difference to them and others in their lives. This happens when we simply ask the client to engage in meaning-making with us.

For example, when clients state that their goal is to be happier, solution-focused therapists ask who will notice this, what the reaction will be to the diffe-rence, and what the client's reaction will be in turn. In this way, "being happier" takes on meaning that both the client and the therapist can envision.

Wittgenstein (1958, p. 153) writes that "an inner process stands in need of outward criteria". Asking clients how others will know that they are "being hap-pier" requires them to transform an internal process into something behavioral.

The Goal is Perceived by the Client as Involving Hard Work

This just makes logical sense. When therapists suggest to clients that change will take hard work, it makes it clear to clients that they are ultimately respon-sible for making their lives better. Furthermore, we tend to value that which we achieve through our own efforts. As De Jong and Berg (2002, p. 84) state, "By suggesting that the client's problem will take hard work to resolve, practitioners, strengthen the client's sense of dignity and self-respect."

In the chapters that follow, we explore the solution-focused tools that help to turn clients' goals into real possibilities.

In Summary

With early roots in the problem-focused solution-development framework of the MRI group, as well as the substantial influence of the hypnotherapist Milton Erickson and the philosopher Ludwig Wittgenstein, solution-focused brief therapy was initially constructed by Steve de Shazer, Insoo Kim Berg and their colleagues at the Brief Family Therapy Center in Milwaukee, Wisconsin. Interestingly, both founders were drawn to therapy from other vocations: music and medicine. It seems somehow fitting that their professional pursuits almost accidentally and simultaneously encountered the field of psychotherapy and they both found themselves following this shared fascination. Their separate and then, later, shared curiosity about how therapy worked led to the formulation of an innovative model of practice that depends primarily on therapists adopting a position of curiosity about the hopes and capabilities of clients. In the next chapters, we present the solution-focusing conversational tools, clarified over approximately 40 years of experimentation, that have proven to be useful to clients and therapists in their work together.

Note

1 In the original introduction to Dolan's (1991) book, de Shazer defined "brief" as "brief therapy simply means therapy that takes as few sessions as possible, not even one more than is necessary, for you to develop a satisfactory solution" (p. x). The authors took the liberty of offering an alternative focus in the desire to emphasize differences over problems.

2 Building Convergent Narratives

In the instruction manuals for self-assembly of furniture and tools, there is usually a picture on the front page of the assembled object along with a list of the tools required for the task. An image of the end result provides an overview to guide the person in completing the individual steps. Often there is an expanded view that shows individual components in a not-quite-attached position, providing some tips that are also intended to show the result coming together. Instructions also usually suggest a sequence of steps that lead from the beginning to the finished product. The authors have found, through the usual school of backward panels and upside-down handles, that one is generally well advised to follow the steps.

Efficient assembly of a physical structure such as a table might well depend on adherence to set steps and sequences. However, assembly of a wooden table is one thing; collaboration with clients to assemble useful human perceptions, plans, actions, and interactions is quite another. It would be folly to suggest that taking a set series of actions in a fixed order will always lead to the desired results in therapy.

The uniqueness and complexity of individual people and relationships demands flexibility and sensitivity in any schema that purports to guide our interventions. With this caution in mind, this chapter offers one possible construal of the objective of solution-focused interviewing. Chapter 3 then presents a review of the conversational tools and some potentially useful sequences for their employment.

Converging Narratives

One way to illustrate the intended result of successful solution-focused interviewing is *converging narratives*.

Therapists rely heavily on clients' verbal accounts of their troubles, hopes, and activities to know the "realities" of their living. We may or may not observe the problem or solution occurring within a therapy session. Clients generally begin

DOI: 10.4324/9781003396703-3

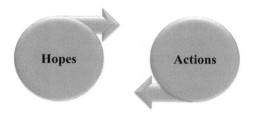

Figure 2.1 Converging narratives.

therapy with a belief that their problems are "real". SFB therapists' responses are based on the assumption that, as much as clients are convinced the problem is immutable, there will be exceptions to the problem that open the door to different perceptions and alternative "realities". To begin hosting a solution-focused conversation, the therapist invites clients to put their hopes into words, to begin creating a narrative of a difference they would value. Utilizing conversational tools, which will be introduced later, the therapist affirms a strengthening of the hope narrative by inviting shifts toward enhanced action-ability, increasing the possibility and probability of corresponding behavioral shifts toward wellness. As the conversation proceeds, the therapist invites increasingly detailed accounts of client hopes, which tend to bring forth more descriptions of actions and events of daily living – what we refer to as the *details of difference*. The therapist selects, promotes and builds client narratives of actions that point in the direction of their hopes.

By way of background, Steve de Shazer (1991, p. 92) quotes the ideas of Gergen and Gergen (1983, 1986), who compared three different kinds of narratives that people may use to describe their experience in the areas of living that bring them to therapy:

1. *Progressive* narratives that justify the conclusion that people, and situations are progressing toward their goals.
2. *Stability* narratives that justify the conclusion that life is unchanging.
3. *Regressive* narratives that justify the conclusion that life is moving away from their goals.

De Shazer (1991) preferred to substitute "digressive" over Gergen and Gergen's original "regressive" because the term "better emphasizes the movement away from the goal" (p. 92). Prompted by this subtly altered distinction, the present authors prefer *divergent*, over "digressive" and the corollary, *convergent* over "progressive".

The language of regressive and digressive seems to connote a unilateral process, implying that the goal is somewhat fixed. "Regressive" seems to suggest that actions are going backwards or away from the goal instead of forward, toward the goal. "Digressive" seems to suggest, similarly, that actions are moving in a direction away from the client's more desirable goal. The shift of language to *divergent* and *convergent* is subtle and important.

SFBT is known for articulating a unique understanding of change; therapy may be effective through altering *either the viewing or the doing* of the problem. De Shazer (1991, p. 96) states:

> [Therapists] want clients to so show some modification of their thoughts, feelings, attitudes, perceptions, and/or behaviors; to point to having substituted something "positive" for something "negative."

Some traditional approaches to counseling tend to suggest that the goal or the better way of doing things lies ahead of the person in the future, and the client needs to take several steps to move there.

SFBT differs from this unilateral approach. At the same time, as we collaborate with clients to move their actions in the direction of their hopes, we also work together to move their hopes into the language of actions. We might suggest that therapy may be effective through altering *both* the viewing and the doing of the problem. To be even more precise, we might suggest therapy succeeds by altering *both the viewing and the doing of hopes*.

One example is asking a person with a nebulous goal such as "to be happier" to identify the first small signs that they were moving in that direction. What do they imagine they would be doing a little more of once they are happier? How will others notice that they are happier? This helps the client to state the goal in terms of actions and events that are more observable and concrete.

Other solution-focusing tools work to help the client appreciate more of what they are already doing effectively. We might think of this as finding small signs of hope in clients' current actions and capabilities. This is at least as important as planning new actions. Desired changes are often initiated by applying existing talents in a slightly different way or with more determination to a scaled-down version of their original hope. The change process is actually fueled by this reciprocity of perception and action – a more bilateral dynamic.

People coming into therapy might initially describe their experience in terms of a *divergent narrative*, where their actions are moving away from their goals, or by contrast, their goals are becoming unreasonably opposite and distant from their current realities. An example is Lance's client who struggled with obesity.

He knew his eating habits were a factor in his condition, but he found himself repeatedly engaging in over-eating of ill-advised foods, particularly as he despaired about his apparent inability to make noticeable progress. At the same time as he was gaining weight, his idea of what he was trying to achieve was drifting farther away from current realities as he mournfully recalled his shape and athleticism from his youth.

Initially, clients may express the idea that their problems are constant, and whatever they've tried has made little difference. This exemplifies the *stability narrative*. An example is a family where parents were separating. They were both hoping to work out the details of co-parenting under these altered circumstances; however, they found themselves repeatedly lapsing back into blame and recrimination over the cause of the separation.

During successful solution-focused interactions, clients increasingly describe their experience in the form of *converging narratives*. The narratives of their hopes and actions are moving closer together, eventually coming close enough so they no longer need therapy. This may be viewed as a working definition of change in SFBT.

Of course, life experience shows us that convergence between hopes and actions is seldom complete. More realistically, we are fortunate when there is appreciable overlap between what we hope for and what we manage to do in the contexts of thoughts, feelings, behaviors, and interactions. In therapy, particularly early in the process, we are equally or more concerned with *movement in the desired direction* than with the degree of convergence.

It should be noted that the *convergent narrative* is the main focus – indeed, almost the exclusive focus – in SFBT. One of the formative realizations in the evolution of SFBT has been that solutions are co-constructed and implemented with little or no attention to the details of the problem. Hence, there will be little or no interest shown in problematic divergent or stability narratives. In fact, solution-focused practitioners would likely take this a step further and suggest that the *stability narrative* is best thought of as an illusion, since human experience is almost never static, and constantly shifting.

For that matter, one common occurrence in solution-focused conversation involves clients coming to realize that they are in fact making small shifts in what they previously considered a "stuck" situation. These small shifts, once detected, then amplified, and brought into the foreground for more appreciative contemplation, can both stimulate hope and become a platform for building further change. These *exceptions to the problem* typically become the focus of intense attention in a solution-focused conversation.

One definition for *exceptions* is *times when the problem could have happened and didn't* (de Shazer, 1991). Solution-focused practitioners are very likely to

Figure 2.2 Convergence is rarely complete.

ask something like, "What did happen when the problem didn't?" Often clients will describe events more consonant with their hopes. Exceptions to the problem are usually synonymous with client narratives shifting, even slightly and briefly, to the convergent form, where what is perceived to have taken place is closer to what the clients would hope for.

Some elaboration is required to bridge the gap between the simplistic graphic representation of the convergent narrative and actual practice of SFBT. Regarding the narrative of "hope", we suggest that clients are better viewed as parts of their various social systems. There may be several *customers for change*: the family, the parent or spouse of the client, a physician, the police, court, probation officer, the school, the child welfare case worker, to name a few possibilities.

"Hopes" may also be construed from the referral by an agency such as the emergency psychiatric unit, victim services, or school. Third-party customers initially included in the composite hopes are those who interact with and have an effect on the client. Accordingly, we embrace the collective, amalgamated hope for change shared to some degree not only by the client who is present, but also others in the client's social context.

As the solution-focused conversation proceeds, it is common for the distinction between first- and third-party hopes to become somewhat blurred with an eventual drift toward more first-party customership, adopting more personal ownership of the hopes for what will be different and better as a result of therapy. An example of this is Joel's client who was admitted to an inpatient psychiatric hospital:

JOEL: So, what are you hoping will be better from being here?

CLIENT: I don't know. It wasn't my idea.

JOEL: Okay, whose idea was it?

CLIENT: My mother. She said I was getting out of control.

JOEL: So, what would she need to see that will tell her that you are in control and it's all right for you to come home?

CLIENT: I don't know. [A pause while **JOEL** waits.] I guess she would hear something from the staff.

JOEL: Of course. What do you think the staff would be saying that would tell her that it's time for you to go home?

CLIENT: I guess that I was more in control.

JOEL: Hmm, how would they know that?

CLIENT: I would be following the rules and going to groups and the program.

JOEL: And when you got home, what would be going on that would tell her, and maybe you as well, that things are better, and you probably will never have to be to a place like this again?

CLIENT: I probably would be listening to her more and helping around the house. I suppose I would also start thinking about the future.

JOEL: Great! What would you be thinking about the future?

CLIENT: I suppose registering for college and deciding what I want to do in life.

(Simon & Nelson, 2007, pp. 97–98)

Clients may present with some persistent condition such as chronic pain, a terminal medical condition, a traumatic childhood, schizophrenia, or other conditions that may be unlikely to dissolve. Of course, they might understandably wish that the unfortunate condition would disappear altogether, but this is not a useful construction of hope for solution-focused therapy. A more useful question is: What does the person hope to do more of *under these admittedly difficult circumstances* – how do we co-construct with the client a practical and possible hope?

"Actions" refer equally to behaviors already performed by the person in the past as well as to actions that may be imagined in the future. SFBT makes elegant use of intentionally blurring the supposed boundaries between the past, present, and future when it comes to constructing solutions. The magnitude of actions also receives unique treatment in SFBT. The tiniest departures from the problem in the direction of possible solutions are given major significance in the conversation. When clients are able to identify small actions that have resulted in exceptions to the problem, they are identifying partial solutions that have already happened.

The "narrative" may partly be expressed overtly in a single therapeutic meeting. It may also be partly thought but not said. It may be thought or spoken in between therapeutic sessions, gradually growing over time. The shifting details of the narrative in the retelling are somewhat similar to the old party game where a story is passed from one person to another along a line.

However, instead of the story deteriorating into the absurd at the party, in therapy the client's accounts grow in richness, relevance, meaningfulness, and wellness. How does the person speak of who they are as they grapple with their challenge? How do we language our experience? Fostering useful shifts in the languaging of our experience is a major part of the business of SFBT.

"Moving" hopes toward actions and vice versa refers both to contexts within the therapeutic conversation, and those outside of the therapy, in daily living. Asking clients to describe hopes being realized in details of actual or plausible events shifts the narrative in a potentially convergent direction. Outside of therapy, doing actions more consistent with the hopes and shifting hopes in the direction of more feasible actions also exemplifies convergence.

At this juncture, it may be useful to remind ourselves that the fabric of solution-focused conversations is the *co-construction of useful difference.* Rather than thinking of some "real goal" that awaits discovery and naming by a professional, we begin with nothing, in a sense, and through sharing language we help clients to construct goals and transform them into possibilities.

Since we know we are developing these ideas in the moment, we embrace the ideas tentatively, allowing the meanings to shift a bit throughout the conversation and in the clients' lives outside the therapist's office. After all, most of the change experienced by clients occurs outside the therapy room.

What Do We Mean by Co-construction?

DeJong et al (2013) summarize Bavelas et al. (2000, p. 18) as follows:

> Bavelas, McGee, Phillips, and Routledge (2000) proposed that the wide range of views about therapeutic communication can be divided into two paradigms. One common view assumes, more or less explicitly, that communication is simply transportation of knowledge, thoughts, and emotions from the mind of one individual to the mind of another. A more recent, contrasting view is that communication is a process of co-construction in which client and therapist collaboratively contribute in different ways to continually evolving versions of the client's history, situation, problems, and solutions.

Clients seek out therapists because they have come to believe that their problems of thought, feeling, behavior and relationship are constant and unsolvable. Most have tried thinking about and discussing those problems without relief. They turn to therapists in the hope that the therapist will help them find a way out of the problem maze.

A long history of psychotherapy seems to suggest that important personal change needs to be approached somewhat indirectly. Otherwise, we would simply ask clients what the trouble is, tell them what to do about it and say goodbye. This improbable scenario is portrayed comically by the well-known comedian Bob Newhart (2023). In the skit, he listens to the client describe in anguished detail the myriad problems she is having and then, at some point, yells at her to "stop it!" Anyone who has spent more than a few weeks in counselling or therapy has learned that this approach doesn't work very well.

The SFBT alternative for assisting clients to make changes is the *co-construction of difference* through conversation. How this is done is the subject of this book, with a special emphasis on the moment-to-moment utterances exchanged between clients and therapists. It is in taking turns to speak that we find opportunities to co-construct difference. DeJong et al. (2013) demonstrate how co-construction can be made visible using microanalysis. They identify four key aspects of co-construction:

> The primary thesis of this article is that the microanalysis of video-recorded therapy sessions can render observable the details of how psychotherapists contribute to co-construction in any therapy session. Moreover, there is basic research on the microanalysis of face-to-face dialogue that applies directly

to the understanding of co-construction in therapeutic dialogues. We demonstrate these proposals with an overview of the recent and growing body of empirical research on microanalysis of psychotherapy sessions. A detailed example from a therapy session illustrates four key aspects of co-construction: grounding between therapist and client(s), therapist's questions, therapist's formulations, and therapist's lexical choices.

(DeJong et al., 2013, p. 17)

One perspective is that our conversation serves to build a *vision of the future* where the trouble moves to the background and preferred experiences move into the foreground. In this way, the practice of SFBT relies on our assumption, affirmed by years of experience, that when clients are able to develop a compelling vision of what they want to be different, they bring their own resources to bear on moving in that direction.

We also speak of this in terms of building converging narratives. Therapists rely heavily on clients' verbal accounts of their troubles, hopes and activities to know the "realities" of their living. We may or may not observe the problem or solution actually occurring within a therapy session. Clients generally begin therapy with a belief that their problems are "real". SFB therapists' responses are based partly on an assumption that, as much as clients are convinced the problem is immutable, there will be *exceptions to the problem* that open the door to different perceptions and alternative "realities". By selective listening, questioning, and affirming of client narratives of their hopes and their actions, we co-create conditions with them to do more of what they hope for. We foster these solutions by inviting clients to think and speak differently about both their visions of a more satisfying future and their day-to-day actions. We create conversational conditions for clients to shift their talk of hopes in ways that make change more probable. We invite clients to shift their accounts of their actions, thoughts, and feelings to select those that orient toward their hopes. DeJong et al. (2013, p. 18) state:

In the 1950s and 1960s, an emerging postmodern movement began seriously calling into question the possibility of understanding essential truths about reality through positivist science and rational philosophy. The postmodern alternative suggested that what is true and real is context – and language-specific, that is, negotiated and arrived at through social interactions (Berger & Luckman, 1966; Garfinkel, 1967; Lyotard, 1984; Wittgenstein, 1958). These ideas have influenced many fields, including psychotherapy, where two streams of postmodern scholarship have contributed to new understandings. One of these came from developments in the philosophy of language, often traced to the work of Wittgenstein (1958), who argued that a proper understanding of how language functions is key to understanding how the meanings held by individuals and larger social groupings develop and change.

Words do not gain their meaning simply because they give an accurate picture or representation of objective reality, analogous to a high-quality photograph. Instead, words acquire their meaning from the ways in which participants learn them and use them in different social contexts. Once these meanings have been created and shared, participants experience their words as meaningful, real, and correct whereas in Wittgenstein's view their meanings continue to be negotiable and flexible. A second, related stream of scholarship, social constructionism, is a theoretical child of postmodernism. This theory, which cuts across sociology and psychology, maintains that individuals using language are in an ongoing process of negotiating meanings about what is true, important, and real in their lives and settings. Individual and institutional meanings are socially constructed in these interactions.

For practical purposes, we suggest the most obvious beginning of co-construction of difference in SFBT is at the point where therapists ask clients "What are your hopes?" Or, "What is it that you hope will be different and better as a result of our work together?" The therapist's part of the co-constructive moment is to ask the question. The clients' part is to eventually answer in a way that shifts from problems to solutions and preferred futures. This collaboration proceeds through speaking turns throughout the session, progressively *building solutions*. At some points, the SFB therapist contribution will affirm client successes. Clients will usually acknowledge the affirmation and often offer their own details, thereby contributing to the co-constructive process. In these ways, therapists, and clients together co-construct narratives of actionable hopes and hopeful actions building into solutions. Ultimately, this co-construction leads to clients doing something that makes a difference in their lives. This is how therapy heals with words; one cannot separate the saying from the doing. Co-constructive conversations incorporate both talk and action.

We have suggested that most clients arrive at a therapist's office anticipating a conversation about the details of their problem. Solution-focused interviewing transforms the conversation from problems to hopes for change. Through exchange of words, we tentatively settle on language that seems to best capture clients' salient hopes for the time being and near future. Five common shifts in language (Taylor, 2005, p. 28) may accompany the conversational progression from trouble to wellness, the swing from narrative divergence to convergence.

1. What I don't want →What I do want
2. When things go wrong →When things go right
3. Beyond my control →Within my control
4. I'm stuck →I'm getting somewhere
5. More troubles to come →Positive possibilities.

These shifts in language map over to common lines of inquiry frequently observed in solution-focused interviews, as presented in Chapter 3. The language of trouble and complaint shifts to the more generative language of solutions.

Rather than approaching therapy as a task of building a "new" narrative from the ground up, it may be more consistent with solution-focused thinking to imagine that we are tapping into clients' existing capacity to make meaning of their life situations in variable and potentially healthier terms. As we listen to clients speak of what brings them to therapy, we regularly detect elements of their narrative that are more convergent with wellness which we refer to as *exceptions to the problem*. We also ask questions that invite a shift in that direction and then build upon their answers, drawing the converging narratives into the foreground.

Contemplating the connection between solution-focused talks in therapy and more satisfactory experience outside of therapy, a potentially useful pair of orienting questions might be:

1. To what extent is therapy successful in bringing clients' possibilities for convergent narratives into the foreground? And then,
2. To what extent do clients shift their perceptions and actions towards convergence in their daily living beyond the therapy setting?

What is Solution-Focused Brief Therapy?

We have referred earlier to conversations between Harry Korman (personal communication) and Insoo Kim Berg. Berg said, "I don't know what it [SFBT] is but I know it when I see it." This idea seemed to suggest that it may be difficult to say exactly what SFBT is and what it is not, but that there is no mistaking the practice as it is observed in action.[1] This line of thinking that component elements to be included or excluded are not easily specified may also embody a theme that was consistent with the early development of SFBT.

Steve de Shazer (personal communication), in particular, argued against becoming formulaic in the practice of the model. He wanted practitioners to be well grounded in the philosophical underpinnings of the model and then to carefully craft their therapeutic interventions based precisely on what clients say in the moment. In this context, there could conceivably be linguistic options as unlimited as there are unique client situations. He also strongly insisted that the model should be considered to be perpetually under development and resisted any conceptualizations that may limit possibilities for future variations.

Those of us who have been fortunate enough to learn the model from de Shazer and Berg, as well as subsequent generations of practitioners, have a keen awareness that the essence of hosting a solution-focused conversation is not as simplistic as knowing a few specific questions. Much more important than any individual question is the attitude or posture from which the solution-focused therapist operates.

In addition, what solution-focused therapists *don't* do is every bit as important as what they do. For example, the conversation is almost never guided in the direction of trying to figure out the history or cause of the problem. We maintain an acute focus on the co-construction of difference as the work of therapy.

The solution-focused therapist orients almost exclusively toward difference in the direction of client hopes, coupled with a virtual certainty that clients have abilities, successful experiences, and creativity that contain the necessary and sufficient resources for the changes they desire. An effective solution-focused interview discovers and amplifies these resources to the point of achieving shifts in the client's experience that is *good enough*.

At this time in the evolution of SFBT, we think we are more able say what it is. If we press ourselves toward careful observation and precise description, when we *know we are seeing it*, we should be able to apply one of our own common lines of inquiry: How do you know that? We should acknowledge that simply asking one of the well-known questions of SFBT does not, by itself, verify solution-focused practice.

It may be one sign, and for that reason we will engage in a brief review of the hallmark and generic questions commonly utilized in SFBT in Chapter 3. As we do that, we invite the reader to entertain the solution-focused questions with a backdrop of the following considerations and dynamics. That will also help determine whether the interview is solution-focused.

- At choice points in the conversation, does the interviewer choose to explore details of the problem or details of hope and capability?
- As the interviewer listens to the client and then responds, do they elect to remain within the context of the trouble or beyond those terms of reference?
- Does the interviewer attempt to install their own, professional language or do they utilize client language?
- Does the interviewer seem to take the position of an expert about life, problems, and wellness or do they seek to elicit the clients' understanding of hopes and possibilities?
- Does the interviewer suggest remedies or conduct procedures designed to fix the problem or do they elicit existing client competencies and capabilities?
- Does the interviewer predominantly give information and advice or lean more toward creating conditions for clients to advise themselves?
- Does the interviewer confront and challenge clients or do they position themselves in a posture of affirmation and collaboration?

For the most part, the solution-focused interviewer chooses the second option in each of these comparisons.

Evidence Base for the Practice of Solution-Focused Brief Therapy

There is a significant body of evidence demonstrating the effective-ness of SFBT that is extensively covered elsewhere (Franklin et al., 2012; solutionfocusedbrieftherapy.com). We will not endeavor to repeat that extensive literature here. What follows is a brief summary of the evaluation research. One of the earliest publications articulating the brief therapy being developed at the Brief Family Therapy Center in Milwaukee, Wisconsin, eventually to become widely known as Solution-focused Brief Therapy, is de Shazer et al. (1986). This group began collecting practice-based evidence in the earliest years – for example, showing that "our average number of sessions per client has declined from 6 sessions for 1600 cases (1978 through 1983) to fewer than 5 sessions for 500 cases in 1984" (de Shazer et al., 1986, p. 207).

Formal research into the effectiveness of SFBT began to accumulate in earnest in the mid-1990s. Between that time and 2022, some 436 published papers were listed in the EBTA compendium (EBTA website evaluation list) and it is apparent that this list is not exhaustive. In summary of this collection, it is noted that:

[Publications exist] in English and at least 12 other languages. Currently 10 meta-analyses; 7 systematic reviews; 325 relevant outcome studies including 143 randomised controlled trials showing benefit from solution-focused approaches with 92 showing benefit over existing treatments. Of 100 com-parison studies, 71 favour SFBT. Effectiveness data are also available from over 9000 cases with a success rate exceeding 60%: requiring an average of 3–6.5 sessions of therapy time.

(Macdonald, 2022)

The first meta-analysis was published in 2006 (Stams et al., 2006), with nine more to follow in the years up to 2021. Groups compiling these meta-analyses are spread internationally from North America to Europe and Asia, reflecting the broad base of interest and scholarship attending SFBT. The specific settings to which these meta-analyses have been oriented include primary medical care, substance abuse, child and adolescent behavior problems, couple's therapy, people with intellectual disabilities, internalizing disorders, group therapy, parent training, and elementary school settings.

The *SFBT Treatment Manual*, published by the Solution Focused Brief Therapy Association, announces that in the United States:

SFBT has been recognized as an evidence-based practice and appears on the Substance Abuse Mental Health Services Administration's National Registry of Evidence-Based Programs and Practices (www.nrepp.samhsa.gov) and the Office of Juvenile Justice and Delinquency Prevention Model Programs Guide (www.ojjdp.gov/mpg).

(Solution Focused Brief Therapy Association, 2013)

Note

1 Joel recalls Harry Korman visiting the clinic Joel was supervising. Harry watched a few minutes of a session from behind a one-way mirror, turned to the other team members and said, "Yes, this is solution-focused."

3 Tools and Maps for Solution-Focused Brief Therapy

Elements of Solution-Focused Interviewing

The host of a solution-focused interview greets their clients and the problems that they bring to therapy with a unique constellation of listening, questioning, and affirming that serves to perpetually encourage convergence of hopes and actions.

Listening

First and foremost, the solution-focused interviewer is listening for client hopes and abilities or signs of difference in that direction. There are several ways in which this intentionally oriented listening works to focus therapeutic interaction on solutions and wellness.

One elegant example is listening to the problem and hearing the hope:

Mother: It's really frustrating you know. The kids come to me for permission to do something. When I say "no", they go to their dad, and he lets them do it.
Therapist: Sounds like you would like to work together better?

In this example, the therapist hears the complaint, shifts their understanding of what they are hearing in the direction of hope and then checks with the clients for accuracy.

Another example is tuning specifically to client language, and key words and phrases in particular. We define "key words" and "phrases" as the things clients say that lend themselves to solution-building.

Recycling the first example:

Therapist: Sounds like you would like to work together better.
Mother: Well, it would be good to have some consistency.
Therapist: Ahh … yes … consistency.

DOI: 10.4324/9781003396703-4

Figure 3.1 Elements of solution-focused interviewing.

The therapist listens for the specific key words used by the client and shifts their own language to match.

Solution-focused interviewers are also listening acutely for any hints of difference, alert to even the tiniest so-called exceptions to the problem, whether real or imagined.

Client: I wish my kids behaved like my brother's kids.
Client: I'm not nearly as active since I moved to the city.
Client: I went on such a binge; I didn't sober up for a week.

In these examples, which have the quality of complaint, the therapist selects the suggestions of difference: how the brother's kids behave, before moving to the city, and when he did sober up.

Equally important as what solution-focused listeners do attend to is what they don't attend to.

Father: Sometimes we just can't find any common ground. We're both strong people. We can dig in our heels, and it just goes from bad to worse.
Therapist: Sure … so there are some times when you do find a bit more common ground?

In this example, the therapist hears the "sometimes", implying that there may also be times when they do find common ground and mentions that as an observational question. In responding this way, the therapist also overlooks – as in looks beyond – the statements of the problem.

These are some examples of how solution-focused therapists orient their listening. In general, it is this solution-focused listening, coupled with paying close attention to visual cues from clients, that determines what solution-focused interviewers select as *opportunities* for further attention. We will be discussing this in more detail in Chapter 4.

Questioning

Solution-focused questioning acts in tandem with selective listening, compounding the focus on solutions. Questions asked by solution-focused interviewers are as diverse as the number of different clients and different life situations. This is partly due to the fact that we construct questions based on the specific language of clients' recent statements. No two clients speak exactly the same, so the details of questions vary appropriately from one person to the next. We aspire to individually fit with each unique client rather than apply general themes across clients in our question construction. We want to emphasize that solution-focused interviewing is not programmed, but rather dependent upon listening carefully and responding to each of our clients as unique individuals.

However, there are a few solution-focused questions that are used more or less similarly by most solution-focused practitioners. These hallmark questions have proven their worth in many interviews, and have become somewhat specifically formatted to achieve maximum usefulness. We present this particular set of questions partly out of respect for the history and evolution of SFBT. These questions have become well known as representative of SF interviewing.

Most SF interviewers will have used some version of many of these questions in the course of developing their personal skill set. We also want to make very clear that, at this stage of evolution of the model – some 40 years since its conceptualization – there are significant differences in whether, when, and how advanced practitioners will deploy these questions. For example, Joel works to get to the Miracle Question as early as he can in most sessions. Lance may or may not use the question in any given session. On the other hand, when each of us asks the question, we ask it fairly similarly. Back to variations: after clients respond to the Miracle Question, Joel may pursue questioning with his adaptation of the pre-session change question, helping clients to realize that change is already underway. Lance will more often pursue extensive detail questioning, to be discussed later under the section *Lines of Inquiry*. We hope to convey to the reader that both the hallmark questions and the more generic lines of inquiry are utilized differently by veteran practitioners. There is no set formula for which questions to use in which sequence.

Hallmark Questions

Invitation Questions

There are many different ways in which solution-focused brief therapists choose to begin a session. Initially at the Brief Family Therapy Center, sessions were begun by asking clients exceptions questions. Later, they asked the pre-session change question (Weiner-Davis et al. (1987): "Many of our clients tell us that, between the time of their initial call to our clinic and this first meeting, some things have already shifted; what have you noticed about your own situation?" Other solution-focused practitioners asked the client about their "best hopes" for therapy (Ratner et al., 2012)). Others asked, "What needs to happen today so when you leave, you'll think that coming here was worthwhile?" Joel's preferred question is "What do you want to be different and better as a result of our work together?" Lance prefers "What are your hopes for this talk?"

Whatever the therapist's choice, all these questions have one thing in common: they serve to invite the client into a solution-building language-game.[1] Many people come to therapy believing that the process involves exploring and resolving problems. Sometimes that is because they have been in therapy before and many of the various models and theories are problem focused. Even if someone has never been in therapy, there is enough information in the popular media that drives the assumption that the process of therapy is talking about problems.

The first job of the solution-focused therapist is engaging clients in a different conversation and deconstructing the notion that what the therapist and the client are going to do together is co-construct problems. Joel has found it useful to conceive of these initial questions as "invitation questions". Once the client has accepted the "invitation" to a solution-building language-game, the context for the Miracle Question is created.

Miracle Question

Suppose that one night while you're sleeping, a miracle happens and the problems that bring us together to talk today are solved. Since you are sleeping when this miracle occurs, you have no way of knowing that it has happened. How would you start finding out the next day that this miracle has taken place?

The Miracle Question serves three different purposes. First, it deconstructs the traditional assumption that problems and solutions are related. That is, that detailing the problem has a direct linear connection to solving that problem. Second, the Miracle Question allows for greater details of differences, and therefore co-constructs possibilities and expectation of change. And third, it gives greater clarity to the client's goals for therapy.

As we have already suggested, this question works best when it includes the five essential elements shown here. It can be asked early in the session. The initial client response is often a period of silence, best affirmed and supported by the therapist's silence, to provide space for clients to construct answers.

Once clients respond to an earlier question about what they want to be different and better in their lives, the therapist can incorporate that as part of the Miracle Question. For example, in response to what she wants to be better and different, Shelly says, "I would want more good days than bad days." That phrase can now be incorporated into the Miracle Question: "Because of this miracle, you begin to have more good days than bad days ..."

Like the pre-session change question, or hope for change question, the Miracle Question is a reliable way to initiate solution-focused conversation. It typically elicits responses that then become the centerpiece of an extended conversation in the session. An intriguing pattern in responses to the Miracle Question is how clearly un-miraculous the answers usually are. That is, clients seldom give exaggerated or unrealistic answers. Typically, they speak about ordinary events of daily living which easily leads into well-grounded talk of change. The value of the Miracle Question lies to some degree in the actual asking of the question and to a major degree in the direction of inquiry created and then pursued by the therapist in response to clients' answers. The Miracle Question quite reliably brings forth preliminary identification of the difference sought by clients in the form of a name or title. Follow-up inquiry elicits the *details of difference*.

Scaling Question

If 10 on the scale represents [the day after the miracle] and 1 represents the opposite, where would you say you are today?

The scaling question is one of the most versatile solution-focused interviewing tools. It embodies some of the most vital solution-focused principles. For example, it inherently erodes less than useful *either/or* thinking and replaces that perceptual stance with *both/and* thinking. A scale of 1 (or 0)^2 to 10 automatically establishes shades of gray. The problem is not on or off; it is more or less present in greater or lesser degrees. Problems and solutions are not mutually exclusive; they coexist in fluctuating proportions. Even at the problem's strongest and worst times, there will be hints of solution. Even after solutions are growing stronger, it is normal for there to be vestiges of the old problem.

The solution-focused model centers around difference. Scaling questions automatically imply difference. Interviewers construct scaling questions to make extreme end answers less likely. A 1 or 0 stands for the worst the problem has ever been, and 10 stand stands for the day after a miracle. This approach, seemingly coupled with other aspects of human nature, leads to client answers that are typically somewhere mid-range, in between 2 and 9. Any mid-range response, whether it be 3 or 7, inevitably represents difference and opens the door to many productive follow-up questions – for example, "What tells you it is 2 rather than 1?" "How did you get that high?" "How do you keep from slipping lower?" "What will be signs of getting to be a half step higher on the scale?"

Another aspect of scaling question versatility is how it can be utilized for many distinct purposes. At first glance it can serve as a measure of progress: "1 stands for the problem when you first came to therapy and 10 is you are doing well enough to stop therapy for a while."

In tandem with this progress indicator, a confidence scale provides a useful package to begin addressing termination: "1 stands for the changes are fairly new and I'm not sure about keeping them going; 10 stands for I'm fairly confident about keeping the changes going."

When ratings are in the top half of both scales, we may gently suggest that clients frequently start thinking about taking a break from therapy. De Shazer (personal communication) stated that when clients scaled 6 or higher, he was fairly certain that they were beginning to think that things were good enough and they may not need to return.

Scaling questions can be used to highlight and reinforce *exceptions to the problem* once the interview has worked to find the exception and establish its significance to the client: "How would you rate your ability to find common ground in that instance, if one stands for no ability and ten stands for pretty successful?" They can also be used to make "brief" explicit: "Where will you need to be on the scale to think that you've made enough progress and can continue making progress on your own?"

No doubt, the creative reader can easily imagine how scales are also used to rate motivation, effort, determination, appreciation, commitment, and an almost unlimited number of other aspects of human experience that may arise in solution-building conversations.

Scales can also fulfill a goal-setting and motivational function. A nice way to introduce scaling in a training environment is to ask participants to predict on a scale from 1 to 10 how enjoyable their evening will be and then, at the beginning of the following day of the workshop, open a discussion about how successful the evening actually turned out to be and what role was played by their prediction. Participants often indicate that they at least reflected on their number, and some will say they tried to live up to or outdo their prediction.

Joel likes asking trainees to rate their experience on a scale after the first day of training where 10 is that their expectations have been met for the overall training. The follow-up question is what it will take to get closer to that 10 by the end of the next day.

Similarly, the scaling question provides an ideal frame for co-constructing next steps with clients. Novice practitioners sometimes move too quickly to this application, when it should come somewhat later after sufficient focus on client resourcefulness revealed by the rating being as high as it is. Careful use of scaling questions also helps orient clients toward small steps in the right direction: "What would be small signs of one-half step higher on the scale?"

The numbers in and of themselves have no meaning until the client and therapist co-construct meanings. Berg and de Shazer (1993, p. 19) write:

> Scales allow both therapist and client to use the way language works naturally by agreeing upon terms (i.e., numbers) and a concept (a scale where 10 stands

for the goal and zero stands for an absence of progress toward that goal) that is obviously multiple and flexible. Since neither therapist nor client can be absolutely certain what the other means by the use of a particular word or concept, scaling questions allow them to jointly construct a way of talking about things that are hard to describe, including progress toward the client's goal(s).

Relationship Questions

Suppose you were to notice one time that your Mom was tired and cranky from her long day but instead of joining her in irritability, you decide to "keep the peace". What would she notice you doing differently? Once she felt you speaking calmly with a kind voice, how might she respond differently back to you?

DeJong and Berg (2002, p. 47) write:

Relationship questions are used in solution building to invite clients to construct descriptions of interactional events as well as their meanings. People live much of their lives in interaction with others, many of whom are tremendously important to them.

As well as acknowledging the fact of relationality in clients' lives, relationship questions serve well in the task of bringing forth details of difference, since they invite clients to see and hear from the perspective of others. It is also common to notice that clients are sometimes more able to express important ideas relevant to their difficulties and hopes through the imagined voice of others.

Coping Question

With things being as difficult as they have been for you, how have you been making your way through your days?

Some solution-focused therapists find this to be a useful default question when they are having trouble eliciting hopes and abilities from clients in any other way. Typically, clients will have something to say about how they are managing that can then become a kernel for identifying and amplifying capabilities.

For example, in the video, *Coming Through the Ceiling* (de Shazer, 1985), de Shazer asks the client, "So, how do you manage to cope with this day after day after day after day?" In response, she wonders about that herself, finally saying, "So I say to myself 'How can I do this?' And sometimes I begin to feel even a little better."

What's Better Question

Most interviews after the first session begin with some version of the "what's better" question. Many practitioners prefer to use the question in its briefest form. Some elect to soften the question slightly with "What are some better signs lately?" or "Since we last met, when have things gone a little better?" or "What are some small signs of things going in a better direction recently?"

Clients are often able to identify recent better events, which are then explored in detail. Not uncommonly, clients are initially unable to think of something better at the outset of the session but then later in the interview do recognize and mention differences in the desired direction. Occasionally, clients will insist that nothing is better, or things are worse, in which case we default to asking about their hopes for this session.

What Else Question

The "focused" element of the title SFBT is very meaningful. Persistent pursuit of details of clients' successful experiences is one of the defining features of solution-focused interviewing. The opening questions are best thought of as initiating a prolonged conversation rather than aimed at eliciting a single answer. Once a client and therapist tap into a significant difference – for example, by engaging the Miracle Question – a sort of conversational matrix often unfolds. Client language identifies a difference. The therapist may choose to mine that idea "vertically" for extensive details and then when the mining has been sufficiently productive, turn to more "horizontal" inquiry: "*What else would be different* the day after the miracle?" When new difference is named, more "vertical" mining is pursued, and so on.

A colleague of ours in the solution-focused community taught a particularly useful version of what else questioning. Yvonne Dolan [personal communication] called it the "miracle day". Beginning with a more or less standard Miracle Question, she would note the first thing that would be different, inquire into the details of that idea, and afterwards ask, "Then what?" Repeating this pattern, Dolan and the client progressively describe a miracle day made up of one specific event after another.

Initiative Question

Of the things that have come up in our talk today, which one stands out to you as something you might consider taking initiative on?

Drawn from the interventive interviewing framework of Karl Tomm (personal communication; Hornstrup et al., 2009), initiative questioning has been integrated with ease into solution-focused conversation. Experience shows it is usually warmly received by clients, both young and old. The question properly belongs in the template category. Its use is not limited to any particular problem or solution context. The question is relevant to the interface between conversation in therapy and client actions in daily living. Ongoing conversations in the SFBT community raise the idea of "homework" or "task". It appears there has been a drift away from assigning detailed behavioral tasks toward more observational suggestions. Most effective solution-focused interviews can co-construct one or more exceptions, which can then become the substance of the session-ending suggestion to *watch for further occurrences*. Initiative questioning, among other benefits, invites clients to be active in either choosing from possibilities already in view or coming up with something original to focus on beyond the session.

As a template, the basic initiative question format can be adapted in numerous ways:

- *Of the things that have come up in our talk today, or previous conversations, or things you have been thinking about on your own ...*
- In family sessions in particular ... *please feel free to say your idea out loud or say it quietly to yourself.*
- As an opening to a live client consultation session ... *of the ideas that you and your therapist have been working on, which ones have you tried to put into action (whether or not they worked as you hoped they would). Even if you haven't actually taken the step yet what's something you've thought about that might be worth trying to do a bit differently?*

Hopefully, this section has provided the reader with a reasonable overview of the kinds of hallmark questions an observer is likely to find cropping up in a solution-focused interview. Of course, each interview is unique and so would be the selection of questions used. One interview may employ many, a few, or none of these specific questions. These hallmark questions may be used in one interview after another, with some – such as the Miracle Question – being quite specifically formatted.

It is important to note that all these questions are templates into which the unique experience of each client is entered. That is, by themselves the questions do not specify certain areas of functioning or life skills. Each of the hallmark questions, in one way or another, orients generically toward *difference in the desired direction*. The details of client answers make the conversation specific to their lives, troubles, and hopes. The authors want to emphasize this in regard to the template concept in order to preclude a danger that, rather than listening to and responding to the client, the questions become formulaic and robotic.

We have suggested that any given solution-focused interview may exhibit many or few of these hallmark questions, depending on client situations and the preferences of the interviewer, as well as many other variables. Subsuming the specific hallmark questions, there are identifiable *lines of inquiry* that the observer will be able to notice in most solution-focused interviews, even though appearances may vary with individual practitioners.

Generic Lines of Inquiry

Several lines of inquiry appear routinely in solution-focused interviews, with questions differing slightly from practitioner to practitioner and from client to client. Within these lines of inquiry are similarities of form and function that unite the questions in a somewhat distinct category or family. The first of these lines of inquiry has to do with getting the interview started along the path of solutions, referred to earlier as *invitation questions*, which typically elicit a general title for the change desired by the client. We might say that when the client begins to generate language of hopes for difference, they have accepted the *invitation into a solution-focused language-game* – at least for the moment.

Titles Questioning: Name the Hope

Beyond the customary meeting-and-greeting exchanges, the first agenda of the solution-focused interview is to immediately start situating the conversation in the language of hopes and solutions. These opening questions usually elicit somewhat general language supplying names or titles for hopes of change.

Most long-standing solution-focused practitioners find that their preferences and habits for starting sessions have evolved over their years. One of the early versions that seemed to be used at BFTC was along the lines of, "What would have to happen, after you left today, for you to say the meeting had been useful?" Some of us became attracted to "What are your hopes for this session?", a question pioneered by the folks at BRIEF in London, England. "What are you hoping will be different after we meet?" is another preference of some.

Another question that seems to have drifted into disuse but is still worth mentioning for academic reasons, for the expectation value it may hold, is, "What would need to happen for you to say you don't need to come back?" It must be noted as well, after these examples of questions carefully constructed to orient quickly toward solutions, that by way of contrast we have an unpublished recording of Steve de Shazer (personal communication) asking a client, "So … what brings you … here … today?" This form of an opening question would likely not be too different from what practitioners of other models would use and might be predicted to elicit more of a problem focus. In Steve's hands, of course, the interview proceeded from this question into a compelling example of focusing on solutions.

Hopefully, the reader might already have recognized that, although it might prove unnecessarily peculiar in actual practice, asking the Miracle Question as an opening could also achieve the same results of beginning a fruitful inquiry into hopes. In this sense, this hallmark question may be considered to be of the same family, to get started with focusing on solutions by eliciting hopes.

In practice, the solution-focused interviewer will often use many questions of the same family as layers of inquiry. This can be a vivid example of what it means to be solution-*focused*. The solution-focused interviewer is so strongly committed to focus intently on client hopes that they usually persist at this level of inquiry until there emerges a successful "languaging" or co-construction of the client's most salient hopes.

Therapist: What are your hopes for this talk … today?

Client: Well, I've just been so depressed lately. I don't know what to do with myself.

Therapist: Hmmm. Sounds difficult … so … what would have to happen sometime after today's talk that would tell it had been a good talk?

Client: I don't know … I've tried everything … nothing seems to help.

Therapist: Okay … so what were you hoping would be a little bit different after we met?

Client: I'm not sure if anything can be done.

Therapist: Um-hmm. So, is it okay if I ask you a strange question?

Client: I guess.

Therapist: I'd like you to suppose that one of these nights, while you are sleeping, a miracle happens and the trouble that brought us together, today, to talk is solved. Since you are asleep when the miracle happens, you don't know that it happens. How would you start finding out in the morning that the miracle had occurred?

Client: Well, maybe I'd feel like getting up for a change …

A key to this manner of interviewing is to be gentle while remaining persistent, or else the client might experience this less as an interview and more as an interrogation. This is easily accomplished by the skilled practitioner. The layered questions, even though they are of the same family, differ enough linguistically that the client can experience each question uniquely, especially if the interviewer delivers that question with novelty, curiosity, and freshness. In most instances, this gentle persistence is quite successful in shifting the conversation so that the client begins to speak of hopes. Following are some additional examples of common initial client responses along with follow-up responses that frequently prove useful in situating the conversation in hope.

Clients may initially decline the invitation to speak of their presence in the meeting in terms of hopes.

Therapist: What are your hopes for this talk?

Client: I never really gave it much thought …

Therapist: Okay …well, now's the time.

It is not uncommon for clients to attribute their attendance to some other party or parties who have recommended therapy.

Therapist: What are your hopes for this talk?
Client: It was suggested to me that I should see a psychologist ...
Therapist: What do they [those suggesting] hope for?

One of the most common initial responses to a hope question is to describe the problem that has prompted engagement in therapy.

Therapist: What are your hopes for this talk?
Client: I've been depressed ...
Therapist: Um-hmm ... so how would you know when our talk did some good?

Another common response is to describe the hope in terms of a process that the client hopes will unfold in therapy.

Therapist: What are your hopes for this talk?
Client: I just need someone to talk to ...
Therapist: Suppose that were to happen, what difference might it make?

It would be neither possible nor desirable to anticipate and categorize all possible client responses to hope questions. It is much more important to pay close attention to what clients actually do say in the moment and then construct useful responses to their responses. The above examples are simply intended to demonstrate the clarity and tenacity with which the solution-focused interviewer issues invitations to focus the therapeutic conversation on hopes.

Events Questioning: The Details of Difference

Solution-focused interviewing is concerned primarily with developing difference in the direction of client hopes. A recurring dynamic in the development of difference is detecting small differences and building upon them. One of the most powerful means of building solutions is focused inquiry into the details of difference. This is achieved in a few different ways.

We gave an example earlier of Yvonne Dolan's miracle day. Repeatedly asking "Then what?", she and the client describe a more desirable state of affairs, the day after a miracle, in terms of a plausible sequence of specific, ordinary events of daily living. This is another opportunity to refer to matrix questioning. When the client says they'll "take the time to sit down and have breakfast for a change", the interviewer chooses between horizontal navigation with a question like, "Then what – what will you do after breakfast?" and a more vertical orientation such as, "What will you have for breakfast?" or "How will that make a difference for you?", pausing to elicit more and more specific observable detail of the experience before moving on to another named event.

Another approach to the building of detail is the question "How would you know?"

Therapist: You said one thing that would be different the day after the miracle is you would be more patient.
Client: Ya.
Therapist: How would you catch on that you were more patient?
Client: Oh ... well there are these three cows at work that are really slow. It takes them twice as long to get out of their stalls after milking. It's really frustrating ... I get mad at them ...
Therapist: And so ... the day after a miracle ...?
Client: Oh ... well ... I would just say to myself "it's okay", go with the flow, maybe give them a pat on the neck.

Hopefully the reader can detect the difference between a more general title, "patient", and a description of behaviors such as "giving them a pat on the neck". This line of inquiry moves the narrative from general terms, possibly referring to internal states, to the terms of events in which outward actions will be readily observable.

A variation of "How would you know?" questioning is "How would others notice?" Oddly enough, clients are sometimes more able to answer our questions using the observations and voice of others.

Therapist: How would your co-workers in the barns notice you were more patient?
Client: Ya ... well I'm always griping about those cattle ... so day after a miracle, maybe I wouldn't complain so much.
Therapist: Ok ... and in place of complaining ...?
Client: I might ask one of them what they did over the weekend.
Therapist: Who is someone you are more likely to ask that?
Client: I guess ... John.

The reader might notice that in the above examples, the interviewer employs a bias toward the details of what would happen instead of what would not happen.

Following nicely from "What would others notice?" is the interactional question, "How would they react differently to you ...?"

Therapist: So ... when you asked them about their weekend ... how might they react differently?
Client: You know, we might enjoy talking more ...
Therapist: And when you and your mates are enjoying talking more ...?

Client: Well, we might do more of it … learn something new about the other person …

Hopefully the reader will notice that detail questioning follows a theme of eliciting a *description of events*, which can then be detailed more and more specifically. It doesn't matter much whether the events are real or not, or whether they have actually been experienced or are imagined. What matters more is that they are at least plausible, possibly realizable and the interviewer focuses on details as though the events were real. A subtlety of some solution-focused interviewing is a blurring of distinctions between verb forms and qualifiers:

Therapist: Now you said you could imagine giving the cows a pat on the neck …
Client: Ya …
Therapist: How do they respond to you differently when you do that?

In this example, the therapist chooses not to strictly keep the conversation in the realm of fantasy by saying, "So … imagining you pat them on the neck, how do you think they might respond differently?" The therapist's language drifts subtly in the direction of realism: "How *do* they respond to you differently when you *do* that?" Other examples of transforming verbs are "would/will" and "could/can".

Detail questioning can proceed productively to surprising depths, until the interviewer runs out of curious questions or until clients show they are tiring of the topic. There are several advantages that accrue from eliciting the details of change:

- Sticking with the difference the client has named by inquiring into minute detail *moves the conversation* in the direction of actions or doings. See the discussion on *convergent narratives* in Chapter 2.
- For those who still find the notion of a goal useful, there is a long history of making goals more attainable by identifying specific details of who, what, when, where, and how.
- Perhaps the most significant result of effective detail questioning is that the process of both pausing and dwelling on a particular point in clients' experience, as well as the actual content of their answers, has the potential to make that experience seem more real, to bring it more into the foreground. Increasing the perceived realism raises the likelihood that clients will recognize some of the expressed details in their own actions in the days following the therapy session. Experienced solution-focused interviewers will recognize a common experience that we may refer to as constructive confusion, where clients seemingly lose track of their timeframe, and begin to speak of some hoped-for events in terms suggesting they have actually happened. This is one of the most client-centered ways of surfacing so-called *exceptions to the problem*. As we persist in asking about the details, clients inevitably begin

to recognize that some of what they hoped for is already happening some of the time. It is up to the solution-focused interviewer to listen carefully for exceptions and then amplify them.

- There is also the possibility that clients may actually be making suggestions to themselves that they may remind themselves of at some timely point in the future. The person who said he might "give them a pat on the neck" may not have ever done such a thing with these three cows that have been so frustrating to him. It may have been a hypothetical invention for him to say that in the conversation. Later, at the barn, he may remember his words and find himself actually doing what he had really only suggested as an example. One possible understanding of this scenario is that a person would somehow cultivate more "patience" prior to getting to the barn and then, because of increased patience, would behave in this new way. Another possible understanding could be that the client finds that they are reflecting on their therapy session, remembers saying "give them a pat on the neck", does that, and finds that they are doing some other things they consider more "patient". This is an example of a potentially useful and creative confusion about cause and effect that would likely intrigue the solution-focused practitioner.

There are two subsets of detail questioning that are worthy of separate attention: *agency questioning* and *movement questioning*.

Agency Questioning: How Do You Do That?

Lance was behind the mirror at BFTC while another trainee interviewed a man who had been kidnapped by thugs at a banking machine, held captive in a basement, and taken each day to withdraw the maximum allowable from his account. He reported nightmares of these events that were so intense he would bolt upright in bed, understandably terrified, until he was able to realize he was no longer in captivity. Behind the mirror, Berg blurted out, "How does he DO that?!" as observing team members often do when they intuit a potentially useful next question.

Berg was responding to the man's language: "realize he was no longer in captivity". As the interview continued, the man explained that eventually he looked across his bed, saw his wife, realized he was with someone who cared for him, glanced around his room at familiar objects, heard the reassuring sounds of the furnace in his home, and thereby brought himself from the past into the present.

Following Berg's example, the solution-focused interviewer has this question ready at all times: "How do you do that?" Consistent with a theme mentioned earlier, the purpose of the question in not so much to elicit a singular answer as it is to start an extended conversation in order to build a narrative. On occasion, however, a poignant, simplistic and useful answer is the result. A client who was trying to stop herself from a years-long habit of shoplifting mentioned that, by the way, she hadn't stolen anything "since last June when she went to court". The author asked her how she did that. She thought for a long time, smiled, and then quietly said, "I stopped carrying big purses". She and the author had a good chuckle about the tiny purse she had with her in the session that day.

It is the authors' experience that clients may not always be naturally inclined to think and speak of their part in successful events. Particularly in the context of troubles of living that bring people to therapy, they are more likely – at least initially – to perceive the circumstances as beyond their control. A key part of building solutions can be restoring and affirming the sense of personal agency. The therapist opens space for this consideration and may employ several versions of agency questions.

Therapist: So … what's better … with you … lately?
Client: Well … I guess my mood is a little bit better.
Therapist: How did you do that?
Client: I didn't really do anything … I went to the doctor and he put me on antidepressants.
Therapist: How did you know to get that help?
Client: My wife … really … she made the appointment.
Therapist: How did you know to go along with your wife?
Client: Well … I guess she was just thinking about what's best for me.
Therapist: So, you think you should try to do what's best for you when you can?
Client: Ya …
Therapist: What are some things you are doing differently now that the pills are helping?
Client: Well … I'm getting back to exercise … and I joined the guys for pick-up hockey.

While agency questions can be useful, they don't necessarily cover all possibilities for change. Such questions only look at changes that happen because of what clients do or might do. Recall from Chapter 2 that one of the corollaries from the change assumption is that change comes from many different directions. Vision of change questions take this into account. By asking clients how a change will make a difference to them and others in their lives, we help them to co-construct a vision of the difference. We trust that the client, holding that vision, will more likely than not do something different that will make a difference.

Movement Questioning: What Difference Does That Make?

There are different ways to initiate inquiry into benefits arising out of small successes or exceptions to the problem, movement in the direction of hopes. The core question is: What difference does that difference make? Clients are asked something such as, "What good things happen as a result of that?" The author's personal choice these days is, "What's the good of that?" (Asked from an affirmative posture) or "What good comes of that?"

Therapist: So ... what's better with your family lately?
Mother: Well ... the first week in September all three boys attended school.
Father: And lately we've been having supper together again.
Therapist (after extended agency questioning): What's the good of getting together for supper?
Father: Well, we seem to drift apart with everybody doing their own thing or eating in their rooms.
Therapist: Right ... so what good comes of getting together at the supper table?
Mother: Well ... we feel like a family again ... a family that does things together ... who care about each other ... we find out what everybody's doing ...

Another way of understanding and utilizing movement questioning lies in the language of importance and motivation. When we initiate conversation about what good comes of taking small steps in a new direction, we create space to build ideas around why it would be worthwhile to do more of that. What serial differences are perceived to be set in motion by the first small changes? What is the value of that?

Common Client Language and Useful Therapist Responses

We have already mentioned that the first order of business in a solution-focused interview is to invite clients to situate the conversation in the language of hopes for difference. It is not uncommon for clients to launch into a description of their troubles in response to initial hope questions. Some examples have been provided for useful follow-up questions to help clients shift their preliminary answers into narratives that refer more to hopes for difference. In terms of interviewing for the purpose of shifting, converging narratives, these earliest exchanges reveal the process to be underway. It is most common if not nearly universal for clients to come to the first session expecting to talk about their problems. They may or may not describe problems before the therapist asks a hope question. Either way, the therapeutic questions create opportunities for clients to move their initial thoughts and narratives from problems to solutions and then from less to more compelling solution talk, with higher potential to converge with actions.

Here are a few patterns of language that occur frequently enough in the process of co-constructing hopes to deserve mention. These common patterns of speaking are paired with examples of follow-up questions that invite clients to further *situate the conversation in hope* and then *shift their languaging of hope* into a more actionable form. Successful navigation of these early exchanges facilitates the beginning of narrative convergence in the immediate session, and then hopefully in clients' experiences beyond the session.

Hear Many, Think One

Clients may come to therapy perceiving themselves to be struggling with several problems at once. Solution-building potential is improved through selecting one area of living – presumably the most salient for the client in the moment – upon which co-construction of hope may begin. One working assumption is that accomplishing change in one area of the client system has the potential to ripple into other areas in a domino effect. In any case, once one area of trouble is addressed effectively, nothing prevents a future second focus of therapeutic attention. See Figure 3.2.

Hear Big, Think Small

We all naturally prefer change to be complete and fast when we have an area of trouble. Supposing that satisfactory change may be down the road, what will be some small signs that beginning steps are taken? Another working assumption is that some troubles may just pass, and more persistent difficulties are best overcome by taking small steps in the right direction that can grow into larger changes. See Figure 3.3.

Figure 3.2 Hear many, think one.

Figure 3.3 Hear big, think small.

Hear Stop, Think Start

Understandably, our first instinct in response to a troublesome experience or pattern in life, such as emotional disturbance or relationship conflict, is that we want it to stop. A useful shift in this initially expressed hope is to what will be happening in place of the problem. Hoping for something to happen is usually more actionable and productive than hoping for something to end. A well-chosen difference with the capacity to replace or crowd out the initial problem is the essence of solution-building. See Figure 3.4.

Hear Internal, Think Interactional

When clients begin to articulate hope for internal change in sensation, cognition, perception, or emotion, we ask how that difference will show externally in interaction. Observable difference is more useful for clients and those around them to identify and track change than guessing about internal states or relying on an individual's attempt to convey elusive private experience. See Figure 3.5.

Hear Others, Think Self

Clients may understand their troubles to be caused by others and then, not surprisingly, construe their earliest hopes in terms of someone else making changes first. Our systemic assumptions say that change in any part of a system, such

Figure 3.4 Hear Stop, Think Start.

Figure 3.5 Hear internal, think about interactional.

as a family, will likely provoke changes in other parts of the system. In this regard, the solution-focused therapist is likely to look beyond traditional notions of cause and effect in favor of an opportunity to build a sense of personal agency with clients. Suppose they shift their behavior in that way, how will you respond differently? See Figure 3.6.

Figure 3.6 Hear others, think self.

Hear General, Think Specific

Early in therapeutic conversations clients may need time to talk their way into describing their troubles and translating into hopes. General language such as *happier, more peaceful, more confident, facing loss* and *grieving*, are common points of departure that are general in nature. Building on the desirable narrative shifts described above, we reflexively request detailed description of specific observable events – equivalent to the journalist's "who", "what", "when", and "where".

As we have said, it would be neither possible nor desirable to anticipate and categorize all possible client responses to hope questions. It is much more important to pay close attention to what clients actually do say in the moment and then construct useful responses to their responses. The above examples are simply intended to demonstrate the clarity and tenacity with which the solution-focused interviewer issues invitations to focus the therapeutic conversation on the language of hope and actions.

Navigating Solution-Focused Conversations: Thumbnail Maps

Given these lines of enquiry typical of solution-focused interviewing, with both hallmark and generic questions, how do interviewers decide what to do and when? We have described solution focusing interviewing in terms of conversational tools. From a position of overview, how do interviewers know which tool to use and when? How do they find their way? What do we do first? What

Figure 3.7 Hear general, think specific

are logical or productive sequences? Over the years, different groups have developed their version of maps or guidelines to follow in the navigation of solution-focused conversation.

The TEAM Map

The TEAM map is depicted in the following diagram. The center of all inquiry is facilitation of convergence between clients' hopes and what they actually do. The core organizing principle is developing narratives of hope and actions partly by accessing four different categories of inquiry or angles from which change may be addressed:

- Titles or names for the hopes.
- Events – the kind of specific detail that arises in description of *occurrences.*
- Agency – what clients do to contribute to difference.
- Movement – the perception of small successes leading to further changes.

There may be a natural linearity to the flow of questioning in an interview. Once the hope has initially been languaged in the form of a title, it is usually productive to inquire about details of events that would involve that hope being realized. If clients do not automatically mention their own agency, then it is useful to ask about that. Working through conversation about agency can

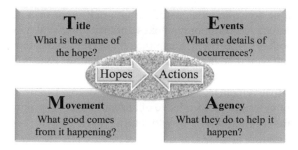

Figure 3.8 Lines of inquiry: the TEAM map.

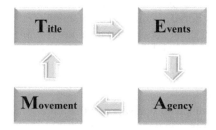

Figure 3.9 Possible flow of inquiry.

naturally lead into identifying benefits or movement in the right direction. The combined inquiry into agency and movement is roughly equivalent to what some refer to as capacity-building: developing clients' perception of their ability to make a difference in their own lives.

However, each conversation is unique and may or may not follow a linear sequence. For example, when clients appear to be holding firmly to a perception that "I have tried everything and nothing works," it may be advisable to postpone agency questioning until later in the conversation, moving from detail or event questioning to explore movement or benefits, building upon their vision of change. The topography of the map represents four lines of inquiry that make strong contributions to solution-building, that are worth including in the interview as far as possible and to suggest natural turning points for the interviewer to consider.

A fifth line of inquiry that also contributes to solution-building is, "What's next?" The co-construction of possibilities for next steps may be initiated in several ways. One of the more obvious is the scaling question. Once clients have indicated where they are on the scale right now, and the interviewer has fully explored the resourcefulness revealed in their progress so far, it is common to ask what might be some small signs of being a half point or a point higher on the scale. This exchange commonly evokes another somewhat general reference to a change, another "Title", which can then be usefully explored in the TEAM framework. What would be the details of that happening (Events)? What do you imagine yourself doing to help that happen (Agency)? What good things might result from that (Movement)?

A young pilot in training took a leave of absence from the program because of "nerves" and was trying to find a way to return.

Therapist: What would be small signs of a half point higher on the scale of being ready to resume training?
Client: Well ... if I started to become interested in flying again ...
Therapist: What might be signs of that happening? How would you know?
Client: I'm getting bored at home. I need something to do. I really wanted to fly planes. I think about what the class is doing these days.
Therapist: Just supposing you did start to regain interest, what might be the first small step you might find yourself taking?
Client: Well ... if I went to the hangar ... just to visit ... hang out ... say hello to folks.
Therapist: What difference do you suppose that might make?
Client: Well ... I miss the people ... and I could see how I felt being closer to the action again ... without having to fly ...

The development of SFBT began when de Shazer asked the question, "What do therapists and clients do together that is helpful to the client" (see Chapter 2). One of the author's clients reported back that "I really like that Miracle Question of yours". The author didn't bother to correct him about not being the actual owner of that question. Evidently it was useful to him to simply recall the miracle conversation from time to time as a reminder of what he and his wife were trying to accomplish in their relationship.

It is the authors' experience from a number of years of practicing SFBT that the transitions represented in the TEAM framework often lead to noticeable shifts in client behaviors in interviews. When inquiry moves conversation from a more general title of change to highly specific details, the tone of talk typically becomes more personalized and animated. This drift into seemingly more hopefulness continues to grow as details of agency, effectiveness or movement, and next steps are drawn into the conversation.

It may be reasonable to suggest that *converging narratives* stimulate hopefulness. Perhaps a more realistic dynamic might be one of reciprocal enhancement (Taylor & Fiske, 2005). The more someone finds their hopes converging with their actions, the more hopeful they become; the more hopeful they become, the more inclined they are to take actions toward wellness.

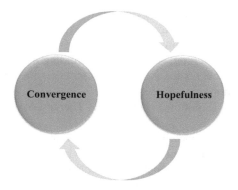

Figure 3.10 Convergence hopefulness reciprocity.

EARS

EARS is another acronym that some have found to be useful guide for solution-focused interviewing:

- E = elicit difference
- A = amplify the difference
- R = reinforce the difference
- S = start again to elicit another difference

Listen Select Build (LSB)

A third map or schema for guiding the solution-focused interview, LSB, has been clarified and articulated by DeJong and Berg (2013). The SFBT manual summarizes it in this way:

> The signature questions and responses by therapists in solution-focused interviews are intended to initiate a co-constructive process which De Jong and Berg (2013), following the lead of de Shazer (1991; 1994; de Shazer et al., 2007), called listen, select, and build.
>
> In this process, the SFBT therapist listens for and selects out the words and phrases from the client's language that are indications (initially, often only small hints) of some aspect of a solution, such as articulating what is important to the client, what he or she might want, related successes (e.g. exceptions), or client skills and resources. Once having made the selection, the therapist then composes a next question or other response (e.g., a paraphrase or summary) that connects to the language used by the client and invites the client to

build toward a clearer and more detailed version of some aspect of a solution. As the client responds from his or her own frame of reference, the therapist continues to listen, select, and compose the next solution-focused question or response, one that is built on what the client has said. It is through this continuing process of listening, selecting, and building on the client's language that therapists and clients together co-construct new meanings and new possibilities for solutions.

(Solution-Focused Brief Therapy Association, 2013, p. 5)

There is substantial resonance between the LSB framework and that of opportunities. Literally speaking, one listens and watches for opportunities, or hints of solutions around which to construct a therapeutic response. What we have entitled *solution-focused listening* and *listening with solution-building ears* undoubtedly equates with the "listen" in LSB.

The "select" component of LSB maps over to our opportunities analysis, which perhaps renders the selection process somewhat more explicit. In an opportunities analysis, we harvest and record multiple opportunities contained in one utterance, rendering the terrain from which "selections" are made. In the opportunities analysis, we generate numerous possible interventive constructions for each opportunity, further elaborating the field from which the eventual selection is made. Selecting in the opportunities framework amounts to choosing a preferred pairing of opportunity and intervention.

The rationale section in an opportunities analysis attempts to make explicit some of the criteria upon which the selection is made. We would suggest that there is room for more research, possibly using a detailed analysis of "rationales" to elaborate in more detail the criteria upon which solution-focused practitioners base their opportunity/intervention pairings.

As the above quote from the SFBT manual suggests, one further intersection with other ideas quoted earlier is that of "preserve, omit, preserve with addition" schema for therapist response construction. In all likelihood, the opportunity selected for "building" will most often be "preserved" in the eventual therapist response. The "building" aspect of solution building refers to several concurrent processes. As suggested earlier, it is primarily client accounts or narratives of hopes and actions that are the substance of solution-focused conversation. Creating conditions for clients to build useful narratives is the objective. Useful narratives are particularly those about hopes, healthy actions, and the convergence of the two. Asking "What are your hopes?" and eliciting any narrative of hope is a unit of building. Asking and answering additional questions to improve the action-ability of the hope amounts to more building blocks, as does focused inquiry and responding along the four lines represented by the TEAM map and the fifth line of inquiry oriented toward next steps. Affirmation absorbed by clients for useful shifts in their narratives is another potential unit or pathway in building. The pragmatics of all these solution-building tools simply taking up space, in addition to having instrumental effects, create the experience of "building" by virtue of the sheer mass or conversational space taken up by solutions in the therapy session.

What are Questions For?

Bavelas (2022, p. 183), in her most recent compendium of theory and research regarding face-to-face dialogue, quotes Tomori and Bavelas (2007): "A question is an "utterance that requests information that the therapist does not have." This definition would seem to apply to many clinical therapeutic environments, and indeed the vast majority of instances of human communication. Implicit in this definition seems to be that the questioner perceives the questionee as having information that the questioner does not have, wants to have, and expects the questionee to deliver – presumably so the questioner will then have that information.

In SFBT, perhaps as well as other post-modern approaches that aim to co-construct shifting perceptions, questions tend to serve a subtly and significantly different purpose, which we articulate as follows: A question is an utterance that invites clients to narrate or give voice to their experience of thoughts, feelings, actions, and interactions. A question with therapeutic intent invites clients to narrate their experience in a way that favors solutions and wellness, bringing their wellness to the foreground. The intended audience for clients' response to the therapeutic question is the clients themselves. The best outcome is for clients to witness themselves articulating new possibilities for ways to think and behave in the context of their troubles and hopes for solutions.

A common occurrence in solution-focused interviewing is extended questioning about the details of difference, or what we have labelled "Events" questioning. Once the clients' hopes for change and their vision of difference has been identified and named, therapists ask numerous questions about the details of either remembered or imagined events that would occur. There is reliable fallout from persistence in this line of questioning. Client description of details leaves identifiable tracks that may in turn lead to recognizing exceptions in the past, potentiate noticing exceptions in the future and result in creating specifics for future reference that clients may remember to try taking useful actions. Interviewer motivation to persist in this line of questioning is entirely about creating narratives rich in specific sensory detail that increases likelihood of clients observing and performing difference. The questions create conditions for clients to provide new information for themselves.

Affirming

To some extent, most therapeutic approaches likely incorporate an element of affirmation of the client. From many years of assisting sessions from behind the mirror, it seems that some therapists appear to rely on concentrated kindness as a primary tool. The notion of unconditional positive regard grew out of client-centered therapy. Emotion-focused therapy appears to make a particular point of affirming emotion. Cognitive behavioral therapy (CBT) appears to focus on less-than-helpful patterns of thinking and the affirmation of more healthy alternative patterns. Differing slightly from other approaches to affirmation, SFBT usually orients affirming interventions fairly specifically to solutions, hopes, and capabilities.

One of the most prominent ways by which the solution-focused interviewer affirms client experience is through the consistent selection of solution-related utterances over problem-related speech. This covertly and continually conveys to the client that this focus can be productive and useful.

More overtly, solution-focused therapists deploy carefully constructed and timed compliments. Guidelines for effective compliments include:

- Specific to actions related to solutions
- Appropriate and accurate
- Tempered to avoid the possibility that the client finds the compliments excessive
- Lean towards complimenting effort over intelligence

Supposition and Pre-supposition

Berg (personal communication) states that "you can suppose anything". In fact, SFBT has often been referred to as a "therapy of suppose". The word "suppose" itself frequently appears in solution-focused interviews:

- Suppose that some night while you are sleeping … a miracle happens …
- Suppose you were to become more patient – how would you notice the difference?
- Suppose you were to find yourself a half point higher on the scale – what might be some small signs?

There is another level at which supposition, or more accurately pre-supposition, plays an important role in SFBT. An interesting exercise is to entertain a specific question and then speculate freely about what "realities" are presumed to be "true" in the asking of the question.

Question: What's better?
Pre-suppositions:

- Something is better
- Clients are capable of noticing and reporting difference
- Attuning to "better" is useful

Question: On a scale of one to ten …?
Pre-suppositions:

* Clients will be able to place themselves on the scale.
* The number is meaningful.
* Higher is better.

To the extent that therapy of different styles likely includes an element of per-suasion, it is worthwhile to reflect on what the persuasive agenda might be in solution-focus and what the role of pre-supposition is in that process. Let's first consider what ideas a SF therapist might wish upon a client and hope the client will embrace. Possibilities include:

* Change is not only possible, it is entirely possible. Beyond that it is inevitable. Let's steer it in a useful direction.
* You [client] have capabilities. You can do things that make a difference.
* Watching intently for progress is powerful.
* You don't need so much to understand or get rid of the problem as you need to start doing something better to replace it. The latter is not dependent on the former.

It is a rarity to see a seasoned solution-focused interviewer engage in any extended overt attempts to persuade clients of a particular idea. Indeed, the reality is quite the contrary: the solution-focused interviewer mostly appears to take a position of deference to clients' understandings of their situation and their hopes. And yet there is therapeutic intent in virtually every act by the interviewer, all the way from selecting a focus on solutions over problems to a specific behavioral compliment suggested to clients. The dynamics of pre-supposition have a repu-tation for strong persuasive effects. It might well be that pre-supposition serves an important persuasive agenda in SFBT.

Persistence and Focus

Steve de Shazer was part of the team behind the mirror while an experienced ther-apist was interviewing a client who presented with what might be referred to as chronic mental illness. The client exhibited a strong habit of repeating his troubles with thoughts and feelings. The interview may not have progressed beyond pre-liminary "languaging" of the client's hope for something to be different. In post-session discussion, Steve complimented the therapist for her "doggedness". He was impressed that, against considerable odds, the therapist never resigned from the task of gently leading the conversation over to ideas of difference.

It is a typical feature of solution-focused practice that the interviewer focuses intently on:

- Client language for hopes.
- Exceptions to the problem.
- Details of difference.
- Extensive follow-up to opening questions such as the Miracle Question.

Part of defining the intensity of focus is what solution-focused interviewers choose not to explore. With little or no attention being paid to the details of the problem, the experience of the focus on solutions is singular and intense. There is additional singularity in the exclusive focus on eliciting client resourcefulness uninterrupted by the therapist performing procedures or giving advice. Giving advice would seem to pre-suppose that the client needs outside resources for success. SFBT pre-supposes internal and social resources are sufficient. That focus could easily be distracted by the switch in positions, potentially creating confusion and diluting the focus.

Customership

It may be said that a good start for a solution-focused interview is a question in the back of the interviewer's mind: "Who is the customer for change and for what?" The conversational process of inquiring into this question brings clarity and detail to an unfolding answer to the question.

In the section introducing the *convergent narrative,* we spoke of the aggregate "you" who wants change. This includes the clients themselves as well as those around them who care about them or are trying to provide care to them. The solution-focused interviewer welcomes all customers included in the aggregate to make an appearance in the conversation, at least initially, in order to determine how they may contribute to solution. Of course, some of these customers will not be in the session. They may be thought of as absentee customers. We create space for the clients present to speak for the absentee customers: "What would the probation officer say she hopes comes out of therapy for you?" As we noted earlier, clients are more than capable of speaking for others and, in doing so, introduce different and frequently useful perspectives into the conversation.

A young man appeared at a community mental health walk-in clinic one day. He had just been to court and immediately after that to an interview with a probation officer, which was located just down the hall from the community clinic. Both recommended he seek mental health services, so he wasted no time in following up. Lance was struggling to find some good questions to get at what the client's hopes were for the session. Finally, the client rescued[3] him with a speech roughly quoted here.

Client: Look … I'll tell you how it is. These days they send everybody for counselling. And you know what … half the time they are right. Some guys are back in court over and over again. They need to get their head straightened out. Now … me … I'm in the other half.

Therapist: So ... what does the court hope will be different with counselling?
Client: Well ... they think I have a problem with booze.
Therapist: What would have to happen for them to start thinking booze wasn't so much of a problem for you anymore?
Client: Stop getting arrested I guess.
Therapist: And you went along with the suggestion?
Client: Ya ... well I have a suspended sentence, so I have probation for six months ...
Therapist: So how is it useful to go along with the probation officer?
Client: So, I don't get a breach of probation and have to go back to court.

A couple was discussing the apprehension of their children by Children's Services:

Therapist: So ... if 10 on a scale stands for we are ready to have our children come home and 1 is when they were removed from the home, where are you today?
Mother: 10!
Father: Ya ... I think so ... they shouldn't have come in to start with.
Therapist (after extended conversation about what the family had done that suggests to them they are at 10 in readiness) : Where would the case worker put you on that scale?
Client: Oh ... she would say something like 4.
Therapist: What would the case worker say she would need to see happening to rate it more like 5?
Client: They want us to get a bigger house ...

Normalizing

A number of years ago, Lance was assisting a session from behind the mirror when a client said she "wasn't 100 percent confident all the time". The therapist's response was something along the line of "How come?" The author would have strongly preferred a response along the lines of "Of course not!". This preference has a basis that may be worth some elaboration.

Recalling the earlier comments about solution-focused listening, the time has come for further discussion of how solution-focused practitioners position themselves for listening and reflection. For the sake of contrast, we might consider positioning adopted in a more traditionally oriented mental health model, where practitioners adhere to problem-focused models. Under those circumstances, in which the authors worked for many years, one adopted the interviewing posture of listening for the problems and inquiring into further details with the question in mind, "What problems does the client present that will become the focus of treatment?"

The positioning of the solution-focused interviewer couldn't be more opposite from this example. One might say that the solution-focused posture is based on quite a different question: "How might the problem reported by the client be re-languaged as a trouble of daily living, and what does the client want to be different and better?" There are several implications of casting the troubles that people bring to the therapeutic conversations in more normalized terms.

- To start with, solution-focused practice does not pay much attention to the problem itself. We do not devote a lot of interviewing time to it, and we do not try to give it a professional name to distinguish it from other problems. Those are activities more consistent with problem-focused practice.
- We are in the business of cultivating hope and are of the opinion that, when comparing "clinical depression" with "feeling down", the latter is a more hopeful beginning for conversational co-construction of change than the former. We are inclined to language both troubles and hopes in terms that encourage optimism. We are much more interested in the name clients give, for when "feeling down" is less of a problem for them. Solution-focused interviewing works to bring wellness into the foreground. We cultivate positive naming of successes and allow troubles to drift unnamed into the background.
- We work from an assumption that clients already have capabilities and perceptions that can be the foundation for the changes they desire. When we see their problems as parts of daily living, it is natural to understand their solutions in the same language. Change will be sufficiently underway once some different things start to occur in their daily living. One option for cultivating these differences is to go directly to them without an intervening phase or procedure of diagnosis and treatment planning for the problem.
- None of this line of reasoning is meant to deny that clients may be challenged by some profound disturbances in cognition or affect such as dementia, schizophrenia, compulsive behaviors, or social isolation. However, in the context of therapeutic conversation, it is the troubles of living clients face as a result of these conditions and, more importantly, what their hopes are for how they may live more effectively with these challenges, that guides the process.

We would be remiss not to address how solution-focused therapists are oriented to diagnosis. Those practitioners who are dependent upon insurance companies for payment are required to provide a diagnosis. Insurance companies follow a medical model, and therefore require practitioners to demonstrate that therapy is medically necessary, which often means there is a valid DSM diagnosis. As solution-focused therapists, we certainly advocate that practitioners follow the dictates of insurance requirements and the policy of the agencies for which they provide services. However, we would point out that a specific diagnosis, and indeed the language of pathology, will often have little or no role in conversational co-construction of difference.

First Session–Second Session and Beyond

The first session in SFBT starts with "languaging" the client's hopes for change. A one-hour session may be divided roughly into three components with the proportions approximately as follows:

- Beginning – first 40 minutes[4]
  - Utilizing lines of inquiry as in the TEAM framework or EARS or LSB
  - Clients do most of the talking
  - The therapist is careful to let the client set the pace for the session. This has been called "leading from behind".
- Middle – session break
  - 10 minutes.
  - Review notes, key words, opportunities, compose closing summary including normalizing, restructuring statement, compliments, bridging statement, and suggestion.
- End – session closing
  - Deliver closing summary.
  - Deciding with the client whether scheduling another appointment would be useful or whether this one session is sufficient.

The main difference in second and later sessions is that we start with the "What's better?" question in place of "What are your hopes?" In terms of function, these two questions have the same purpose: to start the ball rolling in the direction of solution conversation. If clients say nothing is better, after giving them time to change their mind about that, we revert to "What are your hopes for this session?" Whichever way the conversation is initiated, we proceed with the same basic structure of the first session.

The Thinking Break and Closing Summary

The traditional solution-focused interview format includes a break in the session about three-quarters of the way through the time. We announce that we will be taking a short break to think over the client's situation. Prior to stepping away, we ask whether there is anything else that should have come up in the first part of the session as a safeguard against missing something important. For the break, the therapist leaves the room and either works on their own or with the observing team if there is one.

The task of the interviewer during the break is to compose a closing summary for delivery and ending the session upon returning to the therapy room. These summaries are typically complimentary of the clients' efforts so far in their pursuit of change. There also tends to be some normalizing commentary in the closing summary languaging clients troubles as challenges of living as opposed to symptoms of disease or disorder. To summarize, the closing summary includes:

- Two or three potent compliments.
- A brief normalizing summary of how the therapist understands the clients' situation.
- A suggestion for something to try or watch for in the days following the session.

Example

The team is impressed with your decision to get some help with this trouble of feeling down and being irritable because it shows you care about your health and are willing to take real steps to improve things. We are also impressed with your deep caring for your family and your determination that your physical condition is not allowed to "cast a constant cloud over everybody". We were particularly struck with the effort you made to go to the school Christmas pageant, especially knowing how much extra effort that required on your part.

It seems to the team that your situation is a good example of how a physical condition presents a lot of extra challenges for a parent and for family life. We admire your position of making the best of it. We would like to make a suggestion for you for the coming days. That is, we suggest that you take notice of times when you make the extra effort to do something the family wants to do together. In particular, we would like you to notice which family member is most grateful for you coming along.

Introducing the thinking break has already indicated to clients that we are coming to a close. While clients will often comment on what the therapist says after the break, the main focus during this stage is on the therapist's message. Certainly, all indications are that we are not beginning anew the more interactive format of the first three-quarters of the session.

A Note on Complimenting

It is worth noting that within the community of solution-focused practitioners there is a range of opinion about the use of compliment. Some prefer not to use compliments, taking the position that clients should be presumed to be capable of complimenting themselves or at least appreciating on their own what is good for them. In this school of thought, the therapist relies in the interventive power of interviewing, leaving judgment or evaluation up to the client. Some may suggest this maintains a higher level of client-centeredness, keeping the therapists' opinions to themselves.

Other practitioners find value in complimenting clients. Compliments about client resources, strengths, and successful efforts serve to encourage the client to do more of what is working already and instills hope and expectations for a better and more satisfying future. Sometimes compliments may be *indirect*, possibly in the form of a question: "How were you able to figure that you should do that?"

Campbell et al. (1999) suggest that there are five elements to be considered when thinking about providing feedback to the client. *Normalizing* as stated above suggests to client that what they are experiencing makes perfect sense, and therefore they are not "crazy". A *restructuring statement* attempts to deconstruct the problem into something more solvable. The authors expand on this:

> Many clients define the problem in ways that limit solutions, such as chemical imbalance, abusive partners, misbehaving children, or a diagnostic label. Solution-focused therapy uses questions to create awareness of options. Restructuring statements are effective tools in this process. We have found recurring themes that can be presented to the client as more useful ways of thinking about the problem.
>
> (Campbell et al., 1999, p. 28)

Compliments, as stated above, direct clients' attention to their resources, strengths, and actions that have already been taken – especially those that have been useful. The *bridging* statement simply makes it logical how the foregoing is connected to the suggestion. The *suggestion* is something that the client might think about, notice, or try once they leave the therapy session.

In summary, actions of the host in a solution-focused conversation will usually be found in one of three categories: listening, questioning, and affirming. These categories of intervention are dynamically linked and concurrently engaged to stack the deck in favor of hopes, possibilities, capabilities and solutions. Listening particularly for these aspects of client experience begins to orient the conversation in the direction of solutions. Questions are then constructed to further focus and expand on possibilities on the solution side, which are then explicitly affirmed as well. This coordination of listening, questioning, and affirming increasingly draws solutions into the foreground and relegates problems to the background. Solution-focused therapists are known to suggest that problems are not so much solved as dis-solved in SFBT.

Notes

1 See Chapter 1 for a definition of "language-game".
2 Whether to use 0 or 1 to define the low end of the scale has been the subject of some discussion among SF practitioners. Rationales have been offered for each position.
3 Gale Miller (personal communication) says he's positive that there is a secret society of clients who want to be helpful to therapists if therapists will only let them. This certainly supports Miller's thesis.
4 These times are intended as guidelines and will fluctuate according to clients.

4 Microanalysis and Opportunities

Microanalysis

Janet Beavin Bavelas (2022, p. 67) lists the requirements for a formal microanalysis:

- Spontaneous face-to-face dialogue.
- Video recording with all interlocutors on screen.
- Analysis linked to video (preferably annotation of digitized video).
- Analysis of moment-by-moment details, often in fractions of seconds.
- Analysis takes into account the accumulating conversational context.

The authors are not claiming that microanalysis of opportunities, as detailed in this book, represents a formal analysis as described by Bavelas. Given this, we debated whether our use of the term "microanalysis" was accurate.

In our original paper (Taylor & Simon, 2014, p.71) we stated:

> We want to emphasize the difference between this study and research methodology. While most microanalysis research strives for agreement, a study such as this one embraces the differences. These differences provide the fodder for discussion and mutual learning.

In his Foreword to this book, Peter DeJong wrote:

> The value of this book, I believe, lies in the authors' step-by-step methodology and detailed illustrations of doing an *applied microanalysis* of opportunities for constructing SF therapist responses. (italics added)

Finally, in her book, Bavelas (2022, p. 199) addresses the application of microanalysis tools beyond the formal research:

DOI: 10.4324/9781003396703-5

Our approach to dialogue turned out to be applicable to a wide variety of important dialogue settings: computer-mediated communication, communication with an autistic infant, medical consultations, and psychotherapy dialogues. The benefit was not a simple one-way transfer of basic research knowledge to applied research. It soon became clear that what was happening in non-lab settings both validated and expanded the lab research.

We conclude that microanalysis of opportunities describes an application of microanalysis tools as a way of enhancing clinicians' ability to listen and respond to client utterances.

The authors were fortunate to be active in the solution-focused community when the affiliation between the leading developers of microanalysis and solution-focused brief therapy rapidly gained momentum in the early 2000s. Key aspects of the two disciplines fostered a natural synchrony.

While somewhat of a tradition in psychotherapy and problem-solving in general, getting to the root of the problem holds little interest for solution-focused practitioners. Instead, we orient toward getting to the surface of solutions. What do people do that increases wellness in their thoughts, feelings, behaviors, and relationships? Microanalysis also orients toward the surface of the interaction between clients and therapists. What exactly do the participants in the conversation say and do that can be observed and objectively confirmed by multiple observers?

Smock and Bavelas (2013, p. 14) state:

If effective practice is the ultimate goal of evidence-based research, then it is logical and practical that some research should include studies of actual practice, that is, direct observation of what practitioners do in their sessions.

In our original article (Taylor & Simon, 2014, p. 75), we wrote:

Echoing this sentiment, Janet Bavelas (personal communication), advised the authors that while some research orients toward measuring effectiveness of therapeutic interventions, there is also benefit to studying what it is that actually happens in a given intervention. The authors would say that this remains the most useful application of the study of opportunities. As two veteran practitioners of solution focused interviewing, we are still continually delighted and informed by the close examination of the moment-to-moment exchanges between client and interviewer as viewed through the lens of opportunities.

In combination, the two disciplines enable the question of what clients and therapists say and do together that fosters wellness. Because microanalysis observes and describes therapeutic interaction, it is a perfect fit with a question that guided the early years of development of solution-focused brief therapy: What do therapists and clients do together that helps clients move past the difficulties that brought them into therapy? The Miracle Question, scaling questions, and other typical solution-focused patterns of interviewing earned their place in the practice through recurring successes, both observed and reported.

Solution-focused practitioners value description over explanation. Microanalysis provides the quintessential tools for description. With the proliferation of smartphones, we have the capacity to observe and record the moment-to-moment exchanges between clients and therapists. Slipping into explanation is always a possibility, but dedication to the surface of the conversation is a reliable benchmark for restoring description.

One distinguishing feature of SFBT is that the interviewer typically adopts client language. Korman et al. (2013) showed that SFB therapists' formulations significantly preserved client words (46 percent).[1] Reporting the results of their research, they state:

> Our first hypothesis was that there would be a higher proportion of pre-
> serving the clients' exact words in SFBT formulations than in CBT/MI
> formulations. The results confirmed this hypothesis with 46% of the words in
> the formulations of the SFBT therapists being exact preservations compared
> to 23% of the CBT/MI therapists. The second hypothesis was also supported:
> the CBT/MI formulations included proportionately more additions by the
> therapist (35%) than did the SFBT formulations (10%).
>
> (Korman et al., 2013. p. 40)

As the solution-focused therapist constructs questions and affirmations to stimulate the conversation, they can repeatedly be observed preserving and utilizing certain client words and phrases. Is this a general rule to practicing SFBT – something practitioners are expected to do – or is it just good practice? This contrasts with more professional-as-expert approaches, where the therapist may privilege their own language and information.

Froerer (2009) hypothesized that a microanalysis of solution-focused therapeutic dialogues (Bavelas et al., 2000) would find that the therapist preserved a significant proportion of client language. Interestingly, his close analysis determined that somewhere in the range of 5 to 7 percent of actual client words were preserved in therapists' formulations. Some 93 to 95 percent of the total number of actual words that clients uttered were omitted.

In their article, DeJong et al. (2013) demonstrate through microanalysis research how co-construction occurs in psychotherapy. The current authors, both practicing solution-focused therapists, agree that the essence of SFBT is co-constructing possibilities and differences with clients in their own language. Korman et al. (2013) developed four distinct varieties of therapist preservation of client words: preserving exactly; preserving deictically;[2] preserving in altered form; and preserving with addition. It followed from several of the microanalysis studies (Froerer, 2009; Froerer & Smock, 2013; Korman et al., 2013) that selection factors must determine which client language was preserved by the interviewer and carried forward in the conversation.

Perhaps there are key words – key clues to solutions – that seem to promise particular usefulness in the construction of difference. One clue certainly is identified by Smock et al. (2013), who found that SFB therapists used positive content significantly more frequently than CBT practitioners, with "positive content" referring to positive aspects of the client's life. The present authors were curious to discover what other keys guided therapist choices of client language for preservation.

Following is a dialogue between one of the authors and a client providing a typical example of this selection process.

LANCE: Let's say you woke up in the morning after the miracle without this negative outlook, how would you start catching on that this is different?

CLIENT: Um. rather than waking up and maybe hurriedly going through like my morning routine, maybe I'd just take my time and *relax a little bit more*. [Lance: "Okay" (nods)] There's a pressure in–like all the time–so, maybe I'd just be a little bit *more calm*.

LANCE: Ya, ya. Okay. And, um, since you started out the day that way – *more relaxed,* going a little bit slower, *more calm* – how would the day go differently?

In this dialogue example, Lance preserves the client's language as indicated by the italic type in the dialogue extract as he omits the client's problem statements. Lance uses the client's phrases "relax … more" and "more calm" as keys to construct the next question.

In the initial phase of our study, the authors also used the working framework of microanalysis, examining actual therapy sessions with a view to identifying key words in client utterances. There were two interesting early developments from this process. First, it quickly became apparent that when solution-focused practitioners examine a client utterance, they often find several candidates for key words within one utterance. The first instinct of the authors was to isolate identifying features of key words. What was it about a word or phrase that made it stand out to the solution-focused interviewer?

Some identifiers were obvious. For example, when a client says, "I wish I could be more confident", the therapist hears the phrase "more confident" and asks what might be the details of "confidence". Logically, "more confident" is an indicator that there is already some degree of confidence happening.

Other identifying criteria were more subtle. When a client says, "I've been depressed for most of the summer", the therapist hears the word "most" and may inquire into what was different at those few times when the client was not quite so depressed; logically *most* means "not all the time", implying that there must be some times when depression is somehow less.

Over some time pursuing this course of trying to isolate the defining features of key words, the process became less and less promising. There seemed to be no end of candidates for key words. For the extensive variety of key words, there were correspondingly numerous identifiable features. The list of defining features for key words grew exponentially. Attempts to sort the various criteria into categories also proved challenging and unrewarding.

Opportunities

Janet Bavelas, a world leader in microanalysis of therapeutic conversation, and her team at the University of Victoria in British Columbia, Canada, have generously provided members of our solution-focused community with many rich training and supportive resources. Bavelas offered the authors consulting support for our key words project.

At this early point in our project, we arranged a meeting with her to discuss the problem of too many key words to be manageable. In a most solution-focused fashion, she suggested we consider using the term "opportunities". What if we presumed that in any client utterance heard by a solution-focused practitioner, there may be several opportunities for intervention – several words or phrases that offered possibility for developing solutions?

The results of this conversation were refreshing and pivotal. Among other effects, the authors found themselves reorienting from their in-depth search for defining criteria to a more simplified and surface view of conversations with clients. In place of being perplexed by the number and variety of possibilities for key words, we adopted a position of simpler acceptance of the surface reality that there were multiple possibilities for useful therapist responses.

We established that in solution-focused interviewing, each client utterance may contain several opportunities for interventive action. This development significantly altered our inquiry away from seeking ways to identify *the* key word presented by a client. Instead, we acknowledged the presence of options and the implication that there were welcome choices to be made.

The word "opportunities" seemed to come with another useful connotation. In ordinary English, when we use the word "opportunity", there is usually an implication that the opportunity is *for* something. For example, the menu in a good restaurant presents opportunities for a fine meal; the curriculum in a good school presents opportunities for valuable learning. Translating into the context of the authors' interest, a client-generated opportunity is an occasion to take a solution-focusing action – in the realms of listening, questioning, and affirming.

These developments simplified the study considerably, representing a shift that invariably appeals to the minimalism valued by solution-focused practitioners. The authors, both seasoned solution-focused brief therapists, command a reasonably comprehensive set of interviewing options. We are trained and experienced in the actions of solution-focused interviewing. We returned to our study of actual dialogue with clients with a clearer, more surface-oriented framework for observation. We are now guided by one three-part question: within one client utterance, what are the opportunities; what are the possible therapeutic actions that are available for each; and what are the rationales for the intervention choices we make?

As is so often the case in therapy and other solution-building endeavors, opportunities became a turning point in our project, leading us to a number of years of studying therapy conversations and sharing the idea with others. The work is presented in our initial publication (Taylor & Simon, 2014). To begin a more detailed description of the process, some definitions are required.

Relevant Terms

The authors have found that certain terms help us co-construct with clients the meaning of the words that they use to express their hopes for therapy.

Utterance

"We define 'utterance' as a speaking turn – a stretch of speech typically followed by silence and/or a change of speaker" (Taylor & Simon, 2014, p. 65). For example:

THERAPIST UTTERANCE:	What are your best hopes for our work together?
CLIENT UTTERANCE:	My best hopes … I know I saw you back in'92, '93 and even though obviously I had good sessions with you, I don't think I got to where I needed to be. If I got to where I needed to be, I wouldn't be here right now.
THERAPIST UTTERANCE:	So, where is that? How would you know that you were at where you wanted to be?

In this example, the division of utterances is clear. This is an example of turn-taking where each participant expresses a complete thought before the next responds.

In the normal course of a conversation, often the dialogue is marked by interruptions and incomplete thoughts. Following is another example where the divisions of utterances may not be as clear.

THERAPIST UTTERANCE:	When we talked on the phone, I asked you a question – your best hopes. How would you know when you leave – today, tomorrow, the next day – this is something useful?
CLIENT UTTERANCE:	To explore and get something, that's what I'm looking for.
THERAPIST UTTERANCE:	What is that something?
CLIENT UTTERANCE:	Just an experience of life. My biggest problem is my first marriage [therapist: right]. I got married at 21 …
THERAPIST UTTERANCE:	Before you get into that [client: yeah], so you said something about experience of life. Tell me more. What would tell you that there's something about that that's different?

In this example, both the therapist's interjection, "right", and the client's, "yeah", do not directly end the client's or therapist's utterance. However, the therapist interrupts the client in the next sequence. While the client's thought is incomplete – that is, the client's thought is interrupted – nonetheless this would be considered an utterance.

Solution-Building

Solution-building is a therapist–client collaborative and co-constructive process that focuses on a client's personal and social resources, problem exceptions, and the client's vision for a more satisfying future. Solution-building is a key concept in SFBT. As trainers, the authors are often asked whether a given intervention is or is not solution-focused. Joel's usual response is to suggest that the solution-focused police probably won't come and arrest you for asking what might not be categorized as solution-focused.

The question of whether something is or isn't solution-focused is part of a Theory-based language-game. Within that context, the rules of a given Theory determine what does or does not fit within the given Theory. These rules exist *a priori* to the engagement with the client. In contrast, a solution-focused practitioner determines the usefulness of an intervention by the response it elicits: is the response solution-building? The question of whether something is solution-building is determined *a posteriori* by the response of the client. De Shazer (personal communication) states that we never know what question we asked until the client answers.

The "focus" in solution-focused brief therapy is on listening for and encouraging solution talk through the questions that we ask. The responses that therapists choose are not neutral but based upon the therapist's orientation – the term for this is "lexical choice". The lexical choice of solution-focused therapists is listening to clients for clues to solutions.

These clues serve two purposes. The first is to co-construct the meaning of exceptions – times when problems are less central to the client's life or absent altogether. The other is to clarify, co-construct, and detail the client's goal for therapy. De Jong and Berg (2002, p. 16) state:

> Solution-building interviews are organized, in large part, around useful activities. The first is the development of well-formed goals within the client's frame of reference; the second is the development of solutions based on exceptions.

The following dialogue is an example of the solution-building process taking place.

THERAPIST: [Asks the Miracle Question]
CLIENT: Maybe ... sometimes I wake up a little tight. So now I have to go to work – it'll be busy. If I woke up and I was more relaxed, thinking, "Okay, it's just another day at work. I guess go to work and any stressors ... there are a lot of stresses ...
THERAPIST: [Interrupting] Even before that. So, you wake up and you said you'd be more relaxed, thinking differently about work. So how would you be thinking differently?
CLIENT: Sometimes when I get up in the morning, my mind runs on what I have to do. Maybe just getting up and looking at my wife laying there. I always get up in the morning and take a shower, get ready, get my lunch. Maybe just getting up and thinking, "I'm home, I'm not at work. Things should be calm, things should be good," *which it usually is in the morning. In the morning when I get up, it's usually very quiet in the house. And I like that.*
THERAPIST: So, when you wake up in the morning, you wouldn't be thinking about work. You'd kind of be enjoying the moment, enjoying ...
CLIENT: Enjoying peace and quiet. *I love that.*

In this example, the Miracle Question helps the client to co-construct the small details of a difference. The client incorporates the differences within his normal routine: waking up, taking a shower, enjoying the peace and quiet. At the same time, focusing on this peaceful time in the morning will help him as he prepares for what he characterizes as a stressful job.

It might be helpful to distinguish between solution identification and solution-building. The solution-building that is taking place in this example identifies the exceptions and what the client wants to be different. Beyond identification, the therapist's questions help the client to build on the desired change and exceptions in ways that will make a difference to the client.

As is often the case with the Miracle Question, clients will spontaneously alternate between detailing a preferred future and identifying pieces of the miracle that are already happening. In this client's example, exceptions are noted in italics. Solution-building is a process that therapists and clients do together that makes useful meaning of exceptions and preferred futures.

Solution-Building Compass

Compasses are instruments that help individuals find and maintain direction. No matter what direction a person faces, a compass needle always points north, and therefore keeps us moving in a positive direction and prevents us from losing the path.

We have found this a useful way of thinking about solution-focused conversations. Solution-building is the needle that we use to point us in the direction of co-constructing useful conversations with clients. The advantages of the tools and format of SFBT are that they provide a consistent direction in the conversation and keep us moving along a solution-building path. Gale Miller (personal communication) suggests that solution-focused tools like the Miracle Question and scaling questions are "anchors" (the authors apologize here for mixing metaphors). What he means is that once these tools have been used, they can always be re-established. For example:

THERAPIST:	So, after you got up, what would you do?
CLIENT:	Usually I prepare for classes or something like that.
THERAPIST:	So, what would be the clue the miracle happened with your classes?
CLIENT:	A more normal day – definitely a more normal day.
THERAPIST:	What do you mean?
CLIENT:	I get this anxiety that I'm never going to finish what I'm doing. So, I unload on myself. Then I just stop.
THERAPIST:	So, what would happen on this day after the miracle?
CLIENT:	I would be doing what I need to be doing – school wise.
THERAPIST:	What would you be thinking or doing that would clue you into this miracle?
CLIENT:	Like have better thoughts about it. Instead of thinking, "I'm never going to finish this" – just positive thoughts. That would be the clue – that would be the clue! Just positive thought, positive thinking.
THERAPIST:	What would be "positive thinking"?
CLIENT:	"I'm going to get this done. You'll do this. You'll get through all this."

Later in the session, the client raises an issue. Her ex-boyfriend, who had been abusive toward her, frequently contacts her through texting and she describes how this causes her anxiety.

THERAPIST: I want to go back to the thing about the miracle. If this miracle happened, and this ex-boyfriend contacted you. What then would tell you the miracle happened?

CLIENT: I would really just look at the message, look away, and never think about him again.

THERAPIST: You wouldn't think about him again?

CLIENT: Yeah, I would never think about him again. That happened before, he messaged me and I completely [sweeps hands] …

THERAPIST: How did you think about the message?

CLIENT: Just, he's a horrible person.

Solution-focused conversations rarely proceed linearly; clients often move back and forth between problem and solution talk. The re-anchoring of the Miracle Question is a useful way of converting problem talk to solution-building. It is also an example of this solution compass concept.

The therapist is clear about the direction of the conversation. Even though the conversation begins to move in a different and more problem-focused direction, the therapist uses the "compass" to redirect the conversation and re-establish the solution-building path. This often happens when using scaling questions as well. In this example, the client's husband had died after a long illness.

JOEL: If I had a scale of 0 to 10, and 10 is the miracle, and 0 is the worst things have been, where would you put things right now?

CLIENT: [Sighs] 3.

JOEL: *3 – and how is 3 different than 0?*

CLIENT: You know we took care of my husband at home, but he was back and forth to the hospital, whatever. When we were taking care of him, we didn't even have time to even to think or hardly eat or anything because we were so busy or worried. Now we have time to worry and grieve and think about … so, it seems harder now than when my husband was home.

JOEL: So, three is because you're glad he's not suffering.

CLIENT: He's not suffering.

JOEL: And because you're sure you did everything possible. What else puts you up to 3?

CLIENT: Well, now I can take my own health in hand right now. I can start caring about myself. Before, I didn't care whether I lived or died. Now I think I want to be here.

JOEL: Because?

CLIENT: My children … I have a lot around me.

In this example, the client begins to express the meaning of 3 from a problem-focused stance. Joel first re-anchors the miracle then continuously re-anchors 3 (in italic), co-constructing with the client how 3 is different and better than

0. The end result in this dialogue is the client acknowledging that she decided she has reason to continue living. Because Joel follows the basic solution-focused template – pre-session, miracle, scaling questions – he always knows where he is and the direction in which he wants the conversation to go. This exemplifies how therapists invite clients into solution-building conversations.

THERAPIST: So, what are your best hopes?
CLIENT: I thought about this. This is not the first time I've done therapy. This is the second time I went to see a therapist electively; the previous times I was forced. But I kind of hope to have more good days than bad. I've been diagnosed with OCD. [J: uh hum] and that is what ails me. [J: uh hum] But my anxiety has gotten worse, so I'm kind of hoping to in the end be able to sense my triggers and keep something … keep an anxiety attack from happening. Something of that order there.

The authors contend that every client utterance offers opportunities for therapist responses – even when, at first glance, the client's utterances appear to be problem-focused. In the example above, the client's utterance can be separated into various opportunities:

1. I thought about this.
2. This is not the first time I've done therapy.
3. This is the second time I went to see a therapist electively.
4. The previous times I was forced.
5. But I kind of hope to have more good days than bad.
6. I've been diagnosed with OCD.
7. My anxiety has gotten worse.
8. So, in the end, I'm hoping to sense my triggers and keep an anxiety from happening.

Each of the opportunities offers possibilities for response, and whatever choice the therapist makes will determine how the conversation proceeds. We will expand on this concept in Chapter 5 as we examine how we select opportunities, what choices they offer, and how we decide which option to use in response.

Key Words and Phrases

DeJong and Berg (2002) present the idea of echoing key client words to demonstrate respect for clients, to elicit detailed descriptions of client experiences, and to focus on idiosyncratic words and phrases that clients repeat for their possible extra value in building solutions. The current authors narrow the definition of key words: "The authors define key words as words or phrases spoken by clients that can be used for the purpose of solution-building" (Taylor & Simon, 2014, p. 68).

We think of key words and phrases as central themes as clients speak about what they want to be different and better as a result of their conversations with us. Very often, these key words and phrases suggest a central theme for the session. These are often expressed at the beginning of sessions as clients are asked what their expectations are for positive change.

Following are examples with the key words and phrases indicted in italics:

- "I don't think I got to *where I needed to be.*"
- "I want to have the sense of *moving forward.*"
- "...To not be able to *work through something.*"
- "Have more *good days* than bad days."
- "Maybe *sort together* everything I'm feeling."
- "He would want to help me *get through this process.*"
- "I wouldn't have to go into a [psychiatric] hospital ever again. *I'd be more normal.*"

Key words and phrases provide an opportunity for therapists to expand on expressions of change by co-constructing details of differences. In one of the above examples, "where I needed to be" certainly lends itself to asking for specific indicators of being where he needs to be.

In Joel's work as a director of hospice bereavement services, he very often heard clients use phrases such as "get through the process" or "get back to normal". These phrases are all clues to solution-building. It is then a simple process of co-constructing with clients the details of change – making meaning of key phrases such as "get through the process" and "get back to normal".

Both authors have incorporated opportunities in their trainings. We have had similar responses after the trainees have completed an applied microanalysis of one utterance. Once they see the results in black and white, they are amazed at the richness of possibilities that clients offer therapists who are willing to listen carefully to client utterances.

Conducting the Microanalysis of Opportunities

The following describes the process of our original collaborative work on opportunities. While there is much value in working collaboratively, we also recommend individual analyses. Reviewing video recordings of therapy sessions has long been a rich learning tool. We learn different things reviewing our own work and the therapy of others.

Individual microanalysis of opportunities adds the additional advantages of learning to recognize the opportunities that clients offer for solution-building responses and, with practice, developing a greater capacity for recognizing possibilities and strategizing possible responses. Reviewing one's own therapy sessions without the simultaneous demands of hosting a live conversation in real time offers the advantages of taking our time, making multiple reviews of interesting sequences, and reflecting on individual occurrences in the context of other sections of the interview.

The microanalytic level of magnification offers unique enhancements to video review. Focusing on the minute occurrences in conversation almost always reveals events that we did not notice in real time. Adding an orienting question such as "What are the opportunities?", "How is interruption utilized?", or "How is affirmation delivered and received?" creates even more precise focus. This translates well into specific skill-building.

The exercise of conducting a collaborative microanalysis of opportunities includes the following steps:

1. Select a video recording of a therapeutic conversation:
   - Two or more analysts agree on a section of the recording for analysis.
   - Each completes a transcription divided into separate utterances.
   - The analysts meet, either in person or virtually, to finalize the single working transcription, referring back to the recording to resolve any differences of observation.
2. Each participant conducts their analysis separately:
   - The following chart is used to record the analysis.
   - Note that only the client utterances are numbered.
   - The actual therapist utterances are largely ignored, preferably deleted for this exercise.
   - Working on one utterance at a time the analyst answers the following questions in the chart:
     - What are the opportunities in this utterance?
     - What are the possible therapist responses to each opportunity?
     - Which response is preferred?
     - What is the rationale for the selection?
3. The two analysts meet and share their analysis one column at a time:
   - We adopt a curious tone of conversation to explore each other's findings, not a debate about which answer is more 'correct'.

The following is an example of the format we use to chart an utterance:

Utterance #1: I need to unleash everything. I keep building it up, building it up. I start lashing out at people that I shouldn't be. I get – I wouldn't say angry – I get frustrated very fast and I'm not the best person when it comes to that. I get frustrated. I don't kind of calm myself down. I just … I just get very rash.

Chapter 5 presents an actual analysis conducted by Joel and Lance for demonstration purposes.

Chart 4.1 I need to unleash everything

Opportunities	Possible actions * = preferred choice	Rationale
1. I need to unleash everything.	1a) How does unleashing everything make a difference? 1b) What tells you that you've done enough unleashing? 1c) When are there times that you don't feel the need to unleash? 1d) What would you want to be doing different?	
2. I keep building it up, building it up.	2a) How did you figure out that you want something different than building it up? 2b) Suppose a miracle happened…what would you be doing instead of building it up?	
3. I start lashing out at people that I shouldn't be.	3a) 3b) Etc.	
4. I get–I wouldn't say angry.	4a) 4b) Etc.	
5. I get frustrated very fast.	5a) 5b) Etc.	
6. And I'm not the best person when it comes to that. I get frustrated.	6a) 6b) Etc.	
7. I don't kind of calm myself down.	7a) 7b) Etc.	
8. I just … I just get very rash.	8a) 8b) Etc.	

Notes

1 Note that this number applies to one interview with one client and is not necessarily considered a numerical standard for all solution-focused interviews.
2 Deictic preservations refer to the use of such shorthand words as "that" or "this", rather than repeating the client's words in totality.

5 Microanalysis of Opportunities

Opportunities Analysis Example One

Introduction

This chapter and Chapter 6 describe a microanalysis conducted by the authors. Ten utterances were chosen: five each from two sessions with the same individual client. First, each author independently analyzed each utterance using the procedures described in Chapter 4. In the second stage, the authors met to present, compare, contrast, and discuss their independent analyses. What follows is a side-by-side comparison of the authors' results and the transcription of the conversations over two virtual sessions.

The reader will notice that different analysts generate somewhat different arrays of opportunities. This results partly from individual practitioners construing client utterances differently and partly from slightly different approaches to the exercise, varying from teasing out every possible opportunity to selecting fewer opportunities with a higher probability of use. For the practical purpose of reviewing the analysis, it is important to remember that one analyst's opportunity #4 may contain the same language that the second analyst denotes as opportunity #2.

The reader may wish to use this chapter as an exercise for their own practice in addition to, or as an alternative to, reading it as instruction. If that is appealing, simply cover the analyses of the authors and write up your own selection of opportunities, possible responses, preferred response, and rationale.

Analysis Example: Session 1

Utterance # 1

> I thought about this. So, this is not the first time I've done therapy [J: Okay] Um, this is the second time I've gone to therapy electively. [J: uh hum] Previous times I was forced. [J: Okay] (unintelligible) {Laughs} Um, I kind of hope to have more good days than bad.

DOI: 10.4324/9781003396703-6

Chart 5.1 I kind of hope to have more good days than bad

#	Opportunity Lance	Possible responses (preferred = *) Lance	Opportunity Joel	Possible responses (preferred = *) Joel
1	I thought about this.	1a: Good for you! 1b: What specifically have you found useful to think about?	I thought about this.	1a: I appreciate you taking the time to take my question seriously. 1b: What conclusions have you come to? 1c: What have you thought about that will make a difference? 1d: Based on that, what changes have you already started making?
2	This is not the first time I've done therapy ... Um, this is the second time I've gone to therapy electively.	2a: You've been persistent! 2b: What's so important that you keep at it?	So, this is not the first time I've done therapy.	2a: After that you still chose to try again. 2b: What are you hoping will be different this time? 2c: What was helpful those other times even a little bit? 2d: What needs to be different this time, so you'll say to yourself that this time was the charm?
3	I kind of hope to have more good days than bad.	3a: Miracle question.* 3b: How do you know when you are having a good day? 3c: How do you know when there are enough better days?	Um, this is the second time I've gone to therapy electively. The previous times I was forced.	3a: Ah, so you were forced and yet you decided to do this electively. 3b: What made you decide that this time might be different? 3c: What made the elective choice different and better than being forced? 3d: Which – electively or forced – worked better for you?
4			Um, I kind of hope to have more good days than bad.	*4a: What is happening on your good days? 4b: When are there times that what seems like a bad day, actually becomes a good day? 4c: Beside you, who else notices when you're having a good day? 4d: What do you say or do that gives others the clue you're having a good day? 4e: What helps to keep the good days good?

Session 1, Utterance #1: Discussion

Joel's Chart

JOEL: I learned 1a from you. I thought that was something you might say. Of the four, I chose the fourth opportunity – "I hope to have more good days than bad". Of those, I chose, "What is happening on your good days?" The reason is that it begins the process of inviting the client into a solution-building conversation. Good days are also the exception to the problem and suggests that the process is simple: figure out how to have more good days since they are already happening anyway. Any of the other responses in four would offer useful follow-ups that would keep the solution-building conversation going.

LANCE: It's interesting that 4c and 4d introduce the perspective of the observation of others, which I always find very powerful [J: right]. "So, what's happening on those good days is the most basic of those five responses, I thought. As you say, one leads to another. Once you answer 4a, you can do …

JOEL: I would eventually get to 4c or 4d. Once I get the details of what a good day looks like, and her part of it, I would want to ask what keeps the good days good. I want to focus on 4e too. It has something to do with how I choose to ask the question. Because I could have asked, "What do you do to keep the good days good?" That is another option. My preference – "What keeps the good days good?" – is to open up possibilities. It's not just something that she does. One of our assumptions is changes come from many different directions – not just what people do. That opens up the possibility of what helps to keep it going – maybe her boyfriend, maybe her parents, maybe her job. It could be any number of things that are possible supports for her.

LANCE: When you compare 4a and 4e, 4a is a broader question. It's more open. It leaves more room for the clients to fill in their understandings and observations rather than us narrowing for them.

JOEL: Very often when you ask 4a, the response you get entails 4e.

LANCE: The distinction for me in terms of the way I categorize questions 4a is more of a detail question and 4e is more of an agency question.

JOEL: I've use similar terms too. I teach vision versus agency. "What does it look like?" versus "How does it happen?"

Lance's Chart

LANCE: Your comment about the way I talk – one of my first responses was "good for you". I chose 3a: My rationale is it's the most promising opportunity in the utterance. We seem to agree on that. The Miracle Question offers the most openness for further "languaging" of "more good days than bad", including possibly rolling into miracle day questioning. That resonates with your choice of what are the signs of having a good day.

JOEL: One of the signs I'm ready to ask the Miracle Question is when I get a response like that – "I kind of hope to have more good days than bad". Immediately I would think, "Okay, that's the miracle." I think your instinct is right on with that. That's a possibility of going to the Miracle Question.

LANCE: What makes it so clear of all the opportunities? The other opportunities are interesting but they're not as promising. They don't seem to get so directly at solutions. Whereas "I hope to have more good days than bad" is her saying by herself what she wants out of this.

JOEL: That's simply her vision. When she says she wants more good days than bad, what you hear is "more". The deduction is, "Well, if it's *more*, then some good days must already exist."

LANCE: Possibly. Her distinction is to have more good days than bad. It's still suggesting that she has good days even if they're fewer. Her use of "more" stood out for me too. One of my possible questions is, "How do you know when there are enough [good days than bad]?" We then don't have to have the illusion that all days have to be good days.

JOEL: I suppose you could ask, "How many would be enough that you might think you don't have to do this anymore?" We're not looking for you to have all good days – what's good enough?

LANCE: It's an opportunity that points out the vagaries of language and how we need to process it. If you just stop with what she says – "I kind of hope to have more good days than bad" – privately I can't resist questions like, "What's the ratio right now?", "In the past seven days, how many were good and how many were bad?" Until you get to that level of detail, her way of talking about herself is pretty self-limiting. She seems to be saying – almost without evidence – that she has more bad days than good. We really don't know that.

JOEL: Unless you're going to ask that which you wouldn't if you're solution-focused. You wouldn't ask, "Tell me more about the bad days." I'm curious why you hadn't chosen "previous times I was forced".

LANCE: That just seemed more problem-focused to me.

JOEL: I'm looking at my responses, "What made you decide this time might be different" and, "What made the elective choice different and better than being forced?" It is useable.

LANCE: Oh, yeah. My use of the related utterance was along the same lines. So, my possible response to that is a compliment, "You've been persistent," and, "What's so important to you that you keep at it?"

JOEL: "You must have thought it was a good idea to try it again" [both laugh].

LANCE: I agree there are things you can do with and without "being forced".

JOEL: What I like about this exercise is to really work my brain and take even the most improbable possible opportunity and look for possibilities. It exercises the brain.

LANCE: We present this as an exercise foremost.

JOEL: I had a lot more difficulty with the second session from an opportunities analysis point-of-view. In general, first sessions tend to be more problem-focused. That's the expectation most clients come in with. They're going to be talking to you about the problem. The second one, at least in this case – it doesn't always work this way – was more solution talk. How many times am I going to note, "Don't say anything" – "Just let her talk."

LANCE: When you hear this from another perspective – this business about being forced – it starts to raise the level of interest for me. You would think that somebody who had been forced to do something, the last thing that they would want to do later on is do it again. It raises questions about how do you place such a high value on this and, by inference, on making some changes that you're willing to go ahead and do something that you were forced to do in the past. Your question is what made the elective choice different and better. Once you hear someone's thinking about an opportunity and the meaning they took from it, it raises possibilities.

JOEL: If she hadn't made that last statement, "I hope to have more good days than bad", I might have gone with that one.

LANCE: "Now that you're choosing to do this," it really potentiates the hope question, "Now that you're making a deliberate choice to do this, what do you hope comes out of it?"

Utterance #2

I've been diagnosed with OCD. [J: uh hum] and that is what ails me. [J: uh hum] But my anxiety has gotten worse, so I'm kind of hoping to in the end be able to sense my triggers and keep something … keep an anxiety attack from happening. Something of that order there.

Chart 5.2 I have been diagnosed with OCD

#	Opportunity Lance	Possible responses (preferred = *) Lance	Opportunity Joel	Possible responses (preferred = *) Joel
1	So I'm kind of hoping to in the end be able to sense my triggers and actually keep something … some anxiety attack from happening.	1a: Very good to start having a plan! *1b: What do you suppose happens instead when you keep an anxiety attack from happening?	I have been diagnosed with OCD. [J: uh hum] So that's kind of what … ails me.	1a: What are you hoping will be better and different about that? 1b: Despite how someone else has diagnosed you, what do you think? 1c: What would be the smallest sign that it is beginning to no longer ail you? 1d: When have there been times when it didn't ail you?
2	Something of that order there.	2a: I appreciate your flexibility that progress could take different forms! 2b: What would be the first small sign that you were moving in that direction?	But my anxiety has gotten worse.	2a: When has there been times when it initially has gotten worse and then better? 2b: What would be a small clue that it's just starting to get better?
3			So, I'm kind of hoping to in the end be able to sense my triggers.	3a: How would sensing your triggers be helpful? 3b: When you've sensed your triggers in the past, how has that made a difference? 3c: What tells you that sensing your triggers is even possible?
4			And actually keep something … some anxiety attack from happening.	4a: Similar to 2a. 4b: Similar to 3c 4c: "Some anxiety attack from happening"? 4d: What would be the smallest sign that you were just starting to prevent something from happening?
5			Something of that order there.	5a: Right, something of that order – what else? 5b: OCD diagnosis, triggers, anxiety – these are what you're hoping to be better and different? *5c: Similar to 5b but add: of those issues, which is the one that is most likely to change first?

Session 1, Utterance #2: Discussion

Lance's Chart

LANCE: I chose to respond to opportunity number one and of the two possible responses, I chose 1b. My rationale was that opportunity one points most strongly toward a meaningful difference. I would probably use a combination of 1a and 1b. The choices introduce an important shift to what would be present instead of what would be absent. In our work, I consider that one of the more powerful distinctions that we make. When she says that she wants to keep an anxiety attack from happening, that's what she wants to stop. We help clients to think about what will be happening in place of the problem – when the problem could happen but doesn't. That line of questioning addresses that.

JOEL: I also like the fact that you could take your second opportunity ["something of that order"] as insignificant. You turn it into something useful [see 2a and 2b].

LANCE: I don't see something useful in that statement [Lance, opportunity 2], but it's good practice. I don't consider it as close to an opportunity that I would respond to. For the sake of the exercise, it's fun to say, "What could you do with that?"

Joel's Chart

JOEL: I chose, "I've been diagnosed with OCD." I had trouble with this utterance since there were several responses I liked. I chose 5c as my response. I think either opportunity three or four would be my second choice since they point to a difference. However, they are still embedded in the problem. What I like about 5c is that it creates an illusion of choice[1] around change. I've used this "smorgasbord" of problems with solution-building responses before as a way of deconstructing problems as solvable with a follow up of "Which one would have the most impact?" I've often used that intervention when clients come in with a list of problems.

LANCE: I would add to that beside an illusion of choice, it's one of our principles that we think we should try to get a small change happening. Once it starts it tends to snowball and leads to other changes. It's part of screening for opportunities: which of these opportunities is liable to lead to some difference most directly, and most quickly so we can get into change.

JOEL: We tend to do this intuitively. Which choice is going to get where the client wants to go as quickly as possible?

LANCE: It could be an interesting research question: what is our list of criteria or our collection of criteria for what makes a good opportunity? I think we are guided by that principle.

JOEL: It might be interesting to take the choices and rationales separately and see what the connections are.

LANCE: It might start to reveal what we're being guided by. I think that's part of the reason we have the rationale section. When I write my rationale, I usually have one or two reasons why I make that decision. When I talk about what you did, I can see your reasoning. So it seems more criteria come to the surface.

Utterance #3

I guess my anxiety's not that bad. [J: Oh really?] Yeah, I guess I … I. Okay, so I guess I … um … some days … so I knew I was coming here today. [J: yeah?] So yesterday I prepped for it. I prepared myself. [J: yeah] So I made sure; I went to bed early, yeah, I made sure I knew what I was going to do in the morning, I knew … um … I guess I'm more regimented that way. I'm happier when I'm regimented in that way. [J: uh hum] Versus I'm going to stay up late and watch TV – watch a movie or play video games, and then go to sleep really late, and then not enjoy the next day.

Chart 5.3 I guess my anxiety's not that bad

# Opportunity Lance	Possible responses (preferred = *) Lance	Opportunity Joel	Possible responses (preferred = *) Joel
1 I guess my anxiety's not that bad.	1a: Tell me what's better about it? 1b: How can you tell it's not that bad?*	I guess my anxiety's not that bad.	*1a: What's different when your anxiety is better? 1b: How do you help your anxiety be better? 1c: When do you first notice that your anxiety is not going to be that bad?
2 I prepped for it. I prepared myself.	2a: Good for you! 2b: How do know what to do for preparation?	So, I guess I … um … some days … so I knew I was coming here today. [J: yeah?] So yesterday I prepped for it. I prepared myself.	2a: Preparing yourself is something that's helpful? 2b: What's different when you prepare yourself? 2c: What do you do to prepare yourself that's most helpful? 2d: Having prepared yourself for today, so far how has that made a difference?

(*Continued*)

Chart 5.3 (Continued)

#	Opportunity Lance	Possible responses (preferred = *) Lance	Opportunity Joel	Possible responses (preferred = *) Joel
3	I made sure I knew what I was going to do in the morning.	3a: How have you come to realize the benefit of planning ahead?	So I made sure; I went to bed early, yeah.	3a: How did you know that that was going to make a difference? 3b: What difference has it made so far today?
4	I'm happier when I'm regimented in that way.	4a: How did you figure out being regimented was useful? 4b: How did you figure out being structured was useful?	I made sure I knew what I was going to do in the morning.	4a: Similar to 3a. 4b: Similar to 3b.
5	Versus I'm going to stay up late and watch TV – watch a movie or play video games, and then go to sleep really late, and then not enjoy the next day.	5a: Good to know how to prevent a bad day! 5b: How did you figure this out?	I guess I'm more regimented that way. I'm happier when I'm regimented in that way.	5a: How did you figure that out? 5b: How are you able to make sure that you're regimented just enough and not more than that? 5c: Similar to 1a. 5d: What are the signs that tell you that you've guessed right so far?
6			Versus I'm going to stay up late and watch TV – watch a movie or play video games, and then go to sleep really late, and then not enjoy the next day.	6a: Similar to 5a. 6b: When you do go to sleep on time, how does that help you enjoy the next day? 6c: When do you begin to notice that you're enjoying the next day? 6d: What do you notice when you are enjoying the next day?

Session 1, Utterance #3: Discussion

Joel's Chart

JOEL: I chose to respond to the first opportunity, "I guess my anxiety's not that bad," and chose 1a as my intervention. She had stated in the beginning that she wanted to do something about her anxiety. This intervention directly addresses that difference. It also suggests an exception–a time when the problem is better–and deconstructs the constancy of the problem. While what follows can be used as follow ups, for the most part they are strategies that address opportunity #1.

LANCE: Looking at your analysis, it's clearly the most solution promising piece of language in the whole utterance. All by herself she begins to deconstruct the problem of anxiety by having an exception.

Lance's Chart

LANCE: For that particular opportunity, I had two possible responses [see 1a and 1b]. I chose 1b because it opens up space for discovering what happens instead of anxiety. It also allows to be amplified with additional details including agency and movement. She says it's not that bad. That presupposes an embedded statement that there are times that it doesn't happen, or doesn't happen as severely, strongly, or destructively. So, I'm drawn to finding out what happens in place of that. What happens instead of anxiety.

JOEL: It's a very similar rationale.

LANCE: I like how your rationale mentions it's a chance to erode that illusion of constancy. I think that it's important when clients offer us exceptions. When they first talk about a constant problem, they later mention it's not always constant.

JOEL: I do use that term "deconstruction" quite often in my rationales. When a client comes in, and offers you a diagnosis, my first question strategically is "How do we (the clients and I) deconstruct that?" How do we de-pathologize?

LANCE: It's pretty funny; somebody put a lot of effort into that diagnosis and we just want it to dissolve.

JOEL: A question I used to ask – I haven't done it in a while – "Let's suppose that diagnosis never existed. Then what would you say about yourself?"

LANCE: That reminds me of a gestalt therapist I knew. His idea in addressing regrets was to say, "What if all that didn't happen?"

JOEL: Or "What if you didn't regret it, what would you say?"

Utterance #4

I … I … I guess he's very … um … reserved and pessimistic because he knows it's going to happen again anyway [J: yeah] So sometimes I bring it up like (unintelligible) "… no problem". But he's so supportive. So, he knows exactly what's going on. But, but I'm sure he's like, "Yeah, but next weekend when we go to do something, it's going to happen." [J: Oh, okay] Never consistent like that. [J: Okay]

Chart 5.4 Small signs of surprise

# Opportunity Lance	Possible responses (preferred = *) Lance	Opportunity Joel	Possible responses (preferred = *) Joel
1 So sometimes I bring it up.	1a: Good for you for opening conversation! 1b: How is it useful to discuss it with him? 1c: What are your hopes for how he responds in these conversations?	I..I..I guess he's very … um … reserved and pessimistic because he knows it's going to happen again anyway.	1a: What would be the first sign that maybe this is just starting to change? 1b: What would he need to see to be convinced that he could be more optimistic? 1c: What would you be doing, or saying that would get him to notice the change?
2 But he's so supportive.	2a: What does he do that you find supportive? 2b: How does his support change what you do?	So sometimes I bring it up like (unintelligible) "… no problem."	2a: You bring it up; what are you hoping that he'll do or say? 2b: What difference would it make for you if he actually acknowledged a difference? 2c: How did you manage to make it not a problem? 2d: What tells you at those times that it might be good to bring it up?
3 So, he knows exactly what's going on.	See 1a, 1b, 1c.	He'll be like; "yeah, yeah I know. Yeah, I know, I know. You know.	3a: Similar to 1a, 1b, and 1c. 3b: Similar to 2b.
4 But, but I'm sure he's like, "Yeah, but next weekend when we go to do something, it's going to happen."	4a: How do you manage to go ahead doing things anyway? 4b: How surprised would he be when it didn't happen? 4c: What would be the first small signs of his surprise when it didn't happen?*	But he's so supportive. So, he knows exactly what's going on.	4a: What does he do that is so supportive? 4b: How has his being so supportive made a difference for you? 4c: When have there been times when you've surprised him even a little? 4d: What would he notice that will be a surprise for him?
5		But, but I'm sure he's like, "Yeah, but next weekend when we go to do something, it's going to happen.	5a: Let's suppose that next weekend he notices that there has been a small but substantial change; how will he notice that. *5b: MQ: the miracle being that next time the change happens.

Chart 5.4 (Continued)

# Opportunity Lance	Possible responses (preferred = *) Lance	Opportunity Joel	Possible responses (preferred = *) Joel
6		Never consistent like that.	6a: So, there are sometimes that he could have noticed that you've broken the pattern? 6b: This part of consistency; is that something you want to change?

Session 1, Utterance #4: Discussion

Lance's Chart

LANCE: I chose the fourth opportunity. Of the choices, I chose 4c ("What would be the first small signs of his surprise when it didn't happen?"). I thought that, of the several weak opportunities in this utterance, this choice seemed to be the strongest possible response. It embodies a presupposition of her succeeding and may lead her to focus on his positive reaction in place of her problem. I had difficulty trying to find anything useful in the utterance.

JOEL: I suppose you could be silent and let her go on, but there is some obligation to respond: communication involves turn-taking.

LANCE: She made a statement and I suppose it deserves a response. We don't see many significant opportunities that might move the session along. It might be more acknowledging what she said without trying to pick up on something or amplifying.

JOEL: The danger is it might lead to problem talk. Even taking the weakest of the lot and having some semblance of a positive direction would lead to a response from her.

Joel's Chart

JOEL: I chose to address the fifth one. We both chose the same one. Of the two choices, I chose the Miracle Question. I thought what you could do is make the miracle the next time the change happens. So, the miracle happens, and he's surprised. I thought that there's enough information about her vision of change, either implicit or explicit, that asking the Miracle Question would drive the conversation toward her future vision of change and co-construct details of that vision.

Both of ours are similar. Basically, you're asking the same question in a different way.

LANCE: My first thought about asking the Miracle Question is you really can't go wrong with it. I like it because it's broader; the Miracle Question leaves the field wide open. My question is a bit more narrowing.

JOEL: Your question could easily lead to asking the Miracle Question.

LANCE: It's interesting to me that in the utterance, "But he's so supportive" [Lance: utterance 2, Joel: utterance 4] neither one of us picked that opportunity when some people, who might be more strongly relationship oriented, might see that as a strong opportunity to bring forth how the changes she's talking about involve others. How it's a resourceful response from a significant other. It's obvious what to do with number four opportunity. We both had similar questions highlighting the relationship questions. What's interesting is that we both didn't chose that opportunity. I think it's because in number four I see more potential for her to make a difference – for her to do things, or notice things, or experience things from her own perspective rather than relying on what someone else is doing to help her.

JOEL: In the one we both chose, our questions encompass the relationship. If you assume he's supportive, then he would notice and support the change. Your question and the Miracle Question use his support but move it toward her change. What would she be doing that would surprise him?

LANCE: I do feel strongly that number four is the prime opportunity in this utterance. I'm interested in what principle is guiding us away from picking my number two and your number four. You could be right that this opportunity encompasses the relational response.

JOEL: Take a look at opportunity number four. I think what I'm hearing is the "but". You can't separate that from what comes after. "So, he knows exactly what's going on." I think that's a problem statement. It's a statement about constancy: "He's been disappointed so many times, it's been so constant, he knows what's going on."

LANCE: In the spirit of doing the exercise, I tried to figure out responses that would transform a problem-ladened response – questions like, "How were you able to be so open and let him know?" and, "How are you and he able to have such clear conversations about this?" I agree that the utterance is more about how the problem is going to continue uninterrupted.

JOEL: In the first session, what I want to do is to figure out what her vision is, where is she going with this? How are we defining our co-construction together? How do we decide when therapy ends? How do we keep this brief? If you think about it in those terms, the question about what she might do that would surprise him gets more to what she wants to be different in the interrelationship that is as a result of that surprise.

LANCE: Both of our selections of this utterance create an opportunity for her taking a stand against the constancy of the problem – of the expectation of it continuing. Our responses are calculated to co-construct that part, presupposing difference. We picked that opportunity as stronger than some of the others, perhaps because of its potential to bring forth her opposition to the permanence of the problem. It serves to elicit from her the details of a difference.

JOEL: Right, the purpose of the opportunity that you chose is to deconstruct his expectation of her: this is going to happen, and it constantly happens.

LANCE: It's curious how we're spending so much time on an utterance that both of us thought of as having little potential for solution-building. I'm interested in 4a. I think that's more of a direct attempt to deconstruct permanence – the all-encompassing prohibition of the problem.

Utterance #5

Well this past weekend ... this is what made me call you. Um (unintelligible) a really long time. But this time, we went out to eat with two other couples, and I did not want to go – a bad day for me ... anxiety wise, and my boyfriend said it would be good for you to go out. You know it would be good for you to go out. [J: uh hum] Trying to convince me, I said fine. I'll do it [J: right]. My boyfriend made plans and I wanted to pull out (unintelligible) and I don't care what they think about me. It's just rude on my values. And we go out, I ordered food, I didn't eat one bite, made up excuses, nothing. [J: uh hum] When we left, I said to my boyfriend "I practically don't remember our conversation." That's how full my anxiety was that night [J: uh hum] And I'm like well I forced myself to go out but I so regret it, and I don't want to correlate those two things together, but it's hard not to. [J: uh hum] And so I give myself credit for leaving the house.

Chart 5.5 Problem talk

#	Opportunity Lance	Possible responses (preferred = *) Lance	Opportunity Joel	Possible responses (preferred = *) Joel
1	[My boyfriend] said it would be good for you to go out.	1a: How did he hope it would turn out? 1b: What tells him it's worth a try even when you are having a bad day anxiety wise?	Well, this past weekend … this is what made me call you. Um (unintelligible) a really long time. But this time, we went out to eat with two other couples, and I did not want to go – a bad day for me … anxiety wise, and [My boyfriend] said it would be good for you to go out. You know it would be good for you to go out. [J: uh hum] Trying to convince me.	1a: What gave you the idea that maybe you were ready to do that? 1b: similar to 1a but add: "especially given that it was a bad day?" 1c: What gave Ryan the idea that it would be good for you? 1d: How was Ryan hoping that it would be good for you? 1e: Since you did agree, what did happen that you were convinced?
2	Trying to convince me.	2a: What so motivated him that he spent time convincing you?	I said fine. I'll do it [right].	2a: Given that it was a bad day, you still said fine, you'll do it. 2b: Despite being a bad day, a part of you still thought that you would do it?
3	I said fine. I'll do it.	3a: How did you allow yourself to be persuaded? 3b: Which part of his idea that it would be good for you did you find hopeful?	[My boyfriend] made plans and I wanted to pull out.	3a: Of course. 3b: Yet you didn't, how come? 3c: Similar to 2a or 2b.
4	I wanted to pull out.	4a: How did you manage to hang in there and go out anyway? 4b: From your experience, what tells you that it is sometimes best to go against that feeling?	I don't care what they think about me. It's just rude on my values.	4a: How did you manage not to care what they think of you? 4b: How did you have enough sense not to care? 4c: What does that say about what you value?
5	And so I give myself credit for leaving the house.	5a: What is it about you specifically that you are giving yourself credit for?* 5b: What difference does it make to give yourself credit?	And we go out, I ordered food, I didn't eat one bite, made up excuses, nothing.	5a: Similar to 2a or 2b. 5b: Given how you were feeling, how did you even have enough presence of mind to make up excuses?

Chart 5.5 (Continued)

#	Opportunity Lance	Possible responses (preferred = *) Lance	Opportunity Joel	Possible responses (preferred = *) Joel
6			When we left, I said to Ryan "I practically don't remember our conversation."	6a: Given what you were going through that makes sense. 6b: What helped to get you through that experience? 6c: What helped to get you over that experience? 6d: What did you learn from that experience? 6e: What would tell you that you're ready to try this again with a different outcome?
7			That's how full my anxiety was that night.	Similar to 6a–6e.
8			And I'm like well I forced myself to go out but I so regret it.	8a: Similar to 2a, 2b, 6a, 6d. 8b: How is it possible that you just regretted it and not worse? 8c: Despite Ryan's convincing you, you realized that it was you that forced yourself.
9			And I don't want to correlate those two things together, but it's hard not to.	9a: Why not? 9b: What would be a more useful way of thinking about this?
10			And so I give myself credit for leaving the house.	10a: Right, you give yourself credit. 10b: Despite everything, you can find a positive in this: you give yourself credit. 10c: Given what happened, how do you have the ability to give yourself credit? *10d: What do you mean: you give yourself credit?

Session 1, Utterance #5: Discussion

Joel's Chart

JOEL: This is her narrative about this horrible supper with two other couples. This utterance is essentially problem talk – except when she says she gives herself credit for leaving the house.

LANCE: The only piece of non-problem talk was the one you chose.

JOEL: I chose to respond to opportunity number ten with 10a. While what went before in this utterance is a description of what was a negative experience for her; this is a simple statement suggesting a positive outcome from that experience and by asking for the details of how she gives herself credit, it co-constructs the meaning of credit. It's similar to a favorite question of mine, "What did you learn from that experience?"

LANCE: This could epitomize solution-focused therapy. This woman talked for an extended time with a long problem-focused utterance with many opportunities to amplify the details of the problem. She squeaks in one tiny little hint of something resourceful and that's what was seized upon.

JOEL: This is a good example of a formulation. They do three things: they preserve the client's language; they delete some of the client's language; and they transform it. What's deleted is the whole problem narrative. It preserves her language exactly: "you give yourself credit". The transformation is asking her to co-construct the meaning of the statement.

LANCE: Can you give some random speculation to how the client might respond to 10d?

JOEL: "I didn't want to go, but I forced myself to do it"; "I got through this horrible experience, but I survived"; "I didn't lose a boyfriend".

LANCE: Each of those is credible; they're positive outcomes. It would make sense that she would give herself credit for that under those difficult circumstances.

Lance's Chart

LANCE: I'm pretty sure it's remarkably resonant with what you did. I chose the same opportunity as you although mine is number five. Of the choices, I chose, "What is it about you specifically that you are giving yourself credit for?", that's similar to your choice. I suppose I could have also chosen 5b. I thought that this choice was the most attractive opportunity in the utterance because it was the strongest exception. Question 5a could set up 5b as a next and potentially more powerful response.

JOEL: I agree. I saw 5b more as a follow-up. "What does she mean by this?" and then, "What difference does it make?"

LANCE: Your question, "What do you mean by that?" and my question, "What is it that you give yourself credit for?" are very similar.

JOEL: We're both asking her to co-construct meaning of "credit".

LANCE: And by virtue of our choices, we're saying, "Of all the things you said, the only thing worth amplifying here is that you give yourself credit." The other opportunities involve other people: the other couples, her boyfriend. This is the only opportunity in this utterance that addresses things within her control that she can do or not do. It's more powerful and more empowering of the choices she makes.

JOEL: I think that within that utterance, it's the only opportunity that has the probability of getting a positive response.

LANCE: If you contemplate how people work and how experiences build change, what will happen if the next time she were invited to do something, she gave herself credit ahead of time. It might be an important piece of solution-building.

JOEL: I suppose you could follow-up with, "So, now that you give yourself credit, how do you suppose it might make a difference the next time?"

LANCE: I've gotten interested in the past year in what a friend and I have come to call "initiative questions". A good initiative question here might be, "If you think over what we've just been talking about, what would be one thing worth remembering to do again?"

JOEL: That's similar to "what have you learned from this experience?"

Note

1 "Illusion of choice" is an intervention that offers the client choices while at the same time presupposing a primary choice. In this example, the client has a choice of which change will happen first and presupposes that change is going to happen no matter which option she chooses.

6 Microanalysis of Opportunities

Opportunities Analysis Example Two

Utterance #1

Okay … um [J: in terms of what your best hopes are] ya I guess I'm not … I'm trying to be a little bit more observant when things are going well … [J: are going well] ya [J: oh okay] so I'm trying to do … you know that was a better night … oh today wasn't that bad … what made it not that bad [J: um-hm] and then kind of follow through with that … I did notice that if I keep myself busy … [J: um-hm] it's not that bad … [J: um-hm] ummm … you notice if … kind of funny but … because I know like I have the to-do list again and I'm not tackling the to-do list in any aspect … I'm having a bad day … but if I'm tackling something in the to-do list I'm having a better day … and I've noticed those types of things.

Chart 6.1 I'm trying to be a bit more observant

#	Opportunity Lance	Possible responses (preferred = *) Lance	Opportunity Joel	Possible responses (preferred = *) Joel
1	I'm trying to be a little bit more observant when things are going well …	1a: Excellent! That can be a key to making a difference! 1b: What's something that went a little better lately? 1c: How do you do this? 1d: Scaling question … if 10 is being very observant?	I guess I'm not … I'm trying to be a little bit more observant when things are going well …	1a: How have you been able to do that? 1b: What are you learning from that? 1c: How has that made a difference for you? 1d: You've been looking for the small changes.

DOI: 10.4324/9781003396703-7

Chart 6.1 (Continued)

# Opportunity Lance	Possible responses (preferred = *) Lance	Opportunity Joel	Possible responses (preferred = *) Joel
2 What made it not that bad.	2a: Another excellent question you are asking yourself– helps us figure out keys to success! 2b: What's one of your discoveries lately about what made it not that bad? 2c: Scaling question… how good was it if 10 is not bad at all?	So I'm trying to do … you know that was a better night … oh today wasn't that bad … what made it not that bad.	2a: And what are you learning about things being better rather than not that bad? 2b: Similar to 1a, 1b, 1c 2c: What told you that it was a better night? *2d: What is the difference in what you are doing, thinking, and feeling on those better nights?
3 And then kind of follow through with that.	3a: Great – put a good idea to work! *3b: What's an example of following through? What else? 3c: What is some follow through you did lately that you may want to do again?	And then kind of follow through with that.	3a: Follow through? 3b: How have you been following through with that? 3c: What happens when you follow through?
4 I did notice that if I keep myself busy … it's not that bad.	4a: What's better when you keep yourself busy? 4b: Is the to-do list one way to keep yourself busy? 4c: What other ways of being busy can you recall? 4d: What does this noticing tell you about how it [anxiety] works?	I did notice that if I keep myself busy … [J: um-hm] it's not that bad.	4a: Really? 4b: How did you come to noticing that? 4c: Noticing that staying busy makes a difference, how has that been helpful?
5 But if I'm tackling something in the to-do list I'm having a better day.	5a: What's something from the to-do list you tackled lately? 5b: What was better about that day? 5c: Scaling question … if 10 stands for a good day?	You notice if … kind of funny but … because I know like I have the to-do list again and I'm not tackling the to-do list in any aspect … I'm having a bad day … but if I'm tackling something in the to-do list I'm having a better day.	Similar to 4a–4c.

(*Continued*)

Chart 6.1 (Continued)

# Opportunity Lance	Possible responses (preferred = *) Lance	Opportunity Joel	Possible responses (preferred = *) Joel
6 And I've noticed those types of things.	6a: Good for you for paying attention to what works!	I've noticed those types of things.	6a: How has that made a difference for you? 6b: Suppose you continue to notice this, what do you suppose it would change how you think, feel, and act? 6c: What else?

Session 2, Utterance #1: Discussion

Lance's Chart

LANCE: I chose to respond to opportunity number three. Of the three choices for responses, I liked the second, "What's an example of following through? What else?" In general, I thought that there were a lot of high-potential opportunities in this utterance. I choose 3b for its double value of moving thinking into doing as well as for its loading on agency – that the client can take an action that makes a difference. "Follow through" might be a title or name for something. I have no idea what it means in real life, but she knows. So, she can tell us when she followed through, and exactly what she did to follow through.

JOEL: I found it much harder doing this second utterance. It seems to me this second session involved much more solution talk.

LANCE: That's a good test for us. In contrast, there was more problem talk in the first session – not surprisingly – and more problem talk in our selection of utterances. It's good to contemplate the differences in opportunities between those two kinds of contexts.

Joel's Chart

JOEL: I also listed six opportunities. I chose to respond to the second one, and of the possible responses, I chose, "What is the difference in what you are doing, thinking, and feeling on those better nights?" I chose that one because I thought that this intervention started with the exception: "better nights" and expanded to the details of acts, thoughts, and feelings. It also put it in the present and implied future tenses. It's a classic formulation: it preserves her language ("better nights"), deletes the phrases "wasn't that bad and" and "not that bad" and adds or transforms with difference and specifics of doing, thinking, and feeling.

LANCE: I agree; this is a nice example of a formulation. Given what you said that in the second session there's more solution talk, it makes sense that we each might choose to respond to different opportunities since there are more choices. Maybe when there are more problem-saturated utterances, and opportunities are fewer and farther between, it makes it easier to home in on them.

JOEL: Perhaps when there is more problem talk, the exceptions stand out even more. If you have more choices about positive statements, there's a greater chance we're not going to choose the same ones.

LANCE: I'm looking at our respective rationales because it seems to me that if there are more choices, then our rationale for picking what we pick becomes a bigger part of it.

JOEL: I think our rationales are similar.

LANCE: Your rationale for choice 2d fits my possible responses. Similarly, I chose 3b using almost the same language you did: "its double value of moving thinking into doing". You said, "What is the difference in what you are doing, thinking, and feeling?" This is one of those utterances that I thought I could use any of the opportunities in there productively. It was a hard choice to select only one.

JOEL: Right, the choices aren't as glaring.

LANCE: There's a point to be made that sometimes it doesn't matter which opportunity you choose when you're headed to the same destination anyway. There are a lot of different pathways to get there.

JOEL: That's also true with the first session, which was more problem focused. Isn't that the point that we could have chosen any one of the various opportunities since the choice would probably result in a solution-building response? I suppose there are some opportunities that are more accessible than others. Basically, if your intention is to ask a question that will yield a higher potential for a positive response, you're probably on the right track.

LANCE: I like that word "accessible". That's the key for me considering opportunities. Which of these opportunities is likely to give the client and me access to the difference they're trying to create? You might be able to get access in some of the more problem-focused statements, but it might be harder work.

JOEL: It's all about probability, isn't it? That's the intuitive part of practicing SFBT. That's the purpose of the opportunities exercise – training the ear to listen for that.

LANCE: There are two lenses through which we view this process: one lens screens for opportunities in solution-focused terms, and the other screens for probability.

JOEL: I think that this is the difference between an experienced practitioner and one who is fairly new to the model. An experienced practitioner tends to hear the opportunities more. It almost becomes intuitive.

LANCE: I remember saying to someone in the midst of a problem-focused conversation, "I don't actually hear problems too well." There are layers in our perceiving what clients are saying: one layer is what are the opportunities within this utterance, and the next layer is what is the most probable of these opportunities. In turn, this leads to our choice.

Utterance #2

I always feel better when everything's done on the list [J: Okay, okay] even if it's something that doesn't need to be done ... two or three weeks from now [J: right] ... I still feel better with that list being wiped clean even though I know [J: sure, sure, sure] it's not on the immediate list [J: sure] but um ... whether mental or physical and ... it feels better ... it just feels better to have everything done [J: oh of course] and ... like even when I was in school [J: um-hm] and you had a ... a ... a report due in a month it was nicer to just have it done and just get it out of the way [J: right] so even say I had a list of ten things and the report was the long term and the other nine were things I should have done that week [J: right, right] let's say I get ... everything done like that one through nine but I still have that report on my table I still wouldn't feel successful [J: right, right, right] cause I didn't do everything [J: right, right]

Chart 6.2 It just feels better to have everything done

# Opportunity Lance	Possible responses (preferred = *) Lance	Opportunity Joel	Possible responses (preferred = *) Joel
1 I always feel better.	1a: Remind me again of what are the first signs of feeling better? 1b: What do you do differently in a day once you notice you are feeling better?	I always feel better when everything's done on the list even if it's something that doesn't need to be done ... two or three weeks from now.	1a: I suppose knowing that about yourself is important? 1b: Know that about yourself, how has that been important. 1c: I suppose that's not something you want to change. 1d: Say nothing.

Chart 6.2 (Continued)

# Opportunity Lance	Possible responses (preferred = *) Lance	Opportunity Joel	Possible responses (preferred = *) Joel
2 Whether or not it's all work and.	2a: What's something that's not all work that still feels better?	I still feel better with that list being wiped clean even though I know it's not on the immediate list but um ... whether mental or physical and ... it feels better ... it just feels better to have everything done.	*2a: Of course. 2b: That makes perfect sense.
3 It just feels better to have everything done.	3a: *Oh, of course!	Like even when I was in school [J: um-hm] and you had a ... a ... a report due in a month it was nicer to just have it done and just get it out of the way.	3a: Similar to 2a and 2b. 3b: How did you figure out that early that this was important to you?
4		So even say I had a list of ten things and the report was the long term and the other nine were things I should have done that week let's say I get ... everything done like that one through nine but I still have that report on my table I still wouldn't feel successful cause I didn't do everything.	4a: Completing the work is important to you. 4b: Similar to 2a and 2b. 4c: Similar to 3b.

Session 2, Utterance #2: Discussion

Lance's Chart

LANCE: Of the three, I chose the third opportunity with one choice, "Oh, of course!" I saw this utterance as primarily problem focused. So, I thought it was best to give a minimal response.

JOEL: That's a Steve de Shazer response (personal communication).

LANCE: Exactly, that's what I thought when I saw it. It seemed pretty obvious to me. I thought that this is the best response to this utterance as a whole. It's a normalizing response. I thought it would likely deconstruct the notion that she could only feel better when everything has been done. I viewed this utterance as an anxiety-laden narrative about why she needs to be so obsessive. I really didn't want very much to do with that narrative. The only way out I could see was a deconstructive response.

Joel's Chart

JOEL: Look what I chose ("of course"). You can tell we were both influenced
             by Steve [de Shazer]. Both 2a and 2b are about what works for her.
             As you suggested, I also thought "simpler is better". I thought that
             either of those responses would make sense and by implication
             deconstruct her assumption that her need to "get everything done"
             is part of her OCD diagnosis. It's just who she is; she likes to get
             things done.

LANCE: I think this is a really interesting utterance. I think that there are some
             dynamics here that are pretty unique to anxiety problems. When
             people talk about their anxious way of living and the things they do
             in the service of that anxiety, I find it difficult to sort out whether this
             is more a restatement of the problem – a justification and rationaliza-
             tion of the problem – versus a narrative about their hopes for a diffe-
             rence, and solution. I think this is one of those client narratives about
             anxiety that has the potential for getting lost. What I like is neither of
             us did get lost. We didn't engage in an anxiety-laden narrative. We
             both just said, "Of course."

JOEL: Right, this is a case where simpler is indeed better.

LANCE: When I hear clients talk about all the anxiety-motivated things they
             do during the day, it seems so complicated. Their day seems so
             complicated, and their reasoning for how they operate days seems
             complicated. It's easy to get lost in all the complicating details. I find
             it important to step back and not get caught up in the convoluted
             talking, thinking, feeling about, "I do this because then if I don't do
             that, then that doesn't lead to this …" So, for me this is a very char-
             acteristic type of utterance.

JOEL: To paraphrase Maslow's (1966) statement, if all you have is a
             hammer, then everything begins to look like a nail. If you have a
             diagnosis, everything that happens seems to fit into that diagnosis.
             Even what would be a normal reaction to the bad luck that happens
             to all of us becomes folded into that diagnosis. Everything becomes
             self-proving.

LANCE: I often find myself wondering, "When doesn't the problem happen?"
             That's one of the doorways that gets us out of this self-fulfilling,
             convoluted narrative. That's what helps to avoid the trap of losing
             ourselves to problem talk.

JOEL: It's not a coincidence that historically the recognition of exceptions
             led to the development of the solution-focused model.

LANCE: As a practitioner, I think it's important to take a stand against
             the way the client currently understands their situation and their

trouble. Otherwise, I don't think I can do them any good if I get caught up in the anxiety-laden narrative. It's too easy to get lost. To be effective, I have to keep myself in a more resourceful position.

JOEL: Right, when you get caught in the client's narrative, all you're doing is serving to co-construct the problem narrative. You end up creating more of what you're trying to resolve – it makes little sense.

LANCE: I imagine practitioners of other kinds of therapy might be quite comfortable operating within a problem narrative, and maybe taking it into some new directions. As a solution-focused practitioner, I just want out of that kind of narrative. I want us to get into more exception talk even if the exception is totally hypothetical and all in the future. I think I have a better chance of helping the client rather than just reiterating the problems.

JOEL: I'm curious about having a conversation with someone who works more of a problem-focused model. I'd like to ask their idea of how you go from problem to not-problem? How do you get to resolution?

LANCE: I can make a guess. I think they could take a line like, "I still feel better with that list being wiped clean," and say that reveals a cognitive structure that perfect completion is essential. Their purpose would be to recruit the client into the idea that there are other cognitive structures for that. For example, partial completion is not only normal but an acceptable part of life: to try to transition from problem to not-problem that way. That's a total guess.

JOEL: It's interesting. Our mutual choice here would not fit into the CBT paradigm. We look for exceptions. Exceptions to problems are viewed as static in problem-focused models and therefore are to be ignored because they don't fall within the problem model. It goes back to Maslow's adage: if my focus is on problems, I assume they exist and then I go about finding them.

LANCE: Reminds me of the time when I considered myself a Gestalt therapist for a while. What you would do with that statement as a Gestalt therapist is you would get them to say that again, "I only feel better when everything is done." "Say that some more; say that louder; tell everyone here about that." "Tell them about everything you have to do fully and ..." So, you would exaggerate and amplify the problem statement until the point of becoming absurd. Then it opens up possibilities for differences.

JOEL: Right, but I think we get to it faster.

Utterance #3

Uh … yeah … it's helpful and hurtful at the same time because I'm like …
oh why do I have to be like that … and then other times I'm like … I'm like
uh … I'm like well … I … I see … you know like the whole OCD thing …
I see what's non-logical about this … so I understand that it's … silly for me
to think … that getting something done where there are a lot of times of the
month … and there usually is a lot of time in the month … you know … try to
think through it logically but then that one part of … you know … my brain's
just like … oh get it done, get it done!

Chart 6.3 You know like the whole OCD thing

# Opportunity Lance	Possible responses (preferred = *) Lance	Opportunity Joel	Possible responses (preferred = *) Joel
1 Oh, why do I have to be like that?	1a: Good to question some of our habits from time to time! 1b: How is it useful for you to question a habit like this at times?	It's helpful and hurtful at the same time.	1a: What is the helpful part of it? 1b: How are you able to see both sides at the same time? 1c: What is helpful about being able to see both sides at the same time?
2 I see what's non-logical about this.	2a: I'm impressed that you look at this from different points of view! 2b: How is it useful for you to realize this can be understood in different ways, from different points of view?	Because I'm like … oh why do I have to be like that?	2a: You must have a good reason. 2b: What's the other side of that thought?
3 That getting something done where there are a lot of times of the month … and there usually is a lot of time in the month.	*3a: What would your hope be for how you would respond differently when you see there is a lot of time in the month?	Then other times I'm like … I'm like uh … I'm like well … I … I see … you know like the whole OCD thing … I see what's non-logical about this.	3a: What is the non-logical? 3b: Seeing the non-logical, how is that helpful? 3c: What's the part of you that can see that? 3d: How do you manage to see the non-logical?
4		So I understand that it's … silly for me to think … that getting something done where there are a lot of times of the month.	4a: Is that this OCD you talk about or something different than that? *4b: You must have a good reason for wanting to get it done even though you have more time.

Chart 6.3 (Continued)

#	Opportunity Lance	Possible responses (preferred = *) Lance	Opportunity Joel	Possible responses (preferred = *) Joel
5			And there usually is a lot of time in the month ... you know ... try to think through it logically but then that one part of ... you know ... my brain's just like ... oh get it done, get it done.	5a: Would you like to have the choice of following the logic? 5b: What part of getting it done would you want to keep?

Session 2, Utterance #3: Discussion

Joel's Chart

JOEL: Of the ones I chose, I chose number four ("So, I understand that it's silly for me think that getting something done where there are lots of times of the month"). I liked 4b ("You must have a good reason for wanting to get it done even though you have more time"). I thought this might de-pathologize her desire to getting work done as defined as her OCD.

LANCE: So, to try and get her to think about or articulate reasons for wanting that outside of OCD – outside of that language – is that what you mean?

JOEL: I think it serves the same purpose as saying "of course." "You must have good reason for doing this." It's implying, "You're a smart person, you don't do stupid things, you're not crazy. Therefore, you must have a good reason for this."

LANCE: That's an Insoo-ism [Insoo Kim Berg] as I recall. She would say any outrageous behavior a client did, they must have a good reason for doing it.

JOEL: That's where I learned it.

LANCE: It's just lovely. It's so affirming on one level, and it allows you to make a distinction between purpose and action.

JOEL: Insoo (private conversation) said that one thing solution-focus does is give people a brain. I think a better way to say that is that it acknowledges that people have brains.

Lance's Chart

LANCE: Of the three opportunities, I chose the same one as you. I only came up with one response (3a). I chose that one because of all the possible opportunities in this utterance, 3a was most promising for its potential for moving a complaint or self-criticism into a hope. I would have a fair amount of optimism for that intervention. It's a little bit beyond the "of course" response. It holds out the possibility that maybe when she begins to overcome her OCD, she'll be able to turn down the urge to do something when there's time left and she doesn't have to do it. I imagine that might open that up. I figure you can't go too far wrong when you pick out a piece of problem talk and help the client transition it into a hope.

JOEL: I think it's similar to my 4a ("Is that this OCD you talk about or something different than that?").

LANCE: I suspect you would get a period of silence after that. She'd probably thinking about what do you mean, what's inside of OCD, what's outside of it? That also holds out the possibility of opening up the non-problem area.

JOEL: It's similar to the question we talked about last time; "Let's suppose the diagnosis never existed. What would you say about yourself?"

LANCE: I think we might be operating with different presuppositions. Yours tended more towards a de-pathologizing urge. On the other hand, mine is more of a pathologizing urge. It's not that I'm trying to pathologize her, but I do see it as troublesome that she is driven to do everything even when there's a lot of time left in the month. I see that as less than a healthy position. So, I'm supposing that there might be a better way of going about things. I think your presupposition is that there could be a way of looking at her urge to get everything done as normal: as reasonable and healthy.

JOEL: That makes sense, "Get the job done. Don't let it be hanging over you."

LANCE: All that's not unreasonable. Our generation taught most of us that. Meat and potatoes first before you get to the apple pie.

JOEL: The idea of de-pathologizing is important to me. Too many people come in thinking that there's something mentally wrong with them. Or they came in because they saw a therapist and they have a diagnosis. They then become their diagnosis. A lot of what I do is to help them think differently about themselves. Years ago, I had a client who self-diagnosed as having panic disorder. He had graduated from a prestigious college and was a really bright guy, yet he lived a limiting life even though he hadn't had an attack in years. I saw him with a team. After I consulted with the team, I came back and said, "It's interesting to us that you still define yourself this way even though you haven't had a panic attack in such a long time." When he returned, he said that he had thought about that and realized that he had made his diagnosis central to his life. He went on to explain that he realized that his diagnosis is only one aspect of himself – not central to how he defines himself.

LANCE: Deconstructing and depathologizing are important to me too. I think I live that out a bit differently. I think I want to get beyond the problem and get to solution development. I expect a stronger approach would be to do both: sabotaging the problem in a sense and deconstructing it at the same time. You tend to be more direct about deconstructing the problem and I tend to be more indirect. I think there are times that being direct would be more advantageous.

JOEL: And the opposite is also probably true. Coming from a more indirect stance might be more useful at times.

LANCE: I don't think I actually used the term OCD in any of my potential interventions. I think that's an indication of how widely I'm steering clear of anything to do with the problem. To use it as you did in 4a, there are a couple of ideas here: you're not phobic of using it – you're comfortable with the language; you're not avoiding it – and you're using it to create a bifurcation between what is in OCD and what isn't. It's a constructive, solution-oriented use of the problem language. That's why it's important to have that as part of one's repertoire.

JOEL: I wouldn't have used it if she hadn't used it. I wouldn't use a diagnosis unless the client used the diagnosis. I suppose I borrowed this concept from a narrative approach. This makes it external as opposed to internal.

LANCE: We were taught, and we teach others, to use the client's language as a way of joining with them – privileging their way of understanding the world over our way.

JOEL: It reminds me of something [Milton] Erickson said. If you accept what the client says as their reality, then you can manipulate it (Rosen, 1982).

LANCE: When somebody says, "I'm bipolar", I find it useful to ask them how being bipolar is troublesome to them in their life. So, you go from this all-encompassing, immutable title into problems of daily living. Once you hear it in terms of problems of daily living, it's much more solvable. It's easier to solve ups and downs of mood more easily than you can solve bipolar. It's a way of grounding it too.

Utterance #4

So ... I realized if I give in to my cleaning tendencies and didn't ignore them... that previous therapist had told me to do ... or ... the whole ... you know ... flooding theory or versus ... versus desensitization and stuff like that whether I ... I just ... versus doing all that ... just give in to it I'm actually happier doing that ... I'm happier ... you know ... you know we have a dog and two cats so ... our house is a little hairy at times [laughs] [J: right, right] so that's one thing that actually drives me completely insane ... and ... uh instead of ... saying ... you know ... the previous therapist had told me ... just let it be ... well I don't want to let it ... leave it be [raised voice] it's annoying and it ruins my whole day if I let it be [J: um-hm] so I clean it up and go on my merry way [J: um-hm] and ... and I'm better for it.

Chart 6.4 I'm just happier doing that

# Opportunity Lance	Possible responses (preferred = *) Lance	Opportunity Joel	Possible responses (preferred = *) Joel
1 Well, I don't want to let it leave it be ... so I clean it up and go on my merry way ... and I'm better for it.	1a: What are some other examples of small things in your day that are better just done when it occurs to you? *1b: On a scale, 10 stands for it's best to follow the lead of my cleaning tendencies, and 1 is it's best to ignore it – where does this task rate?	I realized if I give in to my cleaning tendencies and didn't ignore them ... that previous therapist had told me to do ... or ... the whole ... you know ... flooding theory or versus ... versus desensitization and stuff like that whether I ... I just ... versus doing all that ... just give in to it I'm actually happier doing that.	1a: How did you figure out that those cleaning tendencies actually make you happy? 1b: How did you come to realize that you're more of an expert on yourself than those therapists? 1c: How smart of you to figure that out.
2		I'm happier ... you know ... you know we have a dog and two cats so ... our house is a little hairy at times [laughs] so that's one thing that actually drives me completely insane.	2a: Of course. 2b: Despite that you allow yourself to have a dog and 2 cats.

Chart 6.4 (Continued)

# Opportunity Lance	Possible responses (preferred = *) Lance	Opportunity Joel	Possible responses (preferred = *) Joel
3		Instead of … saying … you know … the previous therapist had told me … just let it be … well I don't want to let it … leave it be [raised voice] it's annoying and it ruins my whole day if I let it be. So, I clean it up and go on my merry way and … and I'm better for it.	3a: Similar to 1b and 1c 3b: Similar to 2a *3c: [Summarize then …] Through all of this, what else are you learning about yourself? 3d: How did you have the strength to listen to yourself and not those other therapists?

Session 2, Utterance #4: Discussion

Lance's Chart

LANCE: I had just the one opportunity. Of the two possibilities, I chose the second, 1b. I thought 1b will likely cover 1a. Inquiry along this line may have multiple benefits including portraying some urges as better followed than others and perhaps opening up conversation about urges that might be better ignored. I think I saw this utterance more as her going over all the battles, troubles, and therapists. There seemed to be more blind alleys to get lost in. She's saying, "To hell with the therapists, and to hell with the OCD. I just don't like hair and I'm going to clean it up." That just seemed normal to me. It's parallel to "you must have had a good reason". I suppose my rationale is that there are some things we should do when it occurs to us. It's not necessarily OCD. There might be some things that are ridiculous to do like going back six times just to make sure that the door is locked. There's a difference between the hair and the door. So, how about if we start creating shades of gray. I find scales helpful in doing that. I guess I have an assumption with this case that she wants to stop doing some of this. I don't know where that's coming from. I wonder if I'm so pathologized that I think, "She must want that." It's clear I'm operating under that assumption.

JOEL: It might be helpful to go back to what precipitated her wanting to call me. Even before that, what is it that precipitated her saying something to her boyfriend, who said, "You should go see this guy?" Was it this incident that happened in the restaurant?

LANCE: Let's look at yours. I think it might give us a window into how you took it.

Joel's Chart

JOEL: Of my three choices, I chose the third one.

LANCE: We chose the same content.

JOEL: Right, I chose 3c ["Summarize then …] Through all of this, what else are you learning about yourself?"). I thought the whole sequence was basically solution focused. She seems to have deconstructed her OCD diagnosis on her own. She also has shown the strength and wisdom to reject what other "expert" therapists have termed pathology, realizing that her cleaning tendencies just make her happy. By summarizing and emphasizing the main positive points, the intervention goes on to imply that this has been a learning process. It assumes that there are additional positive learnings from her experiences. It follows the EARS process ("elicit, amplify, reinforce, start again"). One thing I remember from this case is asking her what pieces of OCD she would want to keep. The other was when she talked about wanting to wear gloves when she touches dirty laundry. The therapist wanted to desensitize her to this. She said, "It doesn't bother me." I said, "Yeah, but it bothers the therapist."

LANCE: This helps me out of my dilemma. I remember watching this sequence several times. I remember there are two contexts in which gloves are mentioned. One is the laundry. I mean I don't put on gloves to do my laundry, but it doesn't seem to me to be that outrageous. The other is she has the urge to wear gloves wherever she goes in the world. She declines that urge at times because for her it's too outside of the norm. It seems to me that this is a distinction between when is it okay to follow – in her language – her cleaning urges, and when is it not okay. I suppose she would like to wear gloves everywhere she goes but realizes it's more trouble than it's worth.

JOEL: It's just not practical.

LANCE: It answers the question you raised: "What part of OCD would you like to keep?" What's interesting about this case are these fine distinctions. I think what you suggest is to normalize what seems like reasonable behavior and leave it to her – after all, she's the client – to figure out what difference she wants, as opposed to you being the expert deciding what is pathology and what isn't.

JOEL: What this points out is the danger of the diagnosis – any diagnosis. The diagnosis becomes part of who you are. "I have no choice because I'm OCD, I have no choice because I'm depressed …" When we make the distinction between what she wants to keep and what she wants to let go, she ends up with more choices and a greater sense of possibilities. "You're not controlled by your diagnosis."

LANCE: I recall a family of an adolescent I was working with. They had waited months to get an appointment with a psychiatrist. When they finally met with the psychiatrist, he diagnosed the boy as depressed. The parents expressed their relief at now having a diagnosis. I asked them how this was helpful to them knowing this. The mother said, "Up to now, we were worried that there was something wrong with him."

JOEL: Right, "It's just depression." There's an Ericksonian story about a patient who was dying, and they didn't know what the problem was. So they called in a specialist who examined the patient, and then used the Latin term which essentially means, "This guy's dying." Of course, the patient didn't speak Latin and had no way of knowing what the specialist was saying. He thought, "Now I have a diagnosis and so I'm going to get better." He did. So maybe there is some value in diagnosis.

Utterance #5

I ... I kind of ... umm ... I mean I don't think about it ... it just ... I'll ... like let's ... we'll go back to the gloves with the washing machine ... I don't think about trying to desensitize myself ... I just go to what I'm comfortable with and I just go for it [J: um-h] and it didn't bother me [J: um-h] ... I'm not thinking...oh I have to do laundry [whispering] ... should I wear the gloves [questioning] ... should I not wear the gloves [questioning] ... trying not to step into that mindset.

Chart 6.5 Trying not to step into that mindset

# Opportunity Lance	Possible responses (preferred = *) Lance	Opportunity Joel	Possible responses (preferred = *) Joel
1 I mean I don't think about it.	1a: Is this a useful sign to you when you don't think about it? 1b: What does it tell you when you don't think about it?	I ... I kind of ... umm ... I mean I don't think about it.	1a: How do you manage not think about it? 1b: What are you thinking about it instead? *1c: How does that change your thinking about what you called your OCD mindset?

(Continued)

Chart 6.5 (Continued)

# Opportunity Lance	Possible responses (preferred = *) Lance	Opportunity Joel	Possible responses (preferred = *) Joel
2 I just go to what I'm comfortable with and I just go for it … and it didn't bother me.	2a: What are some other examples of small things in your day that are better just done when it occurs to you? 2b: On a scale, 10 stands for it's best to follow the lead of my cleaning tendencies and 1 is it's best to ignore the urge – where does this task rate?	We'll go back to the gloves with the washing machine … I don't think about trying to desensitize myself … I just go to what I'm comfortable with and I just go for it.	2a: How had you the wisdom not to listen to those experts? 2b: When was the first time you noticed you were starting to think differently about this? 2c: Since you're realizing that, how has that been making a difference for you? 2d: Let's suppose that you continue to think this way even more, how do you suppose that will change things? 2e: Similar to 1c.
3 Trying not to step into that mindset.	*3a: What mindset do you hope to have in its place?	And it didn't bother me.	3a: See above. 3b: What's happening instead?
4		I'm not thinking … oh I have to do laundry [whispering] … should I wear the gloves [questioning] … should I not wear the gloves.	4a: You thought wearing gloves might be useful? 4b: How did you decide to wear gloves?
5		Trying not to step into that mindset.	5a: Scale 10 = not stepping into the mindset comes easily and 0 is it's the hardest thing for you to do. 5b: What are the signs that you're in a different mindset? 5c: What is the different mindset? 5d: What difference does it make for you when you're not stepping into that mindset?

Session 2, Utterance #5: Discussion

Joel's Chart

JOEL: I separated this utterance into five opportunities. Of those, I chose the first opportunity ("I mean I don't think about it"). There were three choices in that opportunity, of which I chose 1c ("How does that change your thinking about what you called your OCD mindset?"). I reasoned that this was a further blow against her OCD diagnosis: essentially a deconstruction. I thought her statement suggested that she was in a very different language-game – one that excluded the diagnosis.

LANCE: I thought that this was an interesting utterance. I'm looking at the other opportunities – the ones you didn't choose.

JOEL: The choice I made really speaks to something you said before. In this case, I thought that she and I needed together to chip away from this OCD construction.

LANCE: I'm wondering whether it's the "thinking about" that's part of her trouble with OCD. So, she just sees a stimulus and then responds, and then she sees that as effective and then walks away. That doesn't seem like OCD until she starts thinking about it, "Should I do it, or shouldn't I do it?" Or, "Did I do it, or didn't I do it?" That becomes part of the problem talk. So I feel called upon to make a distinction which is what I think you're doing too. When you ask questions like, "Is that part of the OCD or not?" that suggests an important issue for me. Are there some things that she is doing that's just part of life – they don't seem like OCD to me at all: just doing your laundry – some of it is not so acceptable to her. Does she need to have some distinction between these normal things and the abnormal in her language. That's you working on overtly deconstructing the problem.

Lance's Chart

LANCE: Let's look at the first one for a minute. It's the one you chose, "I don't think about it." I also had a strong pull to that one. So, my question was, "Is this a useful sign for you when you don't think about it?" "What does it tell you when you don't think about it?" Yours tended to be a bit more actionable (see 1a–1c). I like the simplicity of those. I chose opportunity three. They're related opportunities: not thinking about it and mindset. I had one possible response (3a). I think it will help her articulate what she wants. I hope we would be able to get a name for this mindset that's different from whatever the mindset she doesn't want to step into – we don't need a name for that. We do need a name for the mindset that she does want instead. Once we have that, we can begin to map out what will be happening differently when she's in that new mindset, when has it taken place, and where the laundry is in that new mindset.

JOEL: What I like about that choice too is that you're basically saying to her, "How do you want to begin thinking differently about this?" How do you answer that question without thinking differently?

LANCE: That's the purple Volkswagen question.

JOEL: Or a pink elephant. By asking her how she wants her mindset to change, you're requiring her to change her mindset.

LANCE: Maybe that's part of the hope question. When you ask the hope question, people can't answer it without slipping into the hope. It works so reliably because it is a simple question that requires shifting perspective just by answering it.

JOEL: You're inviting them to think different without directly telling them to think different.

LANCE: Right, by answering what they hope for, they show you how simple it is to think different.

JOEL: It's a way of getting to it through the back door.

LANCE: When I teach, I find it much more helpful to ask what do you want as a result of this session rather than what do you want different in your life.

7 Applications

Opportunities as a Supervision Tool

Erica is an occupational therapist (OT). She volunteered to be the supervisee for this chapter on the use of microanalysis of opportunities as a tool for supervision. Erica lives in Toronto, Canada. She provided both transcripts and six video clips from her meetings with her client for the two supervisory sessions: June 24 and June 28, 2021. The sessions were conducted virtually using Zoom.

Prior to the first supervision meeting, Erica and Joel completed their separate microanalyses of two clips. They brought their charts containing their analyses to the supervision meetings. For the sake of presenting results here, Joel integrated their two charts to show the utterance, opportunities, and possible responses for both analysts in one chart.

In order to keep the comparisons consistent, Joel selected the opportunities. In Chapter 4, we consistently used the term "utterance". In this case, and because the utterance was much larger, it was decided to separate the larger utterance into sub-utterances.

Session 1: June 24, 2021

Clip 1: Sub-utterance 1

What was it? I think it was seizing the opportunity of energy, my energy has always been varied, and I can't predict, oh, I'm gonna have a good day today or a bad day today. Or today, I'm going to get my ass off my couch. I can't predict those days. So when I realized, hey, today's actually a better day, the sun is shining. The ideas are flowing, I actually it's like, perfect time, place. And execution, like I managed to align all those three. And I'm like, hey, I managed to do that. And then I noticed that when I was doing my art, the focus was not on my pain, or my suffering. It was, hey, I'm using that energy to do something about it. And I have all this restless energy so instead of just you know, twiddling my fingers or trying to find a fidget spinner, or whatever those kids call it, I decided to put into something, that was tangible. That was beautiful. And that kind of got me going.

DOI: 10.4324/9781003396703-8

Chart 7.1 I can't predict those days

# Opportunities	Possible responses (preferred = *) Joel	Possible responses (preferred = *) Erica
1 What was it, I think it was seizing the opportunity of energy, my energy has always been varied, and I can't predict, oh, I'm gonna have a good day today or a bad day today. Or today, I'm going to get my ass off my couch. I can't predict those days.	1a: What were the first signs you had this energy? 1b: When did you first notice that it was going to be a good day? *1c: What constitutes a good day? 1d: On a scale of 0 to 10 where 10 is the best day imaginable, where would you put those days? 1e: On a scale of 0 to 10, how confident are you that this could happen again?	1a: When are other times in the past month that you have seized that restless energy and used it towards something meaningful to you?
2 So when I realized, hey, today's actually a better day, the sun is shining. The ideas are flowing, I actually it's like, perfect time, place.	2a: When did you first realize it? 2b: What were the first signs of this better day? 2c: What ideas were flowing? 2d: What did you do to sustain that perfect time, place?	2a: When have there been other times when your ideas have been flowing?
3 And then I noticed that when I was doing my art, the focus was not on my pain, or my suffering. It was, Hey, I'm using that energy to do something about it.	3a: What are you learning from that experience? 3b: What would need to happen to have that happen even more? 3c: What were you doing about it? 3d: Was that a big surprise or a little surprise?	3a: Despite your pain, when have there been other times that you have been so focused on something? 3b: What is something you would like to do when you are able to seize the opportunity of energy? 3c: On an ideal day, when you're able to seize that energy, what's the first thing you might do? *3d: Could you tell me about the last time you seized that opportunity of energy and put it into something tangible? 3e: What is another activity that gets your mind off of your pain and into creating something tangible?
4 And I have all this restless energy so instead of just, you know, twiddling my fingers or trying to find a fidget spinner, or whatever those kids call it, I decided to put into something, that was tangible. That was beautiful. And that kind of got me going.	4a: How did you transform the restless energy into something more useful? 4b: How did it get you going? 4c: What would happen if that continued and happened even more? 4d: What would need to happen for that to happen even more? 4e: Who noticed this different energy and how?	4a: What was the latest tangible thing you made? 4b: Despite your ongoing pain, on a scale of 0–10, where 10 is your highest level of confidence that you can continue to put your energy into something tangible, and 0 is the opposite, where are you now?

JOEL:	What do you think would be the most helpful?
ERICA:	I'm not sure what would be best.
JOEL:	We could compare charts. See how that goes. What might be useful for you from this conversation?
ERICA:	Maybe knowing whether the questions I asked are good solution-focused questions. Maybe you can point out questions that were more problem-focused or could have been improved.
JOEL:	Okay.
ERICA:	Should I have broken down the utterances even further?
JOEL:	The idea is to break it down into separate opportunities. That's a good point. There's a difference between the utterance and what are the opportunities within the utterances. [Reviews Erica's responses to clip 1, utterance 1]. Your preference was "Could you tell me about the last time you seized that opportunity of energy and put it into something tangible." What's your rationale?
ERICA:	I thought that this question could explore exceptions and times when she has been able to work on an activity or tangible project despite her pain and other symptoms.
JOEL:	I think any one of those would have been fine. I think they're all definitely solution-building responses. [They review Joel's chart]. Do you have any questions or comments?
ERICA:	I went back through all my questions, and I thought, "Where can I add scales?" That's not something I typically do.
LANCE'S COMMENT:	I think this moment demonstrates a particular value of micro-analysis in supervision: one practitioner gets to review possibilities generated by the other and make choices about what they might like to incorporate into their own work, all this avoiding an older 'supervision' dynamic of one person telling another what they should do.
JOEL:	Right, that's a comment I wanted to make on one of the ones you chose. What I like about this one, "Despite your ongoing pain, on a scale of 1–10 where 10 is your highest level of confidence that you can continue to put your energy into something tangible, and zero is the opposite, where are you now" is you essentially reversed the scale. In your chart: clip 4, sub-utterance 2, she has a pain scale where she puts her perception of pain at ten being the highest. You reverse the scale where you take ten as her highest level of confidence.
	[They review Joel's clip 1, sub-utterance (SU) 1.]
ERICA:	I like the question, "Was that a big surprise or small surprise" (3d).
JOEL:	What do you like about that?
ERICA:	I think it more explicitly asked whether she thought it was a big deal or a small deal. Sometimes I just assume. If I can be more explicit about whether it's a big surprise or small surprise, it would be helpful.

JOEL: It's called "the illusion of choice". She has a choice about the size of the surprise. She doesn't have a choice about it being a surprise.

ERICA: That makes sense. I like, "What are you learning from that experience?" What lesson can she take from something? I also like, "What needs to happen to have that happen even more?" I wouldn't have thought of any of the questions from number four [clip 1, SU 1].

JOEL: Look at what she says [clip 1, SU 1, opportunity #4]. Pain is as much a physical as it is a cognitive experience. [Milton] Erickson would get people to move the pain in trance [cf. O'Hanlon, 1987, pp. 67–68).

ERICA: To move the pain?

JOEL: Yes. So, it changes the experience of pain and focuses away from the pain.

Clip 1: Sub-utterance 2

I can actually focus on one thing at a time, which is good. And I noticed it was like, it was really good in terms of what I'm learning is awareness. And I'm aware of what I'm able to do. And I'm not going to fight myself and you know, make myself feel bad and wrong saying I know, I can't do this right now. Before I would just go on and on and feel sorry for myself now. It's like, Okay, you know what? I'm aware today is not a good day to do it. So, I'm not gonna do it. I'm not gonna make myself feel bad. I'm not gonna make myself wrong.

Chart 7.2 I'm not gonna make myself wrong

# Opportunities	Possible responses (preferred = *) Joel	Possible responses (preferred = *) Erica
1 I can actually focus on one thing at a time, which is good.	1a: How is it good? 1b: What difference does it make for you that you're able to focus on one thing at a time? 1c: How are you able to do that?	1a: Can you give me an example of when you focused on one thing at a time? 1b: What are other times that you have been able to focus on one thing at a time?
2 And I noticed it was like, it was really good in terms of what I'm learning is awareness. And I'm aware of what I'm able to do.	*2a: What have you learned about awareness? 2b: Similar to 1b. 2c: What is it that you are now aware of that you can do? 2d: Then what do you do?	2a: When was another time when you honored that awareness?

Chart 7.2 (Continued)

# Opportunities	Possible responses (preferred = *) Joel	Possible responses (preferred = *) Erica
3 And I'm not going to fight myself and you know, make myself feel bad and wrong saying I know, I can't do this right now.	3a: So what do you do instead of fighting with yourself? 3b: How do you have the courage to fight the urge to make yourself feel bad? 3c: What do you do instead?	*3a: Instead of making yourself feel bad or wrong, what would you be feeling/experiencing instead?
4 Before I would just go on and on and feel sorry for myself. Now it's like, Okay, you know what? I'm aware today is not a good day to do it.	4a: On those not so good days, what do you do instead that's helpful? 4b: What are the first signs that the not good days are starting to become a good day? 4c: What helps turn the not good days to good days? 4d: When were there times that what started out as a not good day actually became a good day?	4a: Can you give me an example of the last time you were able to apply this level of awareness? 4b: Say you wake up the next morning with this new level of awareness of what you are able to do, what is the first thing that you would notice?
5 So I'm not gonna do it. I'm not gonna make myself feel bad. I'm not gonna make myself wrong.	5a: What do you do instead? 5b: Where does that determination come from? 5c: How do you have the courage to go on? 5d: What helps you cope until the next good day? 5e: What's different when you tell yourself you're not going to make yourself wrong?	5a: Similar to 3a.

JOEL: Erica's chart: ["Say you wake up the next morning with this new level of awareness of what you are able to do, what is the first thing that you would notice?"]. This is a variation of the Miracle Question. You chose 3a. What's your rationale?

ERICA: This seems to be a common theme for my sessions with this client, she tends to overdo things when she gets excited about an activity and faces exacerbated symptoms the following day. I'd like to focus on what else she would like to feel instead.

JOEL: I'm wondering; is this trying to help her learn how to pace herself?

ERICA: Yeah, that's been a big theme in our sessions. She just gets – it's like a roller coaster. She gets very excited about something. She gets very immersed in it. Maybe she'll try to clean up a large portion of her room. She knows physically she doesn't have the capacity to do the entire room. She may need to do a tiny bit and take a break. When she's in something, she keeps going and pays for it the next day.

JOEL: In terms of pacing, if you were to add something to this opportunity that deals with her pacing herself, how might you do that?

ERICA: You mean what kind of question I might ask?

JOEL: Right. If you were to specifically address pacing.

ERICA: I think I ask that kind of question later on. I asked what she might tell herself before she starts the next activity. She has a lot of strategies that we had discussed together before. She just doesn't remember to apply them. I guess a question I could ask is, "What might you ask yourself or tell yourself before you start an activity?"

JOEL: I want to back up a bit. One thing this doesn't address. I'm curious about what she says is her goal for her work with you.

ERICA: One of the big things is desensitization around transportation. She had a collision when she was on a bus. The bus collided with another vehicle, and she was thrown. Her arm, hand, and wrist were fractured. She has pain all over her body and she gets very fatigued. It also affected her emotional state. So, she complains of depression, and anxiety about going out. She wants to get back to taking public transportation so she can volunteer and return to work. So, the results of the accident are limiting factors for her. She wants to be engaged in self-care activities: brushing her teeth, taking showers. Right now, she spends most of her time sitting on the couch. She's an artist. She's been working on a few projects here and there with encouragement, but she's not doing anything on her own initiative. She had been trained as a chef, so she would like to get back to cooking. She might make an elaborate dish and then pay for it the next day. So, it does have a lot to do with pacing. I think asking her solution-focused questions has helped her to better organize herself and find ways of preparing meals despite her physical limitations. I think if I made those kinds of suggestions, she probably wouldn't have done them – chefs don't use frozen vegetables and pre-made sauces.

JOEL: How many times have you seen her so far?

ERICA: I've been working with her for over two years now. I see her about once a month.

JOEL: What would she say how your work together has helped her move forward?

ERICA: I think she would say that she's learned a lot of strategies even though she doesn't implement them all the time. She says that she keeps falling down but getting back up. She can get back up because she uses the different strategies. I think getting back to bits of her life before the accident. She has returned to her art, she's going out a bit more, she's engaging with people more socially. She had trouble doing all of that just after the accident.

JOEL: This may require some speculation. What would she say needs to be happening for her to think that she's made enough progress with you that she can continue making progress on her own?

ERICA: When I first started working with her, I told her that my job is to work myself out of a job. So sometimes you need help getting out of the valley and on your way. She doesn't want treatment to end. She told me that it's going to be very tough on her when our sessions end. There have been other providers who had to end treatment because her insurance coverage ended. She took that very badly. So, she doesn't want it to end. I guess maybe I can be a kind of voice in her head encouraging her. She said she's heard my voice and others' voices in her head reminding her to do things.

JOEL: Usually, second session and after, I ask a scale where 10 is things are good enough and we don't need to meet anymore. Then I ask where things would need to be on the scale for them to think they are at a point where they can continue making progress on their own. If someone tells me that they want to come back, I have no objection to that. This is not short-term therapy where we say after X number of sessions, they're through. I like to keep "brief" in front of them – co-constructing that there's going to be an end to therapy.

Clip 1: Sub-utterance 3

So, I'm trying to find that balance between, you know, working on something and focus and because it's like a high, the focus is so great on what I was doing that the pain is there. I didn't put my attention on it. But when I'm done with a project, I'm like, oh great, I'm done. And then Oh, shit, my limbs are not following, I actually need to rest.

Chart 7.3 So, I'm trying to find that balance

# Opportunities	Possible responses (preferred = *) Joel	Possible responses (preferred = *) Erica
1 So, I'm trying to find that balance between, you know, working on something and focus.	1a: What will be the signs for you that you've found that balance? 1b: When are there times that you get even close to that sense of balance? 1c: On a scale of 0 to 10, where 10 is you've achieved that balance, where would you scale yourself? *1d: Miracle question where the miracle is achieving the balance.	1a: What helps you find that balance between the high of focusing on a project and taking a rest? 1b: Can you give me an example of the last time you were able to find that balance between focus and rest?

(Continued)

Chart 7.3 (Continued)

# Opportunities	Possible responses (preferred = *) Joel	Possible responses (preferred = *) Erica
2 And because it's like a high, the focus is so great on what I was doing that the pain is there.	2a: How does the pain change when you have that high and focus? 2b: How do you manage to get beyond the pain and focus instead? 2c: How does focusing change the sensations of pain?	2a: What might a future version of yourself say to you as you are focusing on a project?
3 I didn't put my attention on it.	3a: What did you pay attention to instead? 3b: How did changing your attention make a difference? 3c: How did you manage to change your attention?	3a: What did you put your attention on instead?
4 But when I'm done with a project, I'm like, Oh, great. I'm done. And then Oh, shit, my limbs are not following, I actually need to rest.	4a: What are you learning about pacing yourself? 4b: What are the first signs that you're recovering from all that effort and focus? 4c: What's different after you're more rested? 4d: What tells you that you need to rest?	*4a: What advice might you give yourself as you start working on a project?

JOEL: Your strategy here is to help her pace herself. You chose 4a. What's your rationale?

ERICA: I thought that this question might help her to coach herself and elicit strategies around pacing and energy conservation.

JOEL: How come you would choose that over, say, 1a or 1b?

ERICA: I think both of them would have been good options. The reason I chose 4a was that we just had talked about those topics in detail over several sessions. She knows the strategies. She's just not reminding herself or taking the time to reflect before diving into something.

JOEL: I suppose another option is to ask her, "When has there been a time that you've been able to find the balance between how you're focusing on a project and taking a rest?" That's a question that presumes that there was a time. What you're doing that I think works is using her language. She gives you these key phrases and words and you pick up on them. My experience is that it gives the client a sense that you're listening to them when you use their language. Reviewing my chart, is there anything that you might want to comment on or question?

ERICA: I like the question, "What are the signs that you've found that balance?" I haven't thought to ask the question, "When are there times that you get even close to that sense of balance?"

JOEL: That's another example of a presumptive question. I think this is a good time to ask the Miracle Question because she gives you the phrase of balance.

ERICA: So, using the Miracle Question around balance. When you ask the Miracle Question, do you go through an entire day with that or do you ask, "What would be the first thing you would notice?"

JOEL: What I usually ask, "From the time you open your eyes until the time you close your eyes, what would you be doing, thinking, or feeling; what will be happening that will tell you this miracle happened?" And then I wait to see how they respond. Often, I will come back to the question of the very first thing they would notice after they wake up. I prefer to keep it general at first to see what their response is going to be.

ERICA: I think sometimes I've been leading people a whole day and that gets repetitive. I think being more general would be more helpful.

JOEL: You can always ask, "So, what else would be happening on this day after the miracle?" And then "Who would notice it and how would they notice it?" That can be expanded into how they would notice it and what they would be doing in response. It allows for a very rich description of the miracle.

ERICA: I don't think I've ever asked something like your 2a.

JOEL: It would be interesting to hear your thoughts about that as an occupational therapist.

ERICA: I don't usually ask a lot of questions about pain itself. I will ask questions about where the pain is. The focus for me is on compensatory strategies. What they can do to alleviate the pain. Different ways we can modify the environment. So I guess my questions aren't around pain itself. It would be interesting to try asking about how the pain changes.

JOEL: Neither have I [both laugh]. That's what's nice about doing this, "I've never asked that question, but it would be a good one to ask."

ERICA: It focuses on how the quality and location of pain changes.

JOEL: Something we had talked about before is how pain is both physical and cognitive. So, what kind of conversation can you have that could co-construct a different experience? Asking someone where the pain is focuses them on the pain. So what it does is co-construct more pain. As opposed to asking about how the pain changes. That co-constructs the experience of pain as changeable.

ERICA: Would the question about how the pain improves or gets better be appropriate when talking about pain?

JOEL: Yeah, I think anything that co-constructs a different experience of pain. You can't change the physical, but you can certainly change their experience of it.

ERICA: There are some occupational therapists who are experts on pain. You can take continuing education on pain itself. I haven't, so, that's an area of improvement for me.

JOEL: During one of our [Solution-Focused Brief Therapy Association] conferences, we had a physician presenter who was talking about pain experience. She was talking about the use of the typical pain scale where 10 is intolerable pain. She said that when research was done, people were asked about their experience of pain after being asked the pain scale, they reported experiencing more pain. That makes sense to me. If you're asked a pain scale, what you're co-constructing is the experience of pain. I had talked about this during a training session. A nurse told me that she always asks a comfort scale rather than a pain scale.

ERICA: I'll try that.

JOEL: As an OT, it might be useful to think, "What kind of conversation am I having with someone that helps them have a different experience of pain?" I'm curious – as an OT, does this make sense?

ERICA: Yeah, absolutely, because a lot of our questions are around pain and the symptoms. During an assessment, I'll ask what their pain is like – for example, in their lower back – or what their headaches are like. If I'm in a treatment session with a client, I probably should be reframing the pain experience.

JOEL: For me that brings up how we look at assessments. You could look at assessments as being neutral and objective. But I don't think they ever are. What we call assessments are really just another form of intervention. You're still co-constructing realities with them. When I was working in community mental health, we were required as part of licensing requirements to perform an assessment. I thought that we're really not doing assessments, we're doing treatment. We did a solution-focused first session. I never found I had a problem with completing the required assessment form. It might be interesting for you to try that in your work and see how much information you can gather by just doing a solution-focused first session.

ERICA: For me, part of my role is only doing one-time assessments. I'll do an assessment for the legal or medical field. I need to have the symptom-focused questions answered. It's hard to be solution focused when I'm only doing assessments. When I'm doing an assessment with a client who I'm going to be working with, I think there's an opportunity to do a solution-focused session. I do these situational assessments.[1] I get them to do some things in their house: cleaning, or cooking. The second day we go into the community – maybe go to a store and go shopping. Do you think having more of a solution-focused lens on the assessment would result in a different outcome? Would I see different things from the client rather than getting to

	their limit – having aggravating limits? Do you think they might improve?
JOEL:	Did you answer your question? I can pose the question in a different way. From a solution-focused point of view, how would you do it and still get what you needed for the assessment?
ERICA:	I never thought that way before. I started working with a client using solution focus, but when I reviewed my notes, I realized I didn't have enough information. Insurance companies want to know about client deficits – what justifies paying for this client.
JOEL:	You just turn the opposite. A 3 on a comfort scale is 10 on the pain scale. Give me an example.
ERICA:	One client told me she was able to cook once a week during the past month. That was a big improvement for her because she wasn't cooking at all before. I guess I could document that she's been able to cook once a week, but still has challenges around increasing that.
JOEL:	I suppose you could ask her what it would take to cook just one more day. What might she say?
ERICA:	She might respond that she would continue to have support from her family.
JOEL:	I suppose you could note that she has been able to cook one day, but in order to expand that, she would still need supports. There's a difference between doing solution-focus and doing business. Should we get back to our charts?
ERICA:	I haven't used change questions; I think I should start using that.
JOEL:	How do you think that would be helpful in what you do?
ERICA:	I think that's the whole orientation to solution focus: asking about change. I think deliberately using "change" would be helpful. I haven't thought about using 4b. I Think that would be a good conversation with her.
ERICA:	She often brings up the impact of doing activities. If she goes out shopping, she has to sit outside on her doorstep for an hour or two just to be able to recover before she's able to manage the effort of going up stairs and taking a shower. Maybe a conversation about recovery might help her lessen the time for her to recover. I hadn't thought about this kind of question, "What's different after you've rested?"
JOEL:	It seems to me that would address pacing.

Clip 2: Sub-utterance 1

But I'm listening to my body now. More. Does it always happen? No. Am I still trying to be aware?

Chart 7.4 But I'm listening to my body now

#	Opportunities	Possible responses (preferred = *) Joel	Possible responses (preferred = *) Erica
1	But I'm listening to my body now. More.	1a: How are you listening to your body more? *1b: Since you've been listening to your body more, what difference is it making? 1c: How does listening to your body more change the way you perceive pain? 1d: What does listening to your body allow you to do?	*1a: Can you give me five examples of ways that you are listening to your body? 1b: When was the last time you were aware and listened to your body? 1c: What helps you listen to your body?
2	Does it always happen? No.	2a: When does it happen? 2b: What are the signs that it's going to happen? 2c: When it happens, what difference does it make? 2d: What percentage of time do you estimate it does happen?	2a: When does it happen? 2b: When are times that it does happen?
3	Am I still trying to be aware?	3a: When are you successful? 3b: When you are aware, how does that make a difference? 3c: What do you do to become more aware? 3d: What helps you become more aware?	3a: What's different about the times when you are trying to be aware? 3b: What lets you know you can continue to try to be aware?

JOEL: I like 1a. 1b is an example of a presumptive question. Very different from saying, "Is there a time …?" Most of the time they come up with something.

ERICA: So, a presumptive question assumes they've already have had a past experience. Using words like "when".

JOEL: Yeah. Have you ever asked a question like 1a?

ERICA: No, I never thought about asking that kind of question. I'm looking at 1c. I've never asked questions about the perception of pain – I've never asked her about her perception of pain. I think that might be useful to do with her.

JOEL: In your work as an occupational therapist, it would be interesting what would happen if you started thinking of pain as an experience versus physical.

ERICA: What do you think about psychoeducation of pain? Would there be any benefit in talking to her about how pain works, the perception of pain, and how we can change that? Is that going into a different modality?

JOEL: It's an interesting question. What difference would it make – having that kind of conversation?

ERICA: Personally, I like to know a lot of information. I like to know research and the how and why things work. So do you stick with just solution-focused questions or is there room for the education piece?

JOEL: Do you think that's not solution-focus? Saying to them, "There's two parts of pain: the physical part and the experiential part?"

ERICA: The other training I've had is just about asking questions. I like the idea that there's something beyond just questions.

JOEL: I think that if I have information that is going to be useful for the client, why wouldn't I let them know about that? I think it's best not to get into a rigid definition of what SF is. I think that if something works, you do more of it. I certainly think if in the course of the conversation, the client comes up with something supported by research, you can credit the client for knowing something that the "experts" agree with. This allows the client to be smart.

ERICA: This helps because I've been trying to figure out how to meld the practice of occupational therapy with solution-focused practice.

JOEL: In other clips, she gives hints about how pain is affected by perception. She talks about how focusing on other things distracts her from the pain and makes it more bearable. These are opportunities to credit her for knowing that perception changes the perception of pain. Another option is to wait until after the break and use that opportunity to talk about perception and pain. "How smart it is for you to know that there's a difference between pain and the perception of pain." So, you credit her with the knowledge. So, you chose 1a. What's the reason for that choice?

ERICA: She said that she is listening to her body more. So I was interested in the specific ways she is doing that.

JOEL: Right, I chose 1b because it's a presumptive question assuming that she is listening to her body more and then further presumes that it's making a difference.

Before we schedule for our next session, I'm curious about what this experience was like for you and how it's been helpful.

ERICA: It's been incredibly helpful. I often wonder whether I'm asking a solution-type question or is it problem focused. I also ask myself whether there are other types of questions I should be asking – whether I'm being closed-minded about the questions and whether there are more questions I could be asking. I like that I'm able to look at the type of questions you ask and that expands my knowledge of what's possible.

LANCE'S COMMENT:	Another nice example of benefit from opportunities analysis in supervision.
JOEL:	I have to say that looking at what you've done, I haven't seen one problem-focused type of question.
ERICA:	In the past, it's been suggested that I record the sessions and then review the recording line-by-line. I haven't found that to be as helpful. What I like about this process is how it's structured. I like thinking about as many questions as possible, and then thinking about which one I would pick, and why. The whole process has been incredibly helpful, and I can refer back to it. So the more I do this, the more I'll have more potential questions.

Session 2: June 28, 2021

Clip 2: Sub-Utterance 2

Oh, I'm all nice and happy and refreshed, okay. Like this today is going to hopefully be a good day, or some days, I wake up from a nightmare, and I'm like, Oh, fuck, goodbye. Okay, I'm just gonna take it easy today.

Chart 7.5 Like this day is going to hopefully be a good day

# Opportunities	Possible responses (preferred = *) Joel	Possible responses (preferred = *) Erica
1 Oh, I'm all nice and happy and refreshed, okay. Like this day is going to hopefully be a good day.	1a: What makes that a good day? 1b: What is the first hint that it's going to be a good day? 1c: What happens that tells you it was a good day? 1d: Similar to 2d.	1a: What lets you know that you have the ability to handle the days ahead? *1b: What does a good day look like? 1c: What would you do on a day when you woke up happy and refreshed?
2 Or some days, I wake up from a nightmare, and I'm like, Oh, fuck, goodbye. Okay, I'm just gonna take it easy today.	2a: What happens on the other days? 2b: How do you manage to go on during those days? *2c: How do you figure out that you need to take it easy? 2d: What do you do to take it easy? 2e: How does it make a difference when you do take it easy?	2a: What lets you know that you have the ability to handle the days ahead, whether you have woken up from a nightmare or if you wake up feeling refreshed? 2b: What does taking it easy look like for you? 2c: When you wake up from a nightmare, how have you been able to cope and get through the day?

JOEL: Any thoughts left over from last time we met?

ERICA: Actually, I did meet this client on Friday. I asked more questions. I tried using lists with her. That went really well. She went on the whole session filling out an entire list of signs that things are getting better. At the beginning, she said she wants to be able to start climbing the ladder. She imagines that she has a ladder in a deep dark pit. She is slowly building a ladder to get out of that deep dark hole. She talked about the small signs that she is taking that first step. I let her lead and it just kept going.

JOEL: Good, so what were you doing differently? That was a big thing!

ERICA: I was interrupting her more. She has a tendency to go on to different topics. I kept her on track. [Reviewing the chart] I like 1b – it puts it in the present tense.

JOEL: It's looking for the small signs of change. I chose 2c. This is an indirect compliment.

ERICA: I preferred 2c. I like this question because this has been a concern for her lately (increased frequency in nightmares), and I'd like to know her coping strategies.

ERICA: I don't think that I use a lot of indirect compliments. I like that question. She uses the word "nightmare". I guess that can be a negative word. Would you avoid that when asking your questions?

JOEL: It depends how you use it. For example, take a look at your 2c. That's perfectly fine. It's a coping question. What you've done is related nightmare to coping.

Clip 3: Sub-Utterance 1

But I think it kind of comes back from, part of the old me's coming back, because I used to be someone who's constantly volunteering and helping others. And I would always find strategies. So part of that. So I guess the awareness part kind of came in, because I'm more capable than I give myself credit for.

Chart 7.6 I'm more capable than I give myself credit for

# Opportunities	Possible responses (preferred = *) Joel	Possible responses (preferred = *) Erica
1 But I think it kind of comes back from, part of the old me's coming back, because I used to be someone who's constantly volunteering and helping others.	1a: What do you notice about the old me? 1b: So, if the old me returned, what would you be doing, thinking or feeling? *1c: Scale where 10 is the "old me."	*1a: What might your friends notice as the old you comes back? 1b: Could you tell me about the old you coming back? 1c: What part of the old you has been coming back? 1d: When was the last time you've seen the old you come back?

(Continued)

Chart 7.6 (Continued)

# Opportunities	Possible responses (preferred = *) Joel	Possible responses (preferred = *) Erica
2 And I would always find strategies.	2a: What were the strategies that worked for you?	2a: What strategies have you used to get back to the old you?
3 So part of that. So I guess the awareness part kind of came in, because I'm more capable than I give myself credit for.	3a: What tells you that you're more capable than you give yourself credit for? 3b: When you do give yourself credit, what do you credit yourself with?	3a: What lets you know that you are more capable than you are giving yourself credit for? 3b: How have others noticed this capability in you?

ERICA: I hadn't thought about asking a scaling question like in 1c. I like that idea.

JOEL: Yes, that was my preference. When I hear those kind of comments – getting back to the old me – that always screams scaling to me. That's something that's easy to scale.

ERICA: I also like the phrase "What would you be doing, thinking, or feeling?" It gives her different options.

JOEL: It summarizes very nicely the human experience. Feelings, thoughts, and actions – what else do you have? I have to admit I stole this from Harry (Korman). I learned that from Harry. It sums up the full scale of human experience in three words. You chose 1a.

ERICA: She has several close friends, and I would be interested in hearing their perspective about her old self coming back.

JOEL: I would add to your rationale. If she answers that question, she shows the ability to see herself through other people's eyes. Especially when you get clients who stay with feelings, asking them how other people would notice that things are better requires them to describe behaviors rather than feelings. There's a quote from Wittgenstein (1958, p. 153), "Inner process stands in need of outward criteria." I think your question also brings the social context into the mix.

ERICA: She often references her few close friends. She lost a lot of friends after the accident. The friends she does have, she clings on to them. I like what you said: it makes her describe her behavior. I have other clients who have a hard time with feelings. I think getting them to describe behaviors rather than feelings is going to be helpful to them.

Clip 3: Sub-Utterance 2

So when you're in survival mode, you got to do what you got to do. And I also, I think, it was all those times of falling down. It was all those times of oh shit, what am I going to do? I think all the lessons kind of paid off. So all those times when I thought it was a total failure. No, it wasn't. Because I got back.

Chart 7.7 When you're in survival mode

# Opportunities	Possible responses (preferred = *) Joel	Possible responses (preferred = *) Erica
1 So, when you're in survival mode, you got to do what you got to do.	1a: What helps you go on? 1b: What do you do that helps you get back on track? 1c: How do you manage to get through those times?	1a: What keeps you going when you are in survival mode? 1b: How did you cope when you were in survival mode?
2 And I also, I think, it was all those times of falling down. It was all those times of oh shit, what am I going to do?	2a: Similar to 1a–1c.	2a: What lets you know that you can continue to get back up even if you fall down? 2b: What have your closest friends noticed about your ability to get back after falling down?
3 I think all the lessons kind of paid off.	3a: What are the lessons that paid off? 3b: How did the lessons pay off? 3c: How did those lessons get you back on track?	3a: What let you know you can continue to learn from your lessons and get back? *3b: What are some lessons that have helped you?
4 So, all those times when I thought it was a total failure. No, it wasn't. Because I got back.	4a: What finally convinced you that you weren't a total failure? 4b: How did you manage to get back? 4c: What were the first signs you were getting back? 4d: What did you learn from those times when you got back. *4e: How will what you learn help you get back maybe even faster if there is a next time?	4a: When have you been able to get back?

JOEL: I chose 4e. I think this does several things: it highlights her strengths, her capacity to rebound, co-constructs this as a learning experience, and, hopefully, inoculates her from future times she might get off track. You chose 3b.

ERICA: She says that all lessons have paid off, so I'd be interested in the examples she provides regarding these lessons.

JOEL: I wanted to point out something with your 4a. You use a presumptive question as opposed to a closed ended question – one that's answered with either yes or no. You again use her social context as a way of getting her to describe change. Take a look at 3b. How might you do this in a way that leads to description of change rather than just a list?

ERICA: I might ask, "What are some of the lessons that you've learned that helped you to move forward in your recovery?"

JOEL: I think that's still a list.

ERICA: So, reword it in a way that focuses on change?

JOEL: Yes.

ERICA: Should I remove the word "lesson"?

JOEL: No, this is a brain exercise. See if you can keep the word "lesson" but still focus on change.

ERICA: "How will you know that you learned from the lesson?"

JOEL: Yes. She said that she learns from the lessons. I would be interested in knowing what she has learned and how it has been helpful to her.

Clip 4: Sub-utterance 1

because I felt like I was making a huge difference before when I was meditating and yoga and starting to really want to go back to life. Whatever that is. you know, some somewhat normal. But I've been having so much trouble with that. Because like, it wasn't, that was this was one of the first of many nightmares again.

Chart 7.8 That was one of the first of my many nightmares

# Opportunities	Possible responses (preferred = *) Joel	Possible responses (preferred = *) Erica
1 Because I felt like I was making a huge difference before when I was meditating and yoga, and starting to really want to go back to life.	*1a: How did meditating and yoga make a difference? 1b: What was happening that gave you the idea that you were making a huge difference? 1c: What did people notice when you were making a huge difference? 1d: What was happening that told you that you were wanting to go back to life? 1e: What was happening when you were just starting to go back to life?	1a: In addition to meditation and yoga, what else helped you get back to life? 1b: How were you able to manage adding meditation and yoga to your days? *1c: How were you able to get back to doing yoga and meditation?
2 You know, some somewhat normal.	2a: When things are somewhat normal, what's happening? 2b: Scale somewhat normal.	2a: What does somewhat normal look like to you? 2b: When have things been somewhat normal?
3 But I've been having so much trouble with that. Because like, it wasn't, that was this was one of the first of many nightmares again.	3a: How do you go on when you are having so much trouble? 3b: When are there times when things are bit easier?	3s: What lets you know you can get back to meditation and yoga despite your nightmares?

ERICA: I chose 1c. This is something she did prior to the collision, and she started doing these activities in the past few months. I would like to know more about how she was able to get back to these activities despite her symptoms. She often talks about her pain, headaches, fatigue, and lack of attention. She says these interfere with her ability to do her activities. The fact that she's been able to do these at all in the last few months is a big deal.

JOEL: I chose 1a. This follows the rule if something is working do more of it. The intent here for her to come to the conclusion that it's time to return to something that was working for her. I also like 1a on your chart. I think it opens up possibilities.

ERICA: I don't think I would have thought of asking something like 1d. I think if I asked her that she would talk about her pain, her headaches, and wanting to be done with that.

JOEL: So, you think that it might get a problem-focused response.

ERICA: I think with her in particular. She often starts with the problem, but then shifts into something she wants.

JOEL: What I like about your 1a is you used her phrase "get back to life". I see 1c more as a coping question. I think 1a gives more of a sense of direction. I think the difference is rather than the question "how do you face the awful things in your life," 1a asks the question "how do you get on with your life."

ERICA: I suppose as an OT I'm more comfortable with coping questions. It might be helpful for me to think about the other categories.

JOEL: I wouldn't give up on coping questions. It's helpful when you have some clients who have trouble getting beyond their pain and their disability. Coping questions tend to move the conversation in a different direction. In this case, she's talking about something that makes a difference to her: yoga and wanting to get back to life. I don't think you need to ask her a coping question. She's already suggesting a positive direction.

Clip 4: Sub-utterance 2

Like the pain still there like 10 outta 10, but because of the weed and, ya, because of the weed the brain fog and the type of pain was bearable. And now it's back to like, oh my gosh, why am I getting like, those pain spasms again, and I was having so much fun, like, Okay, I'm gonna get back to life. I want to get a job I want to, you know, contribute back to society.

Chart 7.9 Okay, I'm gonna get back to life

# Opportunities	Possible responses (preferred = *) Joel	Possible responses (preferred = *) Erica
1 Like the pain still there like 10 outta 10.	1a: When are there times that the pain is less by just a little bit? 1b: What helps you get through those times?	1a: How are you able to cope despite the ongoing pain? 1b: In what ways have you been able to function despite the pain?
2 But because of the weed and, ya, because of the weed the brain fog and the type of pain was bearable.	2a: Where does the weed take you on that scale? 2b: Weed helps – what else?	2a: What were you able to do when the pain was bearable? 2b: What else helped to make the pain and brain fog bearable?
3 And now it's back to like, Oh my gosh, why am I getting like, those pain spasms again, and I was having so much fun, like, Okay, I'm gonna get back to life.	3a: How do you maintain that determination to get back to life? 3b: What are the first signs that you're just starting to get back to life? *3c: Scale where 10 is getting back to life.	*3a: What would be the first small sign that you were getting back to life? 3b: On a scale of 0 to 10, with 10 being back to life and 0 the complete opposite, where are you now? 3c: What sort of fun were you having?
4 I want to get a job I want to, you know, contribute back to society.	4a: Of course. 4b: Contribute back to society? 4c: How do you hope to contribute back to society?	4a: What sort of job would you like? 4b: In what ways would you like to contribute to society?

JOEL: I chose 3c. I think "getting back to life" is a vision of change for her. Assuming that she places herself somewhere on the scale, it might help to point out exceptions, co-constructs hope and expectations.

ERICA: I liked 3a. I would pick this question to elicit small details. I think asking about a job or contributing to society (4a or 4b) would be too large of a question as we are in the beginning stages of exploring returning to work. I'm wondering about 4a and 4b. Do you think those might be more problem-solving questions?

JOEL: Maybe it's the word "what". I think the word "what" in this context suggests a list. This is different than how you use "what" in 3a. In that intervention, you're asking her for her vision of change.

ERICA: Looking at it now, I think asking her a scale would have been a better choice. What do you think about asking "why" questions?

JOEL: Give me an example of how you might use a 'why' question?

ERICA: I have no idea. I don't think I ever used a "why" question.

JOEL: I don't think that I usually would use "why" either. I think asking "why" is asking clients for explanations about why they do what they do. I'm not sure that's very helpful. I think that's characteristic of a problem-solving approach. I'm more interested in clients describing behaviors rather than explanations of behavior. I think that's the difference between a theoretical approach and a non-theoretical approach. Theoretical approaches ask for explanations. Can we really know why people do what they do?

ERICA: She says that although the weed makes her "foggy", it does make the pain more bearable. I suppose I could ask her where weed puts her on the scale.

JOEL: Do you want to emphasize the weed? Does it take away from her control? She can do yoga and meditation and she says that helps. Those activities are within her control.

ERICA: Yes, she often brings up that she doesn't want to use weed forever.

JOEL: That might be a useful scale. You could ask her, "10 is all her and 0 is all the weed". Even if she replied with a 0, you could ask her how she would know that she was at a 1 – maybe it's just a little bit more her and a little less the weed.

Clip 5: Sub-Utterance 1

Yeah, I went. Yeah, like, it's like, all my it's like, it's like my whole post-accident recovery. I feel like it's like a wash or feels like a wash, maybe it's not a wash. But it does feel because I was doing really well. Like, you know, I was climbing that ladder, I was doing really well. But I feel like that ladder in that hole is like. And I feel like I got, I'm like somewhere down the pit again.

Chart 7.10 I'm like somewhere down the pit again

# Opportunities	Possible responses (preferred = *) Joel	Possible responses (preferred = *) Erica
1 Yeah, I went. Yeah, like, it's like, all my it's like, it's like my whole post-accident recovery. I feel like it's like a wash or feels like a wash, maybe it's not a wash.	1a: There are times that you maybe think it's not a wash? 1b: What tells you that maybe it's not a wash?	1a: What would you call your recovery instead of a wash? 1b: What tells you that your recovery is not a wash?
2 But it does feel because I was doing really well. Like, you know, I was climbing that ladder, I was doing really well.	2a: What was happening when you were doing really well? 2b: How did you manage to do really well? 2c: Climbing the ladder? 2d: Where will that ladder take you? *2e: How high are you right now on that ladder?	2a: What lets you know that you can continue to climb that ladder? *2b: What would be a small sign that you were one step up the ladder? 2c: What might your closest friend say to you as she was coaching you up the next small step up the ladder? 2d: What will others notice about you as you are taking the next small step up the ladder?

(Continued)

Chart 7.10 (Continued)

# Opportunities	Possible responses (preferred = *) Joel	Possible responses (preferred = *) Erica
3 But I feel like that ladder in that hole is like. And I feel like I got, I'm like somewhere down the pit again.	3a: What are the signs that you're climbing out of that pit? 3b: What helps you climb out of the pit? 3c: How do you manage to get yourself out of the pit?	3a: What would be the first sign that you were climbing out of the pit? 3b: How have you been managing to survive in the pit?

ERICA: I chose 2b. This is a noticing question to get small details about the signs that she was moving in the right direction.

JOEL: My choice was 2e. It's essentially a scaling question but it uses her metaphor – her language. I think your 2d is a sophisticated question. I do like that one.

ERICA: She is very close to her family and her friends. I think getting their voices in the conversation would be helpful.

JOEL: Right, what do you think that question does?

ERICA: It focuses on behavior.

JOEL: It certainly does that.

ERICA: It helps her envision that as she's already making the change.

JOEL: It does the same as asking her how she would know that she is one step higher on the scale. It also adds the behavioral piece because she has to describe it from another person's point of view.

Clip 6: Sub-utterance 1

Every time I've meditated even though I've watched the past few days, I've been kind of Let's stop meditating-ish. I, I'm aware, I've been giving myself self-mantras. And at the end of every meditation, I recite three times to myself the things that I want to be.

Chart 7.11 I recite three times to myself the things that I want to be

# Opportunities	Possible responses (preferred = *) Joel	Possible responses (preferred = *) Erica
1 Every time I've meditated even though I've watched the past few days, I've been kind of Let's stop meditating-ish.	1a: When you do meditate, what tells you that you've done enough? *1b: What is different after you've been meditating? 1c: With everything you're going through physically, how do you focus on meditation?	1a: How were you able to continue to meditate on the days when you wanted to stop?

Chart 7.11 (Continued)

# Opportunities	Possible responses (preferred = *) Joel	Possible responses (preferred = *) Erica
2 I'm aware, I've been giving myself self-mantras.	2a: How do you choose your self-mantras? 2b: Which self-mantras works best for you and how?	*2a: What are those self-mantras? 2b: What other self-mantras would be helpful to you? 2c: What might your closest friend add as a mantra?
3 And at the end of every meditation, I recite three times to myself the things that I want to be.	3a: What are the three things that you recite? 3b: Which of the three things you want to be have you come the closest to?	3a: What things do you want to be? 3b: What let you know you can get back to meditating?

ERICA: I chose 2a because I thought it might help her continue talking about her self-mantras. As I look at it now, I think 2a doesn't really focus on direction or change. I just wanted to know more information. She was talking about something about something that works for her. I'm curious to hear what those self-mantras are.

JOEL: I chose 1b. My rationale: it points to her vision of change and explores practical possibilities.

ERICA: I think it focuses on change.

JOEL: How meditation helps her. So, you said that you just wanted to know more.

ERICA: Right, a common thread is that I just want to know more. It might be more helpful for me to focus more on questions that lead to change.

JOEL: That's the difference between looking at conversations as data-collecting versus looking at conversations as a way of co-constructing realities. I don't think there's such a process as assessments. Any conversation with clients – whether you call it an assessment or not – in reality is an intervention. Insoo (Kim Berg, personal communication) said that asking a question does get information, but at the same time it gives information. It tells the client what you're interested in. The term for that is "lexical choice". The questions we ask tell the client how we think of therapy. For example, Harry (Korman) had come to visit the clinic I was working in. At the time, I was working with a client with a team behind the mirror. Harry came in, watched behind the mirror for a while, then said, "Yes, this is solution-focused therapy." He knew this by the questions I was asking.

ERICA: I sometimes tell clients not to read the reports I write. When they have done that, they relate to me that they feel worse even though they thought that they were recovering. That's because the reports focus on deficits.

JOEL: I guess you need to know the difference between doing treatment and doing business.

ERICA: I hear what you're saying is questions need to focus on change. Thinking more about the assumptions behind solution focus might be helpful for me.

JOEL: Were the two meetings helpful to you?

ERICA: Very, yeah. The whole process of doing the microanalysis was very helpful. Having the idea that everything a client says can be useful.

JOEL: As I reviewed your suggested interventions, I thought every one of them was solution-building. I enjoyed working with you.

ERICA: This was an incredible experience.

JOEL: I would be interested to hear how what we've done together changes how you are working with this client. Even if it's just figuring out how to interrupt her.

ERICA: Yeah, that's a big change. Whenever I interrupt her, I hear your voice in my head saying, "This is not a cocktail party."

Conclusion: Post-Session

Joel contacted Erica several weeks after the last supervisory session and asked for her reflections on the experience. She responded with the following comments.

There are Many Takeaways from Our Sessions: Reflection on Our Work

- I feel I need to reread my notes and our conversation over and over again, and I think that shows the importance of ongoing supervision and training.
- I wouldn't have thought to break down the utterances into very small opportunities. For example, I would have broken this utterance into two sections rather than three "But I'm listening to my body now more" and "Does it always happen? No. Am I still trying to be aware?" Instead of just "Am I still trying to be aware?" So, some of the opportunities really challenged me to think harder.
- I am moving away from collecting data versus "looking at conversations as a way of co-constructing realities". This was big for me. I am learning more about what is considered "doing business" versus treatment. I used to focus a lot on collecting data for documentation purposes and finding out what was going on (problem-solving).
- I'm thinking about what to emphasize versus not emphasize (e.g., moving away from emphasizing marijuana as opposed to activities that are within her control).
- The solution focus is fascinating and there's so much to learn. You had a lot of quotes and references in your workshop and in our supervision sessions that made me want to learn more because these were not things that I learned

about in OT – for example, "An 'inner process' stands in need of outward criteria" (Wittgenstein, 1958, p. 153). You talked about lexical choice.

- I'm thinking more carefully about focusing on a direction of change (rather than mostly coping questions when the client is already talking about change).
- I'm learning more about focusing more on presumptive questions instead of close-ended questions (yes or no) and asking questions that lead to description of change rather than a list of things.
- You also talked about using more "when" and "how" questions to move the conversation in a direction of change instead of just "what" when moving away from mostly asking coping questions.
- I'm learning how to incorporate more indirect compliments into my questions.
- I'm interrupting my clients more, which helps me to hold onto important things that they have said rather than getting lost when they go off on a tangent.
- I really like your point about how we are asking our clients to describe what they would be doing, thinking, or feeling differently. It makes what I am looking for more explicit. I think I use the term "noticing" with my clients and directly saying, doing, thinking, or feeling helps clarify what I mean.
- I like your point about seeing themselves through others' eyes because it helps them describe behaviors. Sometimes I have clients who would just get stuck on a feeling like "happier".
- I liked our discussion about not being so rigid about the definition of SF (e.g., including education) because it allows me to be more flexible with incorporating OT, which is more problem and intervention focused.
- I like the different ways you use scales and I have started using them more and listening to terms that could indicate scales. For example, you talked about "getting back to the old me" and that's something very common with my work – getting back to some of their roles and occupations in the past, even though it may be done in a different way (e.g., modifications to the activity or environment, change in frequency, etc.).
- The microanalysis helped me understand that there are many opportunities in every utterance. It allows me to listen more carefully rather than letting them continue to talk or off on a tangent. I'm trying to hold on to the essence of what they're saying. It makes me think of the different directions in which the conversation can go.

Lance's Comment

When I was proof reading this chapter, I made notes to myself to compliment Joel for two elegant distinctions he introduced in his conversation with Erica: "That's the difference between looking at conversations as data collecting versus looking at conversations as a way of co-constructing realities" and "I guess you need to know the difference between doing treatment and doing business".

As I read on to the point where Erica gave feedback about her experience of the supervision, I was intrigued to notice that she specifically mentioned these two comments as having been useful to her. Prompted by this synchronicity, I re-read the feedback and was struck by how many key words Erica preserved from her supervision conversations with Joel. She brought forth words originating with Joel, such as *what to emphasize, in the direction of change, inner process stands in need of outward criteria, lexical choice, presumptive questions, indirect compliments, interrupt, doing thinking feeling differently.*

Erica also preserved words from her client, such as *but I'm listening to my body now more, does it always happen? No. Am I still trying to be aware?* Key words are key words. Whether these words came from the client directly or Joel in supervision, they registered as having particular significance for Erica. She preserved them in responses she included in her feedback.

For practitioners enamored with opportunity analysis, it is also noteworthy that in commenting on a client's situation, Erica quoted the client exactly as one good way of describing the client's circumstance. This is indicative of the extent to which Erica has entered into the mindset of surface-level analysis of opportunities and key words. This resonates with an interesting evolution in teaching that the authors have developed.

We would venture a guess that almost everyone who has endeavored to present a workshop or class in SFBT will have received a question along the lines of, "What would you do when a client ... [fill in the blank with any life challenge, diagnosis, trauma, difficult childhood]?" Rather than try to give expert advice to the client characterization offered by the trainee, the authors will sometimes say, "Would you be willing to hold off on describing the client and just quote something you have heard the client say." This opens space for the presenter to respond to opportunities in the client utterance and is often warmly received by trainees, once again returning to the surface of the interaction.

Live Interview Supervision

Microanalysis of therapeutic conversation was the medium within which the opportunities framework was crystallized. The frame of opportunities has proven to be useful on its own without the systematic step-by-step formal analysis of sequential minute utterances. This may be thought of as a slight shift in magnification to a more meso-position. One example is clinical supervision.

Observation and assistance of live client interviews is one of the most effective learning tools. One possible stance of the supervisor or team behind the mirror is to attend to arising opportunities generated by clients. Free from the immediate responsibility of managing the actual interview dynamics, observers are generally able to notice more opportunities.

It is occasionally useful to phone into the interviewer to alert them to potentially productive listening, questioning, or affirmation. Interviewers' capacity to notice opportunities may be limited somewhat by a number of factors. Hosting the interview requires attending to many conversational dynamics in addition to the core opportunities for intervention. Interview assistance by colleagues of comparable levels of mastery can be highly productive as a second set of eyes and ears. Benefits may be even more numerous when the interviewer, at an earlier stage of skill development, is supported by a more seasoned practitioner.

Sometimes clinical supervision includes post-session conversation. Useful questions can be constructed within the opportunity frame to guide the discussion.

When the intent is to maintain an interviewer centered review:

- What significant opportunities did the interviewer detect?
- What do they like about their therapeutic responses?
- What other options did they consider?
- How did they decide on the chosen option?
- How do they think their choice panned out?
- In the comfortable position of hindsight, what alternatives might they have liked to try?

Compliments should be provided for well-executed interviewing elements of listening, questioning, and affirming specified by opportunity.

Supervisees will sometimes tire of too much affirmation, requesting that the supervisor also provide constructive criticism or suggestions for how they can improve. Supervisors who have monitored the interview from an opportunity perspective are in a position to suggest:

- Additional opportunities they observed.
- Other possible therapeutic constructions that could be tried.

Video-Based Group Supervision

The opportunities framework has proven to be a generative approach to group supervision using video recordings provided by one or more participants. Lance has occasion to meet with groups under a number of different circumstances with various backgrounds:

- Groups of approximately five to ten therapists, most with intermediate and higher levels of mastery of solution-focused brief therapy.
- Groups including students for whom this is their first exposure to SFBT.
- Groups including a variety of post-modern therapists such as narrative, "bringforthist" and solution-focused models, for whom social constructionism is comfortable philosophical terrain.

When circumstances permit, it is usually advisable to adopt a supervisee-centered posture, beginning with inquiry into participant hopes for the exercise. Recently, one group was organized to focus on the question: how to stay solution-focused in the interview. A brief sampling of individual participants at the beginning of the meeting largely echoed this hope.

It is also useful to specify a context within which opportunity may be defined specifically for the current supervisory event. Lance has found the convergent narrative schema presented in Chapter 2 to be fairly versatile in orienting participants in group supervision. It can be presented briefly and seems to focus the group on client hopes, actions, and change. Other more specific topics can be employed just as readily. Affirmations, certain kinds of questions, use of silence, interruption, and question construction are just a few examples of an extensive range of possibilities. Establishing a context for observation is particularly important when therapists are utilizing different models of practice.

It is also important to reiterate the spirit of opportunities study that the different observations are best thought of as options, without the press of deciding the "correct" or "best" choices. This attitude supports an environment of curiosity and collaboration – much more conducive to learning than competition.

The pragmatics of a group video review utilizing the opportunities frame are as follows:

• After the above introduction, roll the video for short segments of the session from three to five minutes or so, depending on content in the conversation. The main objective is to have a few comments from the clinical clients to consider.
• Stop the tape and invite reports from participant therapists on opportunities observed.
• Affirm observations.
• Encourage examples of observations not shared by all participants and create space for those who didn't notice a particular event to think back and resonate with their colleagues' examples.
• Roll the tape for another segment.

This is the most rudimentary form of an opportunities-guided review of therapeutic conversation. One predictable result is that participants are successful in both making rich observations and appreciating the observations of others. A very common reaction is exemplified by a participant comment in a recent event: "I'm amazed at how much useful information can be found in the first few minutes of a session."

Beyond a basic opportunity review, variations are limited only by our imagination. Some examples are:

- In addition to reporting on observations, invite participants to identify responses they may consider, once again encouraging curious absorption of each other's ideas.
- When therapists using different models are present, invite one or more to observe the segment through their unique lens. Contrasting these differing observations can reveal interesting choice points where conversations can be seen to potentially branch into quite different directions.
- For practitioners with reasonable confidence in their skills, who request specific input about what they might have done differently, choice points and opportunities can be useful for making suggestions.

The opportunities mindset can also be a useful planning tool. One team booked a full day of only clients who were attending their second or subsequent sessions and pre-determined that a particular focus for the day of supervision would be employment of "what's better" questioning.

Note

1 Situational assessments are functional assessments that look at how a client has been catastrophically impacted by an accident in terms of their physical, cognitive, psycho-emotional, and psycho-social wellbeing.

8 Applications

Opportunities as a Training Tool

Introduction

The solution-focused model utilizes questions as tools for co-constructing clients' visions of a more satisfying future. As experienced trainers, both authors have focused on the solution-building tools as a major part of the training: invitation questions, future-oriented questions, the Miracle Question, exception questions, coping questions, scaling questions, and the "thinking" break.

Because the model tends to be question oriented, those new to the model often become so focused on asking "the right question" that they forget to listen and to respond to clients. In fact, the most useful questions originate from client responses. One central motivation for the development of opportunities analysis was teaching trainees how to listen and watch for opportunities for solution-building that clients offer in their utterances (Taylor & Simon, 2014).

The following is one example of how opportunities analysis might be used as a training tool to teach trainees how to listen carefully for solution-building possibilities. This is one portion of a two and one-half days, level one, solution-focused brief therapy training. This particular section of the total training took place on November 12, 2021, and was completed in approximately one hour. There were ten trainees; Joel is conducting the training.

Procedure

The actual exercise was preceded by an explanation of microanalysis and of microanalysis of opportunities specifically (see Chapter 4). The training group was then shown a video clip, which included the following utterance example:

> I need to unleash everything. I keep building it up, building it up. I start lashing out at people that I shouldn't be. I get – I wouldn't say angry. I get frustrated very fast and I'm not the best person when it comes to that. I get frustrated. I don't kind of calm myself down. I just … I just get very rash.

DOI: 10.4324/9781003396703-9

This utterance was chosen because it combined both obvious problem statements (e.g., "I keep building it up" or "I start lashing out..."), and potential solution-building opportunities (e.g., "I get – I wouldn't say angry" or "And I'm not the best person ...").

Prior to the training, the group was asked to download and print out the following utterance and chart:

Utterance: I need to unleash everything. I keep building it up, building it up. I start lashing out at people that I shouldn't be. I get–I wouldn't say angry. I get frustrated very fast and I'm not the best person when it comes to that. I get frustrated. I don't kind of calm myself down. I just ... I just get very rash.

Chart 8.1 Chart with opportunities

#	Opportunity	Possible interventions	Rationale
1	I need to unleash everything.	1a: How does that make a difference? 1b: What tells you that you've done enough unleashing? 1c: When are there times that you don't need to unleash? 1d: What would you want to be doing differently?	
2	I keep building it up, building it up.		
3	I start lashing out at people that I shouldn't be.		
4	I get–I wouldn't say angry.		
5	I get frustrated very fast.		
6	And I'm not the best person when it comes to that. I get frustrated.		
7	I don't kind of calm myself down.		
8	I just ... I just get very rash.		

The utterance was separated by Joel into eight different opportunities. The first opportunity was completed by Joel as an analysis example. The group was then divided into five different sub-groups (the training was done virtually). Each sub-group was assigned one or more opportunities and asked to complete an analysis in approximately ten minutes. The analysis consisted of devising at least three different possible responses to each opportunity as in the example provided of the first opportunity. While considering possible interventions, the group was instructed to include only those interventions that were judged to have a high probability of eliciting a solution-building response.

Discussion 1

Upon review, the authors noted that the design of the exercise incorporated several levels of learning, including a didactic part and some hands-on practice. The component of the whole group discussing each sub-group's work together encourages them to deal with differences in perception, listening, and opinion.

Moreover, by bringing them together for a conversation, it is a reflection piece that allows them to engage in a conversation about applying the tool. At the same time, it also presents an opportunity to teach by drawing a distinction between which responses are more liable to elicit problem-focused narratives compared with solution-focused narratives. The goal of this opportunities exercise is to teach solution-focused trainees the benefits of using microanalysis as a learning and teaching tool for listening and responding to clients.

In the introduction to this chapter, the authors wrote, "The solution-focused model utilizes questions as tools for co-constructing clients' visions of a more satisfying future." While that is certainly true, the questions and other tools we use also seek to elicit and amplify exceptions and build momentum towards change.

The focus on creatively considering multiple possible interventions for each opportunity in an utterance emphasizes how solution-focused practitioners design interventions as clinical tools for co-constructing problem exceptions; in turn, that helps clients to engage in a conversation about future possibilities.

Another advantage of using opportunities analysis is that it is a simple concept that is easily performed – especially for those who are new to the solution-focused model. The reactions we have received from groups that have engaged in this exercise suggest they benefit from analyzing client utterances. They learn quickly how to sort solution-probable statements from problem-probable statements.

Once the trainees reassembled from their sub-groups, the chart was completed in full. Joel began by asking the first group to complete the chart's second opportunity. Afterward, the group reported the following analysis:

Chart 8.2 Group 2

2 I keep building it up, building it up.	2a) How is building up serving you?
	2b) Is building it up getting you the results you want?
	2c) When you're at that point, is there anything you can do to slow the building-up process?
	2d: What other approach would potentially work toward your intended goal?
	2e: When you're at that point, what can you do to slow the build-up process?

One of the members of that group, Robert, asked whether there was an alternative to using the word "different". He said, "I try to avoid using the word different." Joel was curious about his rationale for avoiding "different". His response was, "I didn't want to imply that the client's current course of action was not working. I didn't want to point out that there was a problem in the current way of thinking."

Joel responded that in fact the client's current course of action is not getting him where he wants to go. Kimberly pointed out, "That's why he's there." The question then arose whether or not "difference" implies a negative. Joel responded that in a sense it is a positive because it points out that what the client is doing is not working: "I suppose that's a negative in a positive sense."

Discussion 2

Robert is averse to using the word "different", suggesting that in some way difference is negative – implying that it is a criticism of the client. It is important to understand and embrace the idea that difference is core to solution-focused conversations. Beginning the conversation with what the client wants to be different is the first invitation to helping the client envision a more satisfying future. De Shazer (1991, p. 96) reflects this central theme of the model:

In short, therapists want clients to depict their life outside of the therapy situation as being, in some way significantly different at the end of therapy from what it was at the start.

In response, Kimberly states what might be construed as the obvious, "That's why he's here." In a simple but eloquent statement, she points out what might be understood about therapy in general: people come to see the therapist because they want something to be different and better in their lives. We may disagree model by model how to get there, but the bottom line is the client wants difference to happen. This exchange involving Kimberly and Robert demonstrates an elegant collaborative dynamic in the training design where participants listen to and teach each other.

The next group reported on the third opportunity:

Chart 8.3 Group 3

3	I start lashing out at people that I shouldn't be.	3a) When do you first realize you're lashing out? 3b) Why shouldn't you be lashing out at these people? 3c) How would you prefer to interact? 3d) What would it look like when you're not lashing out? 3e) What would have to happen to communicate differently? 3f) When was there a time when you didn't lash out when you were frustrated?

One other suggestion was given in response to 3c, "What would that look like?" The general consensus from the group was that this intervention would be a follow-up question. Joel suggested that you can only ask a question in response to an opportunity: "Because a follow up can only be in response to the client's response to the original intervention."

The original version of 3f was "Was there ever a time when you didn't lash out when you were frustrated?" Joel suggested that this be changed to a presumptive question, "When was there a time …?"

Following is the fourth group's chart:

Chart 8.4 Group 4

4	I get – I wouldn't say angry.	4a) What would you say?
		4b) What difference would that make you feel?
		4c) How do you know it's not anger?
		4d) Would you say you get triggered?

This sub-group originally suggested 4a and 4b. The group as a whole was asked whether they might suggest any additional interventions, and 4c and 4d were added.

The fifth group reported the following interventions:

Chart 8.5 Group 5

5	I get frustrated very fast.	5a) How do you know when you're getting frustrated?
		5b) When are there times that you don't get frustrated so quickly?
		5c) Are you saying you have a low tolerance?
		5d) How do you slow down so you don't get frustrated?
		5e) What are the things that get you frustrated quickly?

That sub-group suggested 5a and 5b. The group as a whole suggested 5c through 5e.

Another suggestion given was "How do you calm yourself down?" Joel pointed out that the client wasn't talking about calmness. Instead, he was using the word "frustration".

Group 6's chart was:

Chart 8.6 Group 6

6	And I'm not the best person when it comes to that. I get frustrated.	6a) What does it mean to be the best person?
		6b) Similar to 5b.

Group 7's chart was:

Chart 8.7 Group 7

7	I don't kind of calm myself down.	7a) What do you need to feel calmer right now? 7b) What would help you feel calmer? 7c) What has worked to get you in a calmer place in the past? 7d) When was there a time you felt calmer, and can you feel that now? 7e) When was there a time you were able to calm yourself? 7f) Why don't you?

Group 8's chart was:

Chart 8.8 Group 8

8	I just … I just get very rash.	8a) What does it look like when you don't get rash? 8b) When are there times you don't feel the need to get rash?

Joel next asked them to review all the responses (2 through 8) and choose those that were more than likely to receive a problem-focused response. There was a general consensus that 3a should be struck because it would most likely get a problem response.

Chart 8.9 Group 3 deletes

3	I start lashing out at people that I shouldn't be.	3a) When do you first realize you're lashing out? 3b) Why shouldn't you be lashing out at these people? 3c) How would you prefer to interact? 3d) What would it look like when you're not lashing out? 3e) What would have to happen to communicate differently? 3f) When was there a time when you didn't lash out when you were frustrated?

There was a question about whether 3b might earn a problem response. The group was then asked what it thought would be a likely response to that question. There was a general consensus that the question would more likely result in a positive response similar to "It's family and I love them" or "My family doesn't deserve it". There was a general agreement that 3b should remain.

Opportunity 4 was reviewed for estimates of likely responses:

Chart 8.10 Group 4 deletes

4 I get – I wouldn't say angry.	4a) What would you say? 4b) What difference would that make you feel? 4c) How do you know it's not anger? 4d) Would you say you get triggered?

The following conversation happened about 4b and 4d:

KIMBERLY: I question 4d. "Triggered" is not a word that he used. I can see that going down a negative path. He might say, "That's not what I said."

JOEL: How might he answer that question?

KIMBERLY: I'd probably say, "No, I get frustrated" or "I get overwhelmed" or something like that.

JOEL: So, there seems to be a general consensus that this will more than likely get a problem-focused response. [Joel strikes through 4d.]

DIANA: I have a question about 4b. It's weirdly worded – I'm not following it. I'm wondering if 4b is a follow up to 4a rather than the actual opportunity 4.

JOEL: How might you change it so that it would be responsive to 4?

KIMBERLY: "What different emotion would you say it is?"

DIANA: I'm still not sure that 4b is relevant.

JUNE: Maybe I can clarify since I was part of that group. I might have thrown that one out as a way of using the template. Maybe it would be better to ask, "How does that make a difference?" I think we were just trying to jam a square peg into a round hole there.

Discussion 3

Kimberly observes that in the suggested intervention, that sub-group had used the word "triggered". This suggests that Kimberly made two important observations: (1) the client did not use the word "triggered"; and (2) by suggesting that intervention, it more than likely would result in a problem-generating response. The former observation notes what is often common to solution-focused practitioners: the tendency to use client language. In a microanalysis of solution-focused therapeutic dialogues, Bavelas et al. (2000) note that solution-focused therapists preserve a significant proportion of client language.

Kimberly's second observation, that using the word "triggered" would more likely elicit a problem response, suggests that at least she, and (hopefully) others, are understanding the differences between solution and problem narratives.

An additional advantage of doing this exercise is the ability to look back at what the client actually said. There is a tendency to mistake what you think the client said versus what was actually said. It is always possible to return to the verbatim dialogue for verification. An important training concept here is the distinction between observation and inference. It is very tempting to infer what the client means versus staying strictly to what is observable.

JOEL:	Again, it seems that the general consensus is we strike that one out. [Group expresses general agreement.]
ROBERT:	I have a question about 4c. He said it's not anger. Why are we asking that question?
JOEL:	I suppose it could be reworded to, "If it's not anger, what is it?"
HELEN:	I think it's a provocative question.
ROBERT:	It's very combative.
JOEL:	I don't think there's anything wrong with challenging his thinking.
HELEN:	The way it's being asked is provocative; it changes the mood and the environment.
KIMBERLY:	How do you think it changes the mood and the environment?
HELEN:	I think people react to the word "anger". It seems accusatory to me.
KIMBERLY:	He uses the word "anger". The question just asks how he would know it's different than anger.
JUNE:	That was our intent: to probe a little bit, to say "it's opposed to angry" might open up other avenues of discovery.
HELEN:	You could ask, "How do you know it's different than angry?"
DIANA:	Or just leave it as "How do you know?"
JOEL:	What do you think about 3a? What do you think would be the likely response?
LYDIA:	I think more about the problem.
SAMANTHA:	It's too open-ended.
JOEL:	Right, more than likely you would get something like, "I start getting angry, I start breathing heavily, and I have my hands in fists!"

Discussion 4

In this sequence, Robert objects to the use of the word "anger". Helen adds that the word is "provocative". This is a discussion of how meanings are co-constructed. Both see the use of that word as having a negative connotation. This is an opportunity to teach how to make the distinction between what a word means to them versus what a word means to the client. It gets the trainees to think about what words the clients use as opposed to those we try to avoid. As solution-focused practitioners, we are committed to using clients' words.

Chart 8.11 Group 5 deletes

5 I get frustrated very fast.	5a) ~~How do you know when you're getting frustrated?~~
	5b) When are there times that you don't get frustrated so quickly?
	5c) ~~Are you saying you have a low tolerance?~~
	5d) How do you slow down so you don't get frustrated?
	5e) What are the things that get you frustrated quickly?

Opportunities 5 is reviewed for predicted response patterns.

JOEL:	What about 5a? What's the likely response?
JUNE:	This might end up getting into the physicality of getting frustrated. So, I think it's problem focused.
JOEL:	Any on 6 through 8 you might have questions about?
JUNE:	I'd like to go back to the previous page – "low tolerance" (5c). It's taunting him.
JOEL:	"Are you saying I have a low tolerance? Yeah, I have a low tolerance! What are you going to do about it?" [General laughter]
DIANA:	Yeah, we are suggesting, aren't we? We're putting words in his mouth.
JOEL:	I have a low tolerance for your low tolerance. [General laughter]
SAMANTHA:	What about number 7, "What do you need to feel calmer right now?" He's not saying that he is or isn't calmer right now.
JUNE:	That could be modified to "in the moment" or something like that.
JOEL:	I'm going to say something that may seem very radical, "I really don't care how he feels *right now*." It's irrelevant to me.
DIANA:	It might be better to ask how "calmer" felt either in the past or in the future.
JUNE:	I wonder if the group was trying to use it as a scale: "In the past" versus "How do you feel now on a scale of zero to ten?"
JOEL:	That's an excellent point. On any of the opportunities, you could ask a scale as a possibility. For example, "On a scale of 0 to 10 where 10 is you're able to calm yourself down, where would you put yourself on that scale?" Or, "Suppose a miracle happened and you were able to calm yourself down …"
DIANA:	Especially number 4 when we had trouble coming up with a response to his anger.
JUNE:	It does cut through all the verbiage.

Discussion 5

Joel makes what appears to be a provocative statement about the role of feelings in psychotherapy. However, he adds that he is not interested in the client's feelings "right now". This raises a distinction that many new to solution-focused work often find difficult: problem-solving versus solution-building. Problem-solving is the desire to find ways of fixing problems. From a problem-solving perspective, this client's anger is a problem that needs to be "solved". Perhaps strategies might be suggested to help the client better manage his anger.

In the context of therapy, problem-solving tends to include a focus on the details of the problem with an intention to find a remedy that can be applied to mitigate the original trouble. This may involve conversation and interpretation to develop insight into the etiology of the problem.

There are also numerous procedures that may be offered and conducted by therapists to solve the problem. In addition, some practitioners may provide information intended to create or raise client knowledge about their problem in the belief that more problem details will result in problem resolution.

In some models, the therapist is expected to help the client demonstrate change *in vivo*. SFBT takes a different tack. We co-construct with clients a preferred future with the expectation that solutions will occur after they leave and be generated by what they do.

Solution-building, as it is conducted within the framework of SFBT, relies almost exclusively on structuring the immediate therapeutic conversation to collaborate with clients in constructing compelling perceptions and narratives specific to their hopes for a more satisfying future. This is a fundamental paradigm shift in practice, which privileges client wisdom and capability to develop living solutions once they are assisted to focus on their hopes and actions.

For the trainees, the distinction between problem-solving and solution-building offers an opportunity to distinguish between performing procedures on clients to "fix the problem" as opposed to helping co-construct hope and possibilities that allow clients to figure it out for themselves. This requires having the faith that clients can create their own vision of a better future and then do something to change their lives after they leave.

JOEL: Here's the next step. Remember, all you can do is choose an intervention. You can't do a follow-up until the client responds. You have to create some formulation. Reviewing all these possibilities, which is the one you would choose?

ROBERT: I would choose 1a. It's open-ended and it allows the client to go where he wants to go.

DIANA: I'm not sure what you mean, Joel. Are we supposed to choose an intervention for every opportunity?

JOEL: No, that's not the way conversations go: he says, "I need to unleash everything," and then you say, "How does that make a difference?" Then 2a and you respond and so on. This is one utterance, so it makes sense that you would have to pick just one of all the possible interventions for that one utterance. He says the whole utterance and then I respond to one of the opportunities.

ROBERT: None of these possible interventions would work because all of these are just specific to that utterance.

JOEL: Any one of these would work, with the exception of the ones we crossed out. They would likely get a solution-building response. It doesn't really matter which one you would choose.

ROBERT: It seems to me that whatever intervention you choose only refers to that specific opportunity and doesn't include all the others.

JOEL: That's right. You choose to intervene with only one of all the opportunities in that one utterance.

CYNTHIA: What is the most important thing he says in the utterance that you would want to respond to?

ROBERT: I would ask the client, "What is the most important thing you need to focus on right now?" I think the client has the right to decide what he wants to focus on.

JOEL: So, you ask me that question. My response: "I want to talk about what gets me angry all the time. You know what gets me angry? I'll tell you want gets me angry …!" Your job as the therapist is to lead the conversation in a useful way as much as possible. The client says something; you have to respond. The best you can do is to pick a response that will more than likely move the conversation in a solution-building way.

DIANA: There's not one that might be the best, but which one would you choose that will move the conversation forward. There might be several possibilities in the same utterance.

JOEL: Right, it's very practical. You have this long utterance. The client stops. You now have to respond.

ROBERT: The question is what do you respond to? You're saying take just one piece that sounds like the biggest problem, and respond to that, and choose out of multiple possible responses.

SAMANTHA: There are many questions that have a similar theme. They're about change, they're about wanting to make a difference. I would go with, "What do you want to do differently?" You're telling me about all these things that have happened in the past; that clearly isn't working for you, and you're not feeling great about it. Then what do you want to happen differently?"

ROBERT: That's my point. You're not picking anyone of these. You're generalizing. Your intervention is specific to the topic of unleashing.

SAMANTHA: It's for the whole utterance. That question wraps it up in a nice, neat package. We have to choose one thing from that whole utterance. We can take that question and put it in to every one of those opportunities: "I need to unleash." "What do you want to do differently?" "I keep building it up." "What do you want to do differently?"

DIANA:	You could also ask, "How is it serving you?"
ROBERT:	Wouldn't it be more appropriate – this is my question – to say something like, "You mentioned a lot here. Which part would you like to focus on first?"
SAMANTHA:	That's opening up a can of worms. It's a potential for him just to get into problem talk – talking about what makes him angry. Then you've lost him.
JOEL:	Yes, you could say, "You mentioned a whole bunch of things: getting angry, getting frustrated" and so forth. "Which one will have the most impact on you when it changes?" Except for the ones we crossed out together, anyone of the interventions would move the conversation in – at least high probability – a positive direction. All you want to do is to generate a solution-building response. Then you build on that.
LYDIA:	I would choose 5b. If he answers, he acknowledges that he knows how to not get frustrated since he's been able to do it in the past.
JOEL:	Also, it's a presumptive question. "How do you do it" presumes he does it.
JUNE:	I'm not sure this is a choice, but I'm intrigued with "What does it mean to be the best person?" as an intervention.
JOEL:	Why do you like that?
JUNE:	I would find that very difficult to answer myself. It would cause a lot of discussion. I guess that is the goal. Now that I see it, it reflects back to opportunity 6. I think the goal here is to hear the utterance, accurately reflect back, and work with it. The thing I should think about is that the client said this, and it gives us the opportunity to respond.
JOEL:	Here's what I think that does. It describes a preferred future. Any other choices?
SAMANTHA:	I think 7d is similar to other ones. I like that one.
JOEL:	What's the reason you would choose that one?
SAMANTHA:	You're doing a couple of different things there. It's having him think about what's worked in the past, and it requires his perception about past situations.

Discussion 6

At this point, there is confusion in the process. We have found this to be very common: do you choose a preferred intervention for each of the opportunities? Joel points out that's not how conversations proceed. The client poses an utterance, the therapist responds to that utterance, the client responds to the therapist's response and so on. So, the question is what is your preference for responding to this utterance? In other words, we listen for opportunities, we consider possible responses to opportunities, we select one combined opportunity-intervention, and with that we respond to the utterance.

Robert poses an interesting proposition: asking the client what he wants to focus on. He reasons, "It's open ended and it allows the client to go where he wants to go." The question this raises is whether, as solution-focused therapists, we want the client to go where the client wants to go. The alternative is for the therapist to take the lead and guide the conversation. Clients choose what they want to talk about; therapists decide how to talk about it.

Joel suggests that any intervention that is chosen is useful as long as it will more than likely result in a solution-building response. As Joel and Lance discussed in this sequence, Lance counters with the idea that there are some interventions that may be better than others. Perhaps, the central leaning concept is deconstructing the idea that there is the "best" intervention as opposed to the "preferred" intervention.

In this portion of the dialogue, Cynthia essentially does Joel's job when she asks, "What is the most important thing the client says in the utterance that you would want to respond to?" She is helping to clarify the concept that the intervention choice is to the utterance and not the opportunity. As trainers, we need to remember that this is a room of smart people. Good trainers create an environment that allows smart people to be smart. In this example, Cynthia addresses Robert directly – she doesn't have to route it through Joel.

It would be easy to see Robert as a provocateur. In his own way, Robert is doing Joel's job just as much as Cynthia does. He's taking on the role of devil's advocate and getting the group to respond to him. For example, he gives Joel the opportunity to point out how a list of problems can be transformed into a solution-building conversation. Joel says, "You mentioned a whole bunch of things: getting angry, getting frustrated," and so forth. "Which one will have the most impact on you when it changes?" Joel might not have the opportunity to suggest that possibility had it not been for Robert. Far from being the resident skeptic, Robert opens up possibilities for discussion and meaning-making.

JOEL: I want you to see what you've done.

Chart 8.12 Finished chart

#	Opportunity	Possible interventions	Rationale
1	I need to unleash everything.	1a: How does that make a difference? 1b: What tells you that you've done enough unleashing? 1c: When are there times that you don't need to unleash? 1d: What would you want to be doing differently?	

Chart 8.12 (Continued)

#	Opportunity	Possible interventions	Rationale
2	I keep building it up, building it up.	2a: How is building it up serving you? 2b: Is building it up getting the results you want? 2c: When you're at that point, is there anything you do to slow the build-up process? 2d: What other approach would work toward your intended goal? 2e: When you're at that point, what can you do to slow the build-up process?	
3	I start lashing out at people I shouldn't be.	3a) ~~When do you first realize you're lashing out?~~ 3b) Why shouldn't you be lashing out at these people? 3c) How would you prefer to interact? 3d) What would it look like when you're not lashing out? 3e) What would have to happen to communicate differently? 3f) When was there a time when you didn't lash out when you were frustrated?	
4	I get – I wouldn't say angry.	4a: What would you say? 4b) ~~What difference would that make?~~ 4c) How do you know it's not anger? 4d) ~~Would you say you get triggered?~~	
5	I get frustrated very fast.	5a) ~~How do you know when you're getting frustrated?~~ 5b) When are there times that you don't get frustrated so quickly? 5c) ~~Are you saying you have a low tolerance?~~ 5d) How do you slow down so you don't get frustrated? 5e) What are the things that get you frustrated quickly?	5b: Presumptive. 5d: Strategy, presumptive question.
6	And I'm not the best person when it comes to that. I get frustrated.	6a) What does it mean to be the best person? 6b) Similar to 5b.	6a: Reflects back to what he said. Describes a preferred future.
7	I don't kind of calm myself down.	7a) ~~What do you need to feel calmer right now?~~ 7b) What would help you feel calmer? 7c) What has worked to get you in a calmer place in the past? 7d) When was there a time you were able to calm yourself? 7e) What don't you?	7d: What worked in the past, rewires his perspective on past.

JOEL: This is one utterance. Take a look at all the possible interventions in just one utterance. The problem here is not having choices; the problem is deciding which one to choose given the number of possibilities. Consider this: how many utterances happen in the course of a conversation? How many of those utterances have multiple possibilities for interventions?

DIANA: No wonder you need to take a break in the session.

JOEL: Right, there's so much to process. What I hope has become clear is how important it is to listen to clients, and not get lost in having to come up with the next question. Instead, "How do I want to respond to the client with an intervention that drives the conversation in a positive direction?" With the exception of those we have crossed out, any of the others could be asked. It doesn't matter which one you choose. Any of these interventions more than likely would have gotten a solution-building response. I'm really impressed with this; as a group, you are new to solution focus; however, you came up with solution-focused possibilities.

Discussion 7

As trainers, we often find that those new to the model have difficulty formulating questions. We have seen new solution-focused therapists bring "cheat sheets" with possible questions when interviewing clients. Because this practice limits the therapist's ability to listen to and respond to clients, and creatively formulate responses, we certainly discourage this practice.

A benefit of using an opportunities exercise as part of training is that once it is complete, the array of response possibilities becomes apparent – it is a visual representation of the richness of possible interventions. As Joel reminds the group, this is just one of many utterances that occur in the course of a therapy session. The opportunities exercise is designed to help the trainees understand how solution-focused interventions co-construct possibilities. The exercise also demonstrates the richness of intervention possibilities that client utterances provide to therapists.

More Training Examples

Over a couple of decades, the authors have developed their individual frameworks for presenting workshops on solution-focused brief therapy. Both of us have incorporated detailed examination of actual conversation between therapists and clients as part of our presentations. Following is one example of introducing trainees to the practice of paying close attention to the specific utterances of clients in order to develop the orientation of noting opportunities and generating possible therapeutic initiatives.

This example is drawn from a workshop conducted with about a dozen participants including several trainees and some senior supervisory staff at a family therapy center. For the most part, the therapists in this group are not primarily solution focused in their practice. However, they have varying degrees of familiarity with the model as well as other collaborative practices. This half-day workshop was included in the weekly theory course that is presented to the group of graduate level trainees who spend the fall, winter, and spring semesters in active and closely supervised family therapy practice at the Center.

On the occasion from which this example is drawn, this exercise was inserted in the workshop program at the point of introducing the three elements of solution-focused practice described in Chapter 3, specifically after the introduction to the elements of solution-focused listening. This workshop was conducted virtually, using the Zoom platform. After an introduction, the video of the "client" speaking is played with subtitles for the participants to observe. Following the completion of the video, participants are invited to contribute their ideas for opportunities to compliment the "client".

Consistent with the perspective of this book, this example from the workshop is presented in transcript format. Lance introduces the exercise. The "client" example is an edited compilation of video clips from a session recorded and seen by the workshop participants. The "client" role is played by an actor. PT represents participants 1–4. Hopefully the following provides the reader with a vivid example of using the opportunities framework as a learning exercise in a workshop setting.

LANCE: So, we should do a little exercise. I'd like to invite some of you to take the position of solution-focused listening. After I play this clip, I will ask: What compliments would you give this man?

CLIENT: Ya, I just went to the doctor and I got some bad news. I'm not sure how to deal with it. I just found out that I'm HIV positive. I don't know what I'm going to do. I don't know what I'm supposed to do. I don't even know why I'm here. I don't want to tell anybody. It's really scary. My job, what's going to happen there if they find out? I don't know, my family and my friends. I'll lose my friends. I don't want to spend a bunch of time in a hospital. I don't want to be a burden to anybody.

LANCE
(to workshop
participants): So, what are your compliments to him?

PT 1 – TERI: I would commend him for even taking the first step to come and talk to somebody so that he's not carrying that all on his own. He's saying I don't know what to do but [L: Okay] he's there in the moment doing something.

LANCE:	Okay, I see you saw it that way and some other people are nodding. They noticed that too. What else?
PT 2 – LARRY:	Similar to Teri, I noticed that and I noticed a few other things. I found that you could try to make a compliment out of almost anything he did. So, the fact that he even went [L: ah ha] to the doctor was something. I got that he was hoping to deal with the fact that he was HIV. Maybe I imposed the word "hope" but there was something like there was bad news and I'm trying to do something about it. Even though he doesn't really know why he's there, he's still there. It seems that he really cares about his family and his friends. He doesn't want to cause them any trouble. So, I'd say that he's very caring. So, I thought that that was something [L: um-hm] that you could compliment him on.
LANCE:	So, I just want to pick and choose among some of Larry's comments. The one that lit my fire was that "you could make a compliment out of just about anything he {the client} said". Ya? Depending on how you position yourself, right? He {the client} said some awful things there and, Larry says you could make a compliment out of any one of them. And then he listed several specific things he would complement him for. But did you hear that guy in the clip mention hope? Did he use that word? [Several PTs shake their head (no)] No, I didn't hear it either. That's Larry's word but it's really relevant. He just decides to hear some of the guy's troubles in the language of hope. It's possible to hear "I don't want to be a burden to anybody" as a hope to go through this without troubling others too much. So, a lot of neat things about your compliments, Larry. It tells me you firmly installed yourself in the position of a solution-focused listener. Anybody else? Any other compliments you've got for this guy?
JOEL'S COMMENT:	Lance points out the difference between observation and inference. The client does not actually use the word "hope"; that is Larry's inference. What I like that Lance does is make that distinction, at the same time complimenting Larry. In doing so, Lance creates a safe environment for sharing thoughts.
PT 3 – KELLY:	I think the first thing he said was "I don't know what I am going to do [emphasis]". Piggybacking on what Teri said, at least we know now that he's thinking he will do [emphasis] something.

LANCE: "I don't know what I'm going to do" tell us that he knows there is something to do. Ya? It can be heard as a way of saying, "I'd like to figure out what to do". One more compliment?

PT 4 – FREDA: He looks really well kept. For someone who's going through something really hard, he got dressed and he took a shower. I also would point out that, like Larry said, he really cares about his relationships. He sounds like he also has very strong relationships, ties with his family, co-workers and friends.

LANCE: Thank you, Freda. So did anybody else think of that? He looks really well kept. There are two things that are pretty cool about that. One is that's an opportunity with no words. It's got nothing to do with the words he {the client} used. It's an opportunity based on Freda making sure she was absorbing with both eyes and ears. She just looked at him. The other thing is I've never heard that comment before. The well of opportunities is nearly a bottomless pit. There's almost always one more. So, it's not a question of whether or not there are opportunities for intervention in what people say. The question is more how are we going to position ourselves to make sure we notice them, and then how are we going to respond to them. In addition to opportunities being supplied directly by the clients, there is the element of how we are listening to a person and how we are able to construe solution-probable openings within their utterances.

LANCE: Okay, thanks for doing that.

Discussion

For the sake of brevity, and partly because the workshop itself was fairly short, this exercise was restricted to a period of about ten minutes. In a longer workshop with more time available, the exercise can be extended in several ways. Repeatedly inviting "one more" example from participants can proceed almost indefinitely, providing an impactful demonstration and first-hand experience of the depth of possibilities and opportunities in client utterances.

It is common for someone whose primary practice model is not solution focused to identify an opportunity for another kind of intervention. For example, a participant may suggest a possibility of inquiring into the trigger or cause of a particular client problem, something a solution-focused interviewer is not likely to do. In a teaching setting, this presents an opportunity to contrast solution-focused practice with other orientations. Making comparisons across different models of psychotherapy – what practitioners employing alternative approaches consider opportunities – goes a long way to defining their approach to client change.

Inviting the group into a post-session reflection on their experience of the exercise is another way to enhance the learning value. Participants routinely express amazement at the seemingly inexhaustible range of opportunities for solution-focused intervention offered by clients. They usually note how readily they are able to switch their listening posture from a problem focus to that of solutions.

The astute reader might have noticed how the author, at another level, was employing the mindset of opportunities in his interaction with participants in this opportunities exercise. One of the participants said, "You could try to make a compliment out of almost anything he did." The author affirmed the participant's observation by compliment, "The one that lit my fire." Lance preserved the trainee's words – "you could make a compliment out of just about anything he (the client) said" – and then added "depending on how you position yourself ... right?" A productive teaching pattern can be to perform the tools live simultaneously in the course of teaching the tools didactically.

This exercise employed the intervention of compliment, one of the methods of affirmation, to orient the listeners toward opportunities presented by the client. This resembles a well-known teaching exercise used by many solution-focused trainers known variously as the "Complaining Exercise" (Lamarre, 2005) and "Moan, Moan, Moan" (Ghul, 2005). In these two exercises, one member of a pair complains and, after a set amount of time, the listening member of the pair gives the complainer compliments.

Here is another example of putting the construct of opportunities to work in a training environment. The trainee in this case raised a question about utilizing the Miracle Question in a family situation where "the mother [exhibited] a pattern of blaming". Below is brief exchange by email that occurred following the class.

LANCE: After class today, I remembered you raising this question [about using the Miracle Question]. Please refresh my memory on your specific point.

TRAINEE: My question is surrounding how to respond when people continue to place blame in their response to the Miracle Question (i.e. a mother responds by saying "everything would be different because my kids would be listening to me and do what I ask the first time").

LANCE: So, how about exploring your question using the "preserve, omit, preserve with additions" schema along with the notion of opportunities. If you look at the mother's utterance: "everything would be different because my kids would be listening to me and do what I ask the first time", what are some opportunities that contain hints of wellness? Which opportunity stands out the most for you? And once you've selected out that bit of language, experiment with preserving those words along with additions to generate some possible responses to the mother. Let me know what you come up with. If it's useful to you, we can swap our analyses of this statement for the fun of it.

TRAINEE: Thank you for response it has provoked a lot of thoughts for me … Some possible responses may be: "So, your kids will be listening to you, how will you respond differently when they are listening?", "What would be better if your children listened to you the first time?" "What does the act of your children listening to you tell you about them?", "What would other family members be doing if the children were listening to you?" Those are some of my initial thoughts. I would love to hear your analysis!

LANCE: Very nice, Marie. Congratulations on provoking yourself into a generative position. I have attached an off-the-cuff analysis of my own. It's interesting to me to note the similarities and resonance in our response possibilities.

TRAINEE: Thank you for sharing this with me. It is so valuable to see how many different possibilities there are based on one utterance. I have shared the document you sent with the rest of the trainees; I hope that is okay by you!

Chart 8.13 Exchanging opportunities analyses

Utterance	Opportunities	Responses (* = preferred)	Rationale
Everything would be different because my kids would be listening to me and do what I ask the first time.	**1.** Everything would be different.	**1a.** What's the first thing that would be different? **1b.** Wow. Sounds like it would be an important difference if it changes everything. **1c.** How would a day go differently then?	
	2. Because.	**2a.** Sounds like better listening could cause a lot of valuable changes. **2b.** On a scale of 1 to 10, where 10 is very valuable, how much good do you think better listening would do?	

(Continued)

Chart 8.13 (Continued)

Utterance	Opportunities	Responses (* = preferred)	Rationale
	3. My kids would be listening to me.	***3a.** What would tell you they were listening better? **3b.** Which of the kids listens better? **3c.** What do you do differently when one of the kids is listening better?	**3a.** This is my first choice partly because my sense is that it is the most specific wellness-promising opportunity in the utterance and partly for its potential to open up a discussion of the details of "listening", out of which drop some exceptions and perhaps also opportunities to ask 3c.
	4. Do what I ask the first time.	**4a.** What's better about the first time? **4b.** What would be the good in your home of more prompt cooperation? **4c.** What do you see as the long-term learning value for your kids to develop strong cooperation skills?	

Conclusion

We have presented examples of training applications for opportunities analysis. In one example, an actual opportunities analysis was conducted within a workshop framework. In other examples, exercises focused on opportunity detection. One exercise invited trainees to answer their own questions by adopting the opportunities posture. Hopefully the reader can imagine other workshop, presentation and classroom applications for opportunities analysis to work.

9 Applications

Opportunities as a Coaching Tool

Opportunities analysis began as collaboration between the authors with the goal of putting our newly acquired microanalysis skills to work on some important aspect of solution-focused interviewing. We started with the idea that key words used by clients play a strong role in therapists constructing their interventions, hoping that more detailed study would enhance our understanding and use of this phenomenon. In Chapter 4, we described how the original idea of searching for key words evolved into the proposition that each client utterance or action may contain multiple opportunities for intervention.

In the exercise of a microanalysis of opportunities, we encourage a liberal, inclusive approach to identifying opportunities. This enriches the practice of construing multiple possibilities for solution-focusing interventions without regard to whether any particular option is likely to be employed in an actual interview.

As the reader will recall, one category in the formal microanalysis is the "preferred response", which is linked to the "preferred opportunity" – the option the analyst would select as the most promising given the array of alternatives in the utterance. This is the selection of language from the client utterance that the interviewer would most likely preserve in constructing the next interventive response.

This element of the "preferred opportunity" returns us to the notion of key words and phrases. For the particular moment in the interview at hand, the preferred opportunity may be thought of as a key word in the client narrative that provides a potential linguistic path forward into solution-building. Guided by our growing understanding of the multiplicity of opportunities, we might be more inclined to emphasize *a* key word or phrase instead of *the* key word or phrase.

The authors have worked in a variety of agencies, including community mental health clinics, child protection services, educational institutions, hospices, family therapy centers, general private practice, and inpatient and outpatient mental health institutions, to name a few. We have inhabited various roles of therapist, supervisor, manager, mentor, consultant, and trainer in these settings.

DOI: 10.4324/9781003396703-10

The study of opportunities increasingly informed the authors' continuing activities as therapists, coaches, and trainers. We were encouraged by the welcoming responses of colleagues, trainees, and workshop participants. The core notions of opportunities and key words/phrases proved to be easily adopted and put to work in other settings beyond therapeutic interviews with clinical clients. Up to this point, we have included brief sections of transcript from client sessions to demonstrate single interventive moments. In this chapter, we present a full coaching interview with opportunities analysis as a backdrop to both the practice and discussion.

Students of therapeutic conversation at varying levels of mastery are occasionally engaged in scenarios designed to enhance their skills. In many of the agencies where we have worked, there are formal arrangements for supervision. Supervisors find themselves in roles that embody varying proportions of teaching, monitoring and evaluation of supervisees' performances.

Following is an example of a conversation with a therapist trainee that is weighted primarily toward the teaching end of the supervision array, in what might be most accurately titled a coaching session. Once again, the medium of presentation here is the transcript format accompanied by discussion sections. The conversation is divided into what might be loosely considered stages of the interview.

Situating the Interview in Hopes – Clip 1

LANCE: Have you given some thought to what your hopes are for our talk today?

TRAINEE: So, I did kind of think of a case that I'm struggling with and some growing edges I've been working on and that sort of thing. So that's sort of what I came prepared for today.

LANCE: So, two things I'm hearing. One possibly case related. And one possibly growing edge related. Where should we start, given that there's probably a chance for us to spend a little time with each?

TRAINEE: Maybe the growing edge one. I think that's probably woven through a lot of my work with clients so that one would probably be good to just start with.

LANCE: And do you have a name for your growing edge these days? What you call it?

TRAINEE: Yeah, it's just kind of like being more firm or direct with clients sometimes when it's needed. So if, for example, there's kind of like a need to set boundaries with parents. Sometimes I struggle a little bit with being firm enough and like interrupting sometimes too like I really struggle with that. So yeah, those are some of the things I've been kind of working on this practicum here and it's been a lot of work.

LANCE: So, let's look at some layers of that interrupting interest. What is your hope or aspiration in a sense? Where you want to try and get to as a therapist with interruption?

TRAINEE: I think, because what I noticed especially more so when I was starting out, I'm getting a smidgen better. But I would just never interrupt. Sometimes things would go on and on and on and a lot of times that's when the PIP[1] (Tomm et al., 2014) would come out and sort of get really solidified or because they could keep talking about it and could keep kind of heading in that direction. And then I noticed like sometimes the other family members would kind of start to pull away a little bit. So, I think kind of my hope in that is to be able to interrupt those PIPs before they get too strong or before they get too far and I lose the other family members but also being able to interrupt in a way that kind of fits with my style. So, still being – what's the word? Like I'm a very tentative person so still being kind of like a little tentative and to be like a little polite but still being able to like stop it before we get too settled in that.

LANCE: That strikes me as a graceful combination – polite interruption.

Discussion

Almost everything that interviewees do, including but not limited to what they say, presents opportunities for intervention. By appearing for the interview, the student practitioner presents an opportunity for the interviewer to situate the conversation in hopes for what may result from the event, a core principle of SF practice. In this example, the trainee presents two threads of interest in the language of "a case" and "growing edge". Lance acknowledges the two possibilities and asks the trainee to pick the starting point, thereby placing the trainee in the lead in the collaborative endeavor. Hearing "growing edge" as a somewhat generic title offers Lance the opportunity to personalize this particular trainee's growing edge in this current conversation, beginning with an invitation to give it his own, more specific title. Toward the end of the clip, the title becomes "polite interrupting".

While there is a clear boundary between supervision and therapy, there is a parallel between SFBT interviewing with clients and using SFBT as a platform for supervision. In both cases, whether client or supervisee, the starting point of the conversation is what the individual wants from the conversation.

Questions

The reader may wish to explore the following questions to spend time in the milieu of opportunities.

- Remembering the example of the actor video exercise in the Training section, what compliments might the reader consider offering the Trainee based on this short clip so far?
- In this brief opening clip, does the reader observe any opportunities that might qualify as a classical exception in the SFBT sense?
- In this and subsequent clips, how does Lance use the concept of opportunities to construct responses to Trainee utterances?

Shifting What We Don't Want to What We Do Want – Clip 2

LANCE: That strikes me as graceful combination, polite interruption. And when you're in that predicament, in a session where the PIP is on a roll, if one sits back and the PIP takes over and begins to be performed or played out or even if it's being described in a second-hand way but with a lot of intensity, the problem is still seemingly in control of the session. What are your present instincts, at this point, in terms of what you would like to see happening, instead of the PIP controlling the session?

TRAINEE: I think instead of that, well I'd appreciate a little more balance in the conversation. So being, of course, able to talk about their concerns but not let it be this entity that is kind of deciding where we're going to go. I find like once we get too far into it, it's really hard to kind of come back from it because everyone's kind of in this place where they feel the heaviness of the PIP. So I kind of want to keep it from getting to that point, and deconstruct it enough, but not fall into it and begin to sort of head towards the PIP. I think I don't want it to be the thing that controls the conversation.

LANCE: Yeah, what you call the deciding entity [Trainee: yes] exactly. Who or what do you want the deciding entity to be there?

TRAINEE: I think I'd like for all of us to sort of decide that. And I think the families sort of decide their hopes and where they want to be so in that sense like I think that aspect of it is them. I think it's also up to me to have kind of like more of maybe like a presence, to be able to kind of support them in that direction. So, I think they sort of decide where we're going and I try and support them in getting there. I think that is how I see it.

LANCE: So, yeah, that kind of maps out what it means to say we all kind of decide. They decide where they're going and I decide how to help them get there. So, yeah, that kind of nicely embodies both the spirit of collaboration, that we're doing this together. And at the same time it kind of maps out roles – your role as the therapist.

TRAINEE: Yeah, definitely.

Discussion

The trainee expresses his observation that the problem can sometimes "take over" the conversation, indicating that he doesn't think it is very useful for this to happen, bringing forth his language of the "entity deciding" the direction of the talk. This presents an opportunity for Lance to ask what he would like the deciding entity to be, with the possibility of co-constructing the more powerful hope of what he wants to have happen to replace the language of what he wants not to happen.

Also exhibited in this clip is an example of shifting gears to other lines of inquiry. The process of giving title to the person's hope may include a number of exchanges, through which a name for the hope – "polite interrupting" in this instance – can gradually take shape and be brought to the surface.

The quality of the "languaging" of the hope has improved sufficiently, from "growing edge" to "polite interrupting", a title that is good enough for now. Having achieved and affirmed a workable titling of what the person hopes for opens an opportunity for selecting other lines of inquiry in the solution-building.

Turning to questions in the movement category, the trainee can bring forth his expectation that getting better at "polite interrupting" may help him more effectively manage the "deciding entity" determining the direction of therapeutic conversations. That begins to answer the core question of what good might come from making this change, or what difference will the difference make. In SF interviewing, we seek opportunities to co-construct differences that make a useful difference.

Questions

- Can the reader articulate how the elements of solution-focused listening, questioning, and affirming work in synchrony in this section of the interview?
- What are some examples in this clip of "omitting" interviewee language in the construction of next interviewer responses?

Registering and Amplifying Exceptions – Clip 3

LANCE: You said just a little while back: I've gotten a smidgen better.

TRAINEE: Mm-hmm.

LANCE: And how did you come to notice that smidgen of improvement or how do you how do you recognize it now? How would you describe it to me?

TRAINEE: So, I think it's been a matter of kind of being more like attuned to my own feelings in session. Previously, if I noticed we were falling into this PIP, I would find myself sometimes feeling frustrated, sometimes feeling very nervous. I'm like, "Oh I need to interrupt,

I need to interrupt them." My nerves kind of keep building and building. So, I noticed now, a little more often, I kind of interrupt at the first sign of those feelings. I'm like, "Okay, I'm starting to feel a little nervous about where this is going to go so maybe I should stop it before it kind of heads down that path." And it's been also a little bit of just trying to figure out what I'm going to say to interrupt it. So, I'm finding that's been definitely an improvement as well. Sometimes I'll just say like: "Can I interrupt you for a second? I just want to make sure I'm getting this right." Or, "Yeah, can we back-track to something you said like a little while ago?" or something like that. So, I think it's been kind of a combination of being aware of what I'm feeling and how that's a cue that I'm worried things are gonna turn into very deep PIP and also I guess just starting to better find the words to interrupt.

LANCE: So, those feelings of growing nervousness and frustration have gone from being kind of an enemy or an impediment to your practice, from being kind of a foe to a friend?

TRAINEE: Yeah. Yeah, that's a nice way to put it. Yeah, it has.

LANCE: I'm guessing, then, do you think it would be reasonable to say that you might have found yourself developing a bit more trust in yourself in the sense that when you notice that something's bugging you, there's probably a good reason for that?

TRAINEE: Yeah, that's a really nice way to put it. Yeah, I think I have been able to just trust myself a little bit more instead of thinking, "Oh, like just put those feelings aside for now" kind of thing. Now I am kind of like, "Oh, okay, these feelings are here for a reason. So, what could that be?" So yeah, definitely I think trusting myself more has been a huge part of it for sure.

LANCE: Yeah, it makes a pretty big difference if those kind of nervous frustrated feelings, if we think they're a sign of limitation. And then, what's the matter with me? As opposed to: "Oh great, here's the sign, here's a clue for me to do something."

TRAINEE: Yeah, exactly. Yeah. Yeah, it's a really cool thing for sure, a cool experience. Yeah, yeah.

LANCE: And also I appreciate this little detail of starting to notice that you're getting perturbed about where this is going and you're getting that kind of useful nervous frustrated feeling. I don't quite know what to do just yet in terms of words but I do know that I want to do something so I might say: "Can I interrupt you for a second?" You might not have even figured out what you're going to do after you say "Can I interrupt you?" but at least you do interrupt number one, and number two you create some space for yourself to then figure out what to do.

TRAINEE: Mm-hmm.
LANCE: I appreciate the practical value and the depth of that tool of interruption.
TRAINEE: Absolutely. I'm definitely coming to appreciate it a lot myself.

Discussion

Referring back to the previous section of transcript covering the beginning of the section, one can see that from the trainee's utterance:

> I think, because what I noticed especially more so when I was starting out, I'm getting a smidgen better. But I would just never interrupt. Sometimes things would go on and on and on and a lot of times that's when the PIP (Tomm et al., 2014) would come out and sort of get really solidified or because they could keep talking about it and could keep kind of heading in that direction. And then I noticed like sometimes the other family members would kind of start to pull away a little bit. So, I think kind of my hope in that is to be able to interrupt those PIPs before they get too strong or before they get too far and I lose the other family members but also being able to interrupt in a way that kind of fits with my style. So, still being, what's the word? Like I'm a very tentative person so still being kind of like a little tentative and to be like a little polite but still being able to like stop it before we get too settled in that.

For the purpose of constructing this next question, Lance selects, "I'm getting a smidgen better" because it preserves the trainee's exact language of "smidgen" and invites him to give details of doing "better", one avenue toward amplifying the exception. Amplification is accomplished by activities ranging all the way from simply holding the conversation on this topic for an extended period, thereby raising its prominence, to the more technically precise lines of questioning into detail, agency, and movement as well as affirming actions such as compliment.

It is also worth noting that in the initial hearing of this trainee utterance, Lance chose to omit the bulk of the speech, including the exception, "smidgen better", opting instead to orient toward the trainee's emerging title for his hopes "polite interruption". While hosting a solution-focused conversation, an utterance may contain more than one key opportunity, offering choices for sequencing the overall conversation. In this example, Lance opted to firm up the title for difference first, knowing that the exception of "smidgen better" remained available for a subsequent return focus. A common phrase that observers notice in solution-focused interviews is "let me come back to something", reflecting the interviewer's process of continually keeping track of opportunities and sometimes choosing to return to something expressed earlier than the most recent utterance.

Questions

- By what reasoning could "smidgen better" be arguably the strongest exception so far in the interview?
- What useful shifts in perception may have been co-constructed in this part of the conversation?

Putting the Exception to Work Using Scaling – Clip 4

TRAINEE: Absolutely. I'm definitely coming to appreciate it a lot myself.

LANCE: Let's ground ourselves in a scale. If 10 is I'm as skilled with interruption and, in your case, with graceful and polite interruption, I'm as skilled as I want to be. And 0 is I haven't yet begun to recognize that it's a skill that I aspire to. Where would you put yourself these days?

TRAINEE: I think when I first started the practicum I was definitely at a 0. I think now I'm at like a 5 – though, as someone who doesn't like interrupting and stuff, that was like a huge leap for me so it's definitely gone up quite a bit.

LANCE: Nice. How would you say you've come to terms with your quiet side, your preference for politeness, in order to progress that far with interruption?

TRAINEE: I think I sort of had this idea before, maybe like a SCIP[2] or something, where I guess this idea that quiet people are polite people or validating people or whatever. They don't interrupt. Like that's not part of what it is. I think that's what I used to really believe. But now I can see like you can have both of those things together. You can be generally a quiet person. You can generally be a polite person or you can be validating and still, like, interrupt from time to time. And interrupting can – I've been starting to learn, interrupting in itself can be something that's polite because it sort of keeps it from getting worse for everybody and it keeps it from someone's feelings really getting hurt. So I think I just needed to sort of begin to shift my idea that you can only be one or the other sort of thing. Now I can kind of understand that you can have both and that sometimes they can even complement each other. So, I think that's helped me a lot in being able to start interrupting people more when appropriate.

LANCE: Some powerful shifts there. Shifting from either/or position to both/and. [Trainee: Exactly. Yeah, definitely.] Well good for you because I know that an either/or position can be strong and can be limiting.

TRAINEE: Definitely.

LANCE: I think this is pretty neat observation that you've developed that there's a way in which interruption can be polite. Do you think, along with that, another one of your values, do you think there's a way in which interruption can be validating?

TRAINEE: Yeah. I think I'm learning a lot too that it's, that it was such a big fear for me before. If I interrupt them, if I cut them off or whatever, then they're going to experience that as me silencing them or telling them to stop or as invalidating. So I've been finding like the way I sort of frame it, it's been able to be validating. So, just as an example sometimes I'll be like sorry, can I interrupt you for a second? You're saying a lot of important stuff and I just want to make sure I'm getting it right. So that in itself can just slow them down with it and it's also very validating, I find. Oh yeah and then I find if it's like – if it's a sort of PIP of blaming or something like that or trying to shift responsibility to be on somebody else entirely, I find interrupting that I'm trying to sort of reframe it to what's within their control. I find that can be kind of empowering and validating too instead of just focusing on like what everybody else is not doing or what they need to do. So I've definitely found that it can actually be quite validating at times.

LANCE: When you get to switch, through a graceful interruption, from in blaming position to out of blaming, what would you say it is that you might be validating there?

TRAINEE: I think it's kind of like validating the frustration or feeling stuck and the position of: it's the other person who needs to kind of do everything. It's kind of like acknowledging that that's a tough position to be in and then trying to explore what sort of control or what sort of strengths that they do have. So I think it is particularly like validating that stuckness and then supporting them in getting unstuck.

LANCE: Kind of stages or layers of validation. First you validate the frustration or feeling of stuckness behind the blaming. And I think if you left it there, I wouldn't be so impressed with it, but I see you take it to the next layer, which is validating the alternative, their own resources and abilities. Yeah?

TRAINEE: Yeah.

LANCE: What would you see as a sign of a little bit of progress? I know you're astute with smidgens so if we got a smidgen above 5 what would tell you?

TRAINEE: Um, I think that would be if I'm noticing, maybe it's a matter of, like I don't know, quantity, the amount of times that I interrupt when appropriate. Of course, I think maybe I'm not always so attuned to when I do interrupt so I think being more like attuned to it and then noticing when I do actually interrupt. I think that would increase the number a little bit. And I also think continuing to trust my feelings and to continue practicing the ways I interrupt and shifting my perspective on interrupting because I definitely noticed like some of my beliefs still linger a little bit. So I think if I could just continue to challenge like that either/or sort of perspective. I think that would really help me to continue to move beyond the 5.

Discussion

There are numerous applications for scaling in SF interviewing. One is to amplify exceptions and bring forth interviewee capabilities. An opportunity for this use of scaling is presented in the trainee's utterance, "Absolutely. I'm definitely coming to appreciate it a lot myself."

Intuitively, the trainee's language of "appreciate it a lot" seems to beg the question of "just how much do you appreciate it?", providing an opportunity for quantifying how "good" it is. The reader may notice that the scale is constructed so that it is unlikely to elicit a response of 0. Anything above 0 implicitly reveals difference. Even if the rating given is 1, we can work with the difference between 0 and 1. How do they detect the difference? What are the details of difference? In our example here, the trainee is able to quantify change from 0, at the "start of the practicum" to "5 at this point in time". The SF approach is to explore both sides of the 5, typically beginning with how the person has progressed that far and then sometimes focusing on next steps, or a "smidgen" higher on the scale.

Questions

- How is the scale constructed to make an answer of zero unlikely?
- What Trainee capabilities are exposed by his progress so far?

Eliciting Details and Agency – Clip 5

LANCE: I found you pointing towards some very important practicalities again. You talked about the ways to interrupt and practicing. That really kind of grounds the whole hope. There are different things we can do to interrupt. And mindful practice, like lots of our activities, our skill level with activities results from practice, right?

TRAINEE: Exactly, yeah.

LANCE: Okay so, just before we leave it, let's focus a bit on the notion of ways to interrupt. If you do kind of a quick check on your repertoire, what comes up for your ways of interrupting?

TRAINEE: I have a few. Usually I'll say, "Can I interrupt you for a second?" or, "Is it okay if I interrupt you for a second here?" Sometimes I say he said something really important. I want to take a second to highlight it. If it's a situation where it's really strongly devolving into a PIP, sometimes if I can muster up enough courage, I'll be a little more kind of firm there. So sometimes it'll start with like, "Can I interrupt for a second?" Then I'll say like, "I'm noticing we're getting a bit too hung up on the details" or whatever, 'cause a lot of times there's debating back and forth about the truth of what happened. So sometimes I'll say that. Sometimes I'll say, "I just want to be aware. I'm just worried about maybe we're losing so and so a little bit here." And then I'll just shift to the other person and see what they have to say. Or sometimes I'll interrupt and try to highlight the PIP. Like sometimes it'll be like, "I'm not sure if you're noticing this but do you notice like sometimes in these conversations you slip into a little bit of this blaming and then the other person kind of feels like they have to defend themselves? Do you notice that happens a lot?" So in those situations where it's the PIP I try and kind of stop it. Shift away from the details and maybe focus more on the process, I suppose. So yeah, those are just some of the things that I like to do if I'm interrupting.

LANCE: That's a good deep repertoire. I noticed one thing about it that I thought might be worth highlighting too. Some of the things you may use to interrupt have the syntax of questions: "Would it be okay if I were to interrupt you?" The interesting thing I think I heard – and I just want to check with you. I think those are statements masquerading as questions. That gives them a little bit more gentleness. Would that be a decent observation or evaluation?

TRAINEE: Yeah, that's 100 percent accurate. I do try and ask as a question to make it a little more tentative but I'm not really asking. I'm going to interrupt.

LANCE: Because, back to that question of whose job is whose. Yours is to help people get to where they're going with their hope. And that means making some choices. Here's one I'm gonna make. I could present it to you gently but I'm still gonna make it.

TRAINEE: Yeah, exactly. Exactly.

Discussion

One reliable way to facilitate the building of client narratives of solutions is to inquire into details – in this instance, of conversational events containing "polite interruption". This line of inquiry exhibits the SFBT principle of building solutions based on existing client resources. What are the interviewee's already established capabilities that could be used and refined even more?

This contrasts with a more expert driven approach of aiming to build skills from the outside in: professional expert education or advice to the student about what they may do that is new or different. This is not to say that an SFBT coach does not contribute some of their own experience that seems potentially useful to the student. The component of the response-building schema we refer to as "preserving (client language) with addition" is one mechanism by which the SFBT practitioner may share their experience in a form remotely resembling giving "advice". The SFBT approach simply privileges or prioritizes client expertise over professional expertise.

Questions

- What might be the value of orienting toward existing interviewee capabilities?
- What examples are there in the interviewer responses of the "addition" aspect of "preserve with addition"?

Encouraging Shifting Titles – Clip 6

If the reader refers back to the previous clip, they will find a trainee utterance:

TRAINEE: I have a few. Usually I'll say, "Can I interrupt you for a second?" or, "Is it okay if I interrupt you for a second here?" Sometimes I say he said something really important. I want to take a second to highlight it. If it's a situation where it's really strongly devolving into a PIP, sometimes if I can muster up enough courage, I'll be a little more kind of firm there.

Once again opting to recall a potential opportunity from an earlier utterance, Lance responds:

LANCE: Yeah. Okay. So if we can back off from the specifics of interruption just for a minute, you spoke of firmness. I really liked the word, thinking about an interviewer being firm. And from what I've heard from you so far my guess is you're interested in a polite version of firmness but still interested in firmness. I don't know if there are other things that fall under that heading for you, other ways you would like to be in a session that equal firmness. Does anything come to mind?

TRAINEE: Yeah. So what comes to mind is sort of under that umbrella term is being more direct at times. And then I also think having a stronger presence. I think is also part of it.

LANCE: Talk a bit more about being direct.

TRAINEE: Hmmm. I kind of mentioned this before. I find I'm a little more tentative, which at times can work quite well. I find sometimes an effort not to kind of like, I shouldn't say hurt feelings because I don't think it would hurt anyone's feelings but to really make sure that I'm not invalidating anyone or that I'm not being impositional, I'll tend to throw in a bunch of words just to sort of cushion it a little bit, but then sometimes I find that kind of makes it lose its effectiveness or like the ability for it to kind of stick. So, I think I'm kind of trying to be more attuned to times when that might not work so well for me and when I just need to kind of be direct and put it out there.

LANCE: Back to both/and again. I can have the choices of being tentative and direct. I can have both available to me, depending on the circumstances. [Trainee: Yeah.] What do you notice about yourself in terms of directness? What are clues? What do you do differently?

TRAINEE: I think it becomes a little more obvious when I'm either a bit more blunt. I don't know if that's the right word but blunt – and also, when I take a bit of a firmer position on something, I think that's when people can really start to notice I'm being more direct.

LANCE: Oh yeah, and earlier you talked about sometimes I cushion things in a lot of words. So one other clue is seemingly fewer words. You might be more blunt, as you say.

TRAINEE: Yeah, exactly.

LANCE: And something else you mentioned along the way under the heading of firmness, or a companion to it, was presence. Could you talk a bit about the presence you aspire to in your position as a therapeutic interviewer?

TRAINEE: I think it's just ensuring that I and the family kind of have like a good understanding of what my role is. So my role is not being to take sides or to, "fix" anybody. But I'm here to support the family in working on their interactions and relationships. So I found like making that super clear from the get go that this is my job, this is not my job. People are aware and they don't kind of fall into this asking for me to do this for them or to do all the work for them or that kind of thing. Yeah, so I think making it clear, being aware that I'm validating people but that I'm not taking someone's side at the expense of someone else kind of feeling excluded. Yeah, I'm not sure if that answered the question.

LANCE: Yeah, it answered the question I asked plus another one that I didn't ask, which I think is kind of interesting too. I got the impression as you spoke about your presence that you are fairly clear about what your place is in the conversation and it occurs to me that that might be a pretty important part of being clear with the family. You better know what you're doing in order to be clear with them what you're doing. [Trainee: Yeah.] Yeah. And I heard good standards there. I heard some clarity about what you don't do. Those weren't random. They have the specificity of what sometimes families want us to do. They may want us to take sides, not usually not out of any malicious intent but in their urgency to get things going better, they want the help of the therapist and maybe that's take my side or do the work for me. And those are those are not uncommon wishes for families to have and so it's neat for me to see that you've developed a position to handle that. And to be aware of what your response will likely be.

Discussion

Hopefully, the reader begins to detect how solution-focused coaching works to build narratives based on opportunities in language, particularly selecting key words and phrases to elevate to the top of the conversation. Some SFBT practitioners find themselves leaving behind the notion of "goal" since it tends to have more of a singular connotation with tradition of specificity and permanence. Joel, for example, favors the concept of vision over goal because visions are fluid and transform with experience and information. In a larger sense, this demonstrates how the model continues to evolve.

SFBT practice tends to favor a more fluid development of language for hopes. In these few clips, the trainee can be seen to have brought forth a number of words or concepts with which experienced therapists and coaches would likely resonate. He aspires to the skill of "polite interruption". He also seeks "firmness", "presence" and the choice of "being direct" as some other aspects of effective interviewing. These words add breadth to the narrative of his "growing edge".

One value of an enriched narrative for difference is that the client co-constructs several appealing possibilities, or perhaps opportunities, by which he may remind himself of his preferred differences in thinking and acting. He has more titles, or subtitles, for hopes and change that may create opportunities for more and varied links to actions and observations in his therapeutic practice.

Questions

- Is the reader able to notice a repeating pattern of affirming and questioning in interviewer utterances?
- Experimenting with another angle on the notion of opportunities, in what way do interviewer responses offer opportunities to the interviewee?

"Supervision" Regarding a Specific Case – Clip 7

The previous section in this coaching interview was oriented primarily toward interviewing skills and patterns of practice. Just as student therapists frequently ask for help with a certain case, this section briefly demonstrates case-focused coaching with a solution-focused stance continuing to rely on opportunities presented by the trainee. The contrast between this form of intervention and a more supervisor-as-expert approach should be apparent.

The authors do not intend to suggest that this is somehow better than the format of more experienced and skilled interviewers sharing their learnings in the form of instruction and advice. It might be better thought of as an alternative, along the previously mentioned lines of building competencies from the inside-out that can complement a more outside-in design of instruction and demonstration.

LANCE: Okay, so, of the other things we talked about, one thing you mentioned was a case that you'd reflected on briefly so if you think it's a reasonable direction to go here, I'd probably suggest we spend the remaining bit of time with that case. Does that make sense? [Trainee: Um-hm, absolutely.] Could you talk about what your hopes might be for how a conversation about that case might be useful?

TRAINEE: So, it's a family where there is a high-conflict separation and they, of course, came into the center because they're concerned about their kids but so many of my conversations with the parents end up being the other parent is terrible and they're ruining our kids. They do this wrong and this wrong and it's all about the other person and how I need to fix the other parent. I don't know where the time went but we're somehow nearing the {unintelligible} with this family and so I'm kind of feeling the pressure. There's been so much back and forth and this is definitely a family where I've had to interrupt a lot more than I'm used to. Or I've had to be a little more firm than I'm used to, so they're giving me lots of practice but I'm finding sometimes it just doesn't stick. So, I'm worried that you know I'll bring up that we're kind of nearing the end. I think they already know but I'm worried that what will come up is we haven't done anything or there hasn't been any change or you haven't changed so and so. Yeah, so that's kind of where I'm at with this family. They're talking {unintelligible} sometimes.

LANCE: Well I'm glad you got them for the practice effect, but I know there can be mixed feelings about that. And I do hear the growing kind of sense or pressure. In a way, endings have a way of doing that. So far I've heard you present two sides of the family's presentation.

You said they're here, they've come to the center, of course, because they're concerned about their kids. And if you can, this might involve a bit of recollection and memory or it might involve some guesswork. Could you try to present each of the parents in that language? What do you think their hopes are for their kids?

TRAINEE: Yeah. So, both parents actually appeared to hope that their kids won't be deeply affected by the parents' conflict. And both really want their kids to feel comfortable talking about their feelings, talking about what's bothering them, being open about it instead of kind of keeping it in. The funny thing is they're both totally on the same page about their hopes. So yeah, that's kind of where they were hoping our work would go.

LANCE: It's both exciting and tragic in a way. It's exciting that they're on the same page because they ought to be able to get what they want and usually the challenge is getting parents to be on the same page. These guys are already on the same page, but tragically they're messing up the congruence or the agreement they have with their bickering.

TRAINEE: Um-hmm.

LANCE: If we were to do layers here could you make some more guesses about what they might say their hopes would be? Since they hope to not have the conflict between the parents affect their children badly, what might be their hopes for how their children would respond to the differences between their parents? What would they hope would happen in place of what they hope does not happen?

TRAINEE: Mm hmm. I think they both seem to hope that the kids don't sort of like internalize or blame themselves for the conflict. They notice sometimes like the kids might get a little bit quiet. Instead of that I think they want, they interpret the quietness as something's wrong, so they want the children to be able to say what's wrong, instead of kind of keeping it in.

LANCE: So, it occurs to me there might still be another layer there. So you don't want the children to blame themselves. They don't want their own parental bickering to quiet the kids, to silence them. They don't want that to happen. Let's use that one for example. When they don't want their resentment or their conflict with each other to silence their children, what do you think would be a sign to them that the healthy alternative was happening?

TRAINEE: Um, I think that would be like if they were maybe communicating their feelings a little bit more, maybe about the conflict between their parents. I think they see that their kids worry a lot about their parents bickering so I think the alternative or something that they would notice that would kind of indicate that it's heading in a good direction is if maybe they feel a little more secure or a little more comfortable. I guess maybe even trusting their parents to be able to talk about stuff without it kind of turning into something related to the parents' relationship.

Discussion

The first thing to note in this section of the interview is that the conversation is once again situated in the interviewee's hopes for how the talk may be useful. The coach does not presume to decide what is best. As is common in responding to hope questions, the trainee enters into a lengthy narrative of the challenges. From that utterance, Lance selects "and they, of course, came into the center because they're concerned about their kids" and asks, "What do you think their hopes are for their kids?"

Lance begins by exploring the trainee's hopes for this coaching session. Presumably, the trainee hopes to facilitate the family meeting their hopes for therapy. This line of inquiry contains the embedded suggestion that it may be most useful to focus less on the mechanical interviewing difficulties and more on the client's hopes. The inquiry employs a common tactic of systemic interviewing, where we ask people present in the interview to speak for people absent from the interview. Endeavoring to speak for the parents, the trainee generates a promising opportunity:

So, both parents actually appeared to hope that their kids won't be deeply affected by the parents' conflict. And both really want their kids to feel comfortable talking about their feelings, talking about what's bothering them, being open about it instead of kind of keeping it in. The funny thing is they're both totally on the same page about their hopes.

The language of "both" catches Lance's attention as a standout exception to the parent's reported pattern of disagreement. Incorporating the resourceful "bothness" – potentially a worthy objective in and of itself – already achieved by these clients, Lance moves the conversation in the direction of what the clients hope will start to happen as the trouble stops happening.

In a sense, Lance is "interviewing" the clients, who are not actually present in the conversation, through the trainee. The trainee either knowingly or unknowingly presents an opportunity in the coaching interview that the clients presented to him in the family therapy session. Perhaps this is another juncture at which solution-building may be usefully contrasted with problem-solving.

The latter might be addressed in terms of the communication challenges and session management. Solution-building orients toward hopes, both of the clients and the trainee, and opportunities, also presented by both, to build narratives of "success", moving toward convergence of hopes and actions.

Another feature of this exchange between Lance and the trainee can be descriptively named layer questioning, another common feature of SF interviewing. This is demonstrated by isolated clips from trainee language interspersed with isolated clips from Lance's responses.

TRAINEE: Yeah. So, both parents actually appeared to hope that their kids won't be deeply affected by the parents' conflict. And both really want their kids to feel comfortable talking about their feelings, talking about what's bothering them, being open about it instead of kind of keeping it in. The funny thing is they're both totally on the same page about their hopes.

LANCE: Since they hope to not have the conflict between the parents affect their children badly, what might be their hopes for how their children would respond to the differences between their parents? What would they hope would happen in place of what they hope does not happen?

TRAINEE: I think they both seem to hope that the kids don't sort of like internalize or blame themselves for the conflict.

LANCE: What do you think would be a sign to them that the healthy alternative was happening?

TRAINEE: If maybe they feel a little more secure or a little more comfortable. I guess maybe even trusting their parents to be able to talk about stuff without it kind of turning into something related to the parents' relationship.

Questions

- What might be the value of interviewing the trainee in such a way as to bring forth the resourcefulness of his client family?
- Based on the developments in this clip, what opportunities are available for next steps in the interviewer's responses?

Before the Break – Clip 8

The authors both continue the practice of taking a break, nearing the end of the solution-focused interview, to reflect on the conversation, gather their thoughts and prepare a closing summary to end the session. As is customary, we ask whether there is "anything else" that we should talk about that hasn't had a chance to come up in the meeting. The following clip also incorporates a form of initiative questioning (K. Tomm, personal communication).

LANCE: Yeah. So, I'd like to take a short break. Are you okay with that? [Trainee: Yeah]. I'll just be two or three minutes and then I'd just like to come back and wrap up with you. So a couple of things before we take the break, is there anything you wish we had talked about, or wished had come up in the talk that we didn't get around to?

TRAINEE: I don't think so. I think the firmness, directness, all that sort of thing, interruptions, I think that's kind of a theme that's woven throughout a lot of my work so I feel like it was like a really nice productive conversation. I don't feel like anything was missed or anything.

LANCE: Let's put one of our initiative questions to work here. Reflecting on the talk we just had and maybe even the talks you had with yourself leading up to it, and the reflections you had about what to talk about, is there any one thing that comes to mind? It's gonna stick with you maybe a little more after the talk today to the point you might be intrigued with taking more initiative on it?

TRAINEE: What really stuck with me from today if I hadn't necessarily thought about it from this angle it's given me kind of a lot more motivation and incentive to sort of keep going with this growing edge. But I think the knowledge now that I am actually trusting myself more, trusting my feelings in session. I'm not kind of shoving them away. I'm trusting my intuition. The skills I've been developing, that piece about trusting myself more, I haven't framed it like that, but I can see that that's really grown in last few months, even alone. So I think that's a huge, exciting thing for me but I think I'm going to really latch on to and hold on to it going forward here.

LANCE: Do you have a speculation about what difference it might make to be more absorbing and embracing of this growing trust in yourself?

TRAINEE: Mm hmm. You know I'm of course part of this therapeutic dynamic with the clients. I'm part of the equation too. So I think I'm understanding that it's gonna bring up feelings for me and I think being attuned to those is even like a way to sort of validate those feelings too because I think I've been very invalidating of my own experiences. So, I think just trusting myself will actually in turn give me more of a presence. When I'm with families too I won't come across as like super uncertain or something. I can lean into my feelings or experiences and skills more. Yeah.

LANCE: Would you be willing to take that one little step further and say how you think an enhanced presence on your part might benefit clients?

TRAINEE: It will also give them a little more confidence in me too. I think it'll also make a little more clear like my role and my position. They'll be more inclined to kind of like accept that, I guess. If I'm showing that I'm trusting in myself and in the process, what I'm doing with them and then they kind of feel like they can trust me to support them on it. So, yeah, I think it can be really helpful too for clients.

LANCE: Okay, let's take a couple minutes' break. I'll be back shortly.

Discussion

More than anything else, this clip reveals how key opportunities in the client's language have become condensed in the trainee's takeaway from the talk. The linguistic path through this conversation may usefully be portrayed by a list of words and phrases delivered into the conversation by the trainee and selected for amplification by Lance:

- Firmness.
- Directness.
- Interruptions.
- Trusting myself more.
- More of a presence.

The astute reader may have noticed that all of the words in this list were initially introduced into the conversation by the trainee except for "trusting myself more". In Clip 3, Lance responds to the trainee's narrative of previously struggling with nervous feelings with the following guess, which the trainee then confirms energetically:

LANCE: I'm guessing, then, do you think it would be reasonable to say that you might have found yourself developing a bit more trust in yourself in the sense that when you notice that something's bugging you there's probably a good reason for that?

TRAINEE: Yeah, that's a really nice way to put it. Yeah, I think I have been able to just trust myself a little bit more instead of thinking, "Oh, like just put those feelings aside for now" kind of thing. Now I am kind of like, "Oh, okay, these feelings are here for a reason. So, what could that be?" So yeah, definitely I think trusting myself more has been a huge part of it for sure.

In terms of opportunities, we usually think of a single word or short phrase. In this example, the opportunity arose from a longer narrative from the trainee about a shift in how he perceived his own nervousness during an interview, from believing it to be a shortcoming to a possibly useful cue for action.

Questions

- What examples of solution-building in this clip have the form of eliciting the difference that the difference could make?

- In this last clip, what opportunities does the Trainee present to help the interviewer construct the closing summary?

After the Break

LANCE: So, just a couple of thoughts to wrap up. I'm impressed that you did this. And I think it says a lot about your congruent pursuit of skills and abilities. As we talked, I was impressed with your clarity about yourself. You know quite a bit about your nature and some of your usual habits, your established ways of being. In that context, I'm very impressed with your adventuresome side and your willingness to open doors into being different, sometimes maybe even being opposite, as a part of building your repertoire of skills for this work you do. Yeah, so willingness to step out right outside of the comfort zone of kind of who I usually am, my usual nature. It really parallels nicely with the fact that a therapeutic conversation is a very different conversation. It's very specialized and has very different rules. You've been willing to challenge one of the rules of ordinary conversation, which is don't be too interruptive. In therapy, by all means interrupt at times. And what occurred to me about that is your position on things like PIPs, and how they can grow in strength, interruption, the strength of presence to do that, what can be the value of it. You could say sometimes we interrupt the problem to validate the person.

TRAINEE: Yeah, I like that way of framing it for sure.

LANCE: And just to close, I'm very impressed with your layers of interests around presence. I think the therapist or counselor's presence is indeed a big deal. And I think firmness is one part of that. I was glad to hear that you consider timely and graceful interruption to be an important part of firmness. You have standards about how you want interruption to be done well, not poorly. So that just seemed like a very good stack of ideas, at one level very important conceptually and at another level very practical. I think they're going to make a difference in each and every talk you have with clients. [Trainee: Um-hm. Thank you!] Yeah, well, so we'll leave that there. Have a good day.

TRAINEE: Thank you and thank you for this conversation. I found it very helpful and productive and encouraging so, yeah, it was a good start to a Monday.

Notes

1 This coaching interview was conducted with a family therapy trainee who is studying the service delivery model entitled the IPScope developed by Karl Tomm and his

colleagues (Tomm, 2014). IP denotes interpersonal patterns of interaction. PIP denotes a pathologizing interpersonal pattern, WIP, a wellness interpersonal pattern, to name a few. "Scope" refers to a relational perspective adopted by the practitioner to "view" these patterns of interaction. By way of analogy, we might say SFBT practitioners adopt the SolutionScope.

2 Back to the IPScope, the SCIP acronym stands for sociocultural interpersonal pattern, a way of interacting that may be partly determined by cultural and social patterns that influence the persons involved.

10 It's Your Turn

If you have made it as far as this chapter, there's a good possibility that you now have a good idea of the opportunities process. This chapter is meant to give you a chance to practice the approach on your own. We have selected an utterance to be analyzed and we will take you through the process step by step.

At the end of the chapter, you will find a blank chart that you can use as a template for your opportunities analysis. The utterance we have chosen is taken from a first therapy session. The client is David. In this sample, David reflects on the impact of the death of his father on his job performance.

In the course of the conversation, he states that he wants "to get to where I want to be". The therapist asks how he would know that he is getting to where he wants to be. This is his response and the utterance that you will be analyzing:

It's been a very frustrating 11 months. Last summer, my Dad committed suicide. I feel like I put pressure on myself to get through it. I haven't resolved my grief. As a result of that, I've had some adverse effects in terms of my performance at work. It's turned to somewhat of an identity crisis for me. I'm used to performing very well at work. Getting frustrated is just making things worse. It's been frustrating to not be able to work through something. I was the guy that could always be counted on. I feel like I'm not that person.

Chart 10.1 Sample chart

#	Opportunities	Possible actions/*Preferred action	Rationale
1	It's been a frustrating 11 months.	1a: I can imagine. 1b: how have you been able to cope? 1c: What will you be doing, thinking, or feeling when you are starting to be less frustrated?	

(Continued)

DOI: 10.4324/9781003396703-11

Chart 10.1 (Continued)

#	Opportunities	Possible actions/*Preferred action	Rationale
2	Last summer, my Dad committed suicide.		
3			
4			
5			

Step 1

Using the chart, continue to divide the utterance into its additional opportunities. There is no wrong or right way to do this. It is totally up to you how you want to divide the utterance. As a guide, following is an example of the first two utterances you might include using the chart. While there are five cells indicated here, you might need to add more cells, depending upon how you divide the utterance.

Step 2

Once you have divided the utterance into its component opportunities, the next step is to create possible interventions for each one of the opportunities. For future reference, the authors have found it useful to number them according to their opportunity number. For example, in the chart above, the first opportunity's possible interventions are numbered 1a, 1b, and so on. The second would be numbered 2a, 2b, and so on.

This step is the creative part of the process. Try to come up with at least three possible interventions for each opportunity. For example, in the first opportunity in the above example, you might notate: "1a: I can imagine; 1b: how have you been able to cope; 1c: what will you be doing, thinking, or feeling when you are starting to be less frustrated". These are only examples – we encourage you to come up with your own ideas.

Step 3

Now review all the possible interventions for all the opportunities in this utterance. Ask yourself the following question, "What is the probability that this particular intervention will more than likely get a solution-building response." It might be helpful to review Chapter 4, and specifically the definition of "solution-building".

For example, for 1d in the example above, the analyst listed, "Tell me more about being frustrated." We can probably agree that this intervention would more than likely receive a problem-focused response. If you decide that any intervention will likely receive a problem response, cross out that intervention, suggest an alternative intervention that would more than likely elicit a solution-building response, and add that to the chart.

Step 4

The way therapy conversations go, the therapist has to decide how they will respond to the client. In general, conversations proceed by taking turns: the client says something, the therapist responds, and so on. In this exercise, for every client utterance the therapist can only give one response. It is important to remember that you're not responding to each opportunity; rather, you're responding to the whole utterance. In the case above, David offers a long utterance. You will not be responding to that utterance with multiple interventions – only one.

Review all your opportunities and their possible responses. Of all the opportunities and interventions, choose only one that would be your preference. For example, when completed, the chart above may have five or more opportunities and each one of those opportunities might have three (or more) possible interventions. That would be a total of 15 suggested interventions. You will pick only one of the 15 as your preferred intervention. Note this one preferred intervention by using an asterisk, underlining, or circling it.

Step 5

Now you have chosen your preferred intervention, what solution-focused principle(s) guided that choice? Note the choice rationale in the indicated space in the chart. For example, in the chart above, let us suppose that 1c was chosen. The rationale might be that the intervention invites David into formulating a goal for therapy.

Future Possibilities

- Choose an utterance from your own work and analyze it using the opportunities' procedure.
- Find a colleague who will be interested and willing to do an analysis. First get them to buy this book (the authors do realize that this is a poor attempt at crass commercialism). Together, select a possible utterance or utterances from some section of this text or from transcript from your own practice. Working separately, divide the transcript into utterances. Meet to negotiate a single uniform list of utterances based on conversational turn-taking. Based upon our experiences, the authors suggest that there be an agreement on how to divide the conversation into its component utterances in order to maintain consistency. Each analyzes the utterance(s) separately. Once the analysis has been completed by both colleagues, meet together to compare and discuss your

work. The authors' experience is that this will lead to some very interesting and thought-provoking conversations.

A Final Word

When we began this book, we said this about our goal:

> Most of all, we have written this book in the hope that it would offer an organized way of listening to and responding to clients that would present a useful addition to practice.

In our own collaboration, both authors began to realize how we grew in our own abilities to listen for clues to solution-building from clients. As we taught others this method, they responded with enthusiasm about their own discoveries. Ultimately, any intervention, any process, and any method need to be validated through utilization in the service of our clients. Only clients can tell us whether what they and we are doing together is making a difference to them. After many hours of research and analysis, we have come to trust that the process that is described in this book is a powerful tool for honing our skills for listening to and responding to clients. Ultimately, this is what solution-focused brief therapy is about: how we as therapists usefully listen to and respond to clients.

> Our job is to create the conditions under which clients find their own solutions, to help clients look into their hearts to find what they truly want and how they might get there.
>
> (de Shazer et al., 2007, p. 156)

Chart 10.2 Blank chart

#	Opportunities	Possible actions/*Preferred action	Rationale
1			
2			
3			
4			
5			

References

Anderson, H., & Goolishian, H.A. (1992). The client is the expert: A not-knowing approach to therapy. In S. McNamee & K.J. Gergen (Eds.), *Therapy as a social construction* (pp. 25–39). London: Sage.

Bavelas, J. B., McGee, D., Phillips, B. & Routledge, R. (2000). Microanalysis of communication in psychotherapy. *Human Systems: The Journal of Systemic Consultation & Management*, 11, 47–66.

Beavin Bavelas, J. (2022). *Face-to-face dialogue: Theory, research, and applications.* New York: Oxford University Press.

Berg, I.K., & De Shazer, S. (1993). Making numbers talk: Language in therapy. In S. Friedman (Ed.), *The new language of change: Constructive collaboration in psychotherapy* (pp. 5–24). New York: The Guilford Press.

Berger, P. L., & Luckman, T. (1966). *The social construction of reality: A treatise in the sociology of knowledge.* New York: Doubleday.

Blundo, R., & Simon, J. (2016). *Solution-focused case management.* New York: Springer.

Brenner, C. (1974). *An elementary textbook of psychoanalysis.* New York: Anchor Books.

Cade, B. (2007). Springs, streams, and tributaries: A history of the brief solution-focused approach. In T. Nelson & F. Thomas (Eds.), *Handbook of solution-focused brief therapy: Clinical applications* (pp. 25–63). New York: Haworth.

Campbell, J., Elder, J., Gallagher, D., Simon, J., & Taylor, A. (1999). Crafting the tap on the shoulder: A compliment template for solution-focused therapy. *The American Journal of Family Therapy, 27*(1), 35–47.

De Jong, P., & Berg, I. K. (2002). *Interviewing for solutions* (2nd ed.). Pacific Grove, CA: Brooks/Cole.

De Jong, P., & Berg, I. K. (2013). *Interviewing for solutions* (4th ed.). Pacific Grove, CA: Brooks/Cole.

De Jong, P., Beavin Bavelas, J., & Korman, H. (2013). An introduction to using microanalysis to observe co-construction in psychotherapy. *Journal of Systemic Therapies, 32*(3), 17–30.

De Shazer, S. (1982). *Patterns of brief family therapy.* New York: The Guilford Press.

De Shazer, S. (1985a). *Coming through the ceiling: A solution-focused approach to a difficult case* (Video). Brief Family Therapy Center. Milwaukee, WI: Brief Family Therapy Center (120 minutes).

De Shazer, S. (1985b). *Keys to solution in brief therapy.* New York: W. W. Norton.

De Shazer, S. (1988). *Clues: Investigating solutions in brief therapy.* New York: W. W. Norton.

De Shazer, S. (1991). *Putting difference to work.* New York: W. W. Norton.

De Shazer, S. (1994). *Words were originally magic.* New York: W. W. Norton.

De Shazer, S., Berg, I. K., Lipshik, E., Nunnally, A., Molnar, W., Gingerich, M., & Weiner-Davis, M. (1986). Brief therapy: Focused solution development. *Family Process,* 25(2), 207–222.

De Shazer, S. & Dolan, Y. (2007). *More than miracles: The state of the art of solution-focused brief therapy.* New York: The Haworth Press.

Dolan, Y. (1991). *Resolving sexual abuse: Solution-focused therapy and Ericksonian hypnosis for adult survivors.* New York: W. W. Norton.

Durrant, M. (2004). Foreword. In Y. Ajmal, & I. Ress (Eds.), *Solutions in schools* (pp. vi–ix). London: BT Press.

Edmunds, M., Frank, R., Hogan, M., McCarty, D., Robinson-Beale, R., & Weisner, C. (1997). Managing managed care: Quality improvement in behavioral health. Retrieved February 25, 2020 from www.nap.eduhttps://www.nap.edu/read/5477

Fiske, H. (2007). Solution-focused training: The medium and the message. In T. Nelson & F. Thomas (Eds.), *Handbook of solution focused brief therapy: Clinical applications.* New York: The Haworth Press.

Franklin, C., Trepper, T. S., Gingerich, W. J., & McCollum, E. E. (2012). *Solution-focused brief therapy: A handbook of evidence based practice.* New York: Oxford University Press.

Froerer, A. S. (2009). Microanalysis of solution-focused brief therapy formulations. Unpublished doctoral dissertation. Department of Applied and Professional Studies, Texas Tech University, Lubbox, TX.

Froerer, A. S., & Smock, S. J. (2013). Identifying solution-building formulations through microanalysis. *Journal of Systemic Therapies,* 32(3), 60–73.

Garfinkel, H. (1967). *Studies in ethnomethodology.* Englewood Cliffs, NJ: Prentice-Hall.

Gergen, K. J,. & Gergen, M. J. (1983). Narratives of the self. In T. R. Sabin, & K. E. Scheibe (Eds.), *Studies in social identity* (pp. 254–273). New York: Praeger.

Gergen, K. J., & Gergen, M. J. (1986). Narrative form and the construction of psychological science. In T. R. Sabin (Ed.), *Narrative psychology: The storied nature of human conduct* (pp. 22–44). New York: Praeger.

Ghul, R. (2005). Moan, moan, moan. In R. Newlson (Ed.), *Education and training in solution-focused brief therapy* (pp. 63, 64). New York: The Haworth Press.

Haley, J. (1973). *Uncommon therapy: The psychiatric techniques of Milton H. Erickson,* M.D. New York: W. W. Norton.

Haley, J. (1990). *Strategies of psychotherapy.* Carmarthen (UK): Crown House.

Hornstrup, C., Tomm, K., & Johansen, T. (2009). "Sporgsmal – der gor en forskel" (Questions that make a difference). In *Erhvervspsykologi* (Business Psychology), 7(3), 2–16.

Joyce, A., & Piper, W. (1998). Expectancy, the therapeutic alliance and treatment outcome in short-term individual therapy. *The Journal of Psychotherapy Practice and Research,* 7(3), 236–248.

Korman, H., Bavelas, J. B., & De Jong, P. (2013). Microanalysis of formulations in solution-focused brief therapy, cognitive behavioral therapy, and motivational interviewing. *Journal of Systemic Therapies,* 32(3), 31–45.

Lamarre, J. (2005). Complaining exercise. In R. Nelson (Ed.), *Education and training in solution-focused brief therapy* (pp. 65, 66). New York: The Haworth Press.

Lyotard, J. (1984). *The postmodern condition: A report on knowledge.* Manchester: Manchester University Press

Macdonald, A. (2022). *Solution-focused approaches: SFBT Evaluation List.* Retrieved April 10, 2023 from https://solutionsdoc.co.uk/sfbt-evaluation-list

Marias, J. (1967). *History of philosophy.* New York: Dover.

Maslow, A. H. (1966). *The psychology of science.* New York: Harper & Row.

Miller, G., & De Shazer, S. (1998). Have you heard the latest rumor about …? Solution-focused therapy as a rumor. *Family Process, 37*(3), 363–377.

Newhart, B. (2023). *Stop It.* Retrieved February 5, 2023 from www.youtube.com/watch?v=jvujypVVBAY

O'Hanlon, W. H. (1987). *Taproots: Unifying principles of Milton Erickson's therapy and hypnosis.* New York: W. W. Norton.

Ratner, H., George, E., & Iveson, C. (2012). *Solution-focused brief therapy: 100 key points & techniques.* New York: Routledge.

Rosen, S. (1982). *My voice will go with you: The teaching tales of Milton Erickson.* New York: W.W. Norton.

Simon, F., Stierling, H., & Wynne, L. (1985). *The language of family therapy: A systemic vocabulary and sourcebook.* New York: Family Process Press.

Simon, J. (2010). *Solution-focused practice in end-of-life and grief counseling.* New York: Springer.

Simon, J., & Berg, I. K. (1999). Solution-focused brief therapy with long-term problems. *Directions in Rehabilitation Counseling, 10,* 117–128.

Simon, J., & Berg, I. K. (2004). Solution-focused brief therapy with adolescents. In F. Kalsow (Series Ed.) & R. F. Massey (Vol. Ed.), *Comprehensive handbook of psychotherapy: Vol. 3. Interpersonal/humanistic/experiential* (pp. 133–152). New York: Wiley.

Simon, J., & Nelson, T. (2007). *Solution-focused brief practice with long-term clients in mental health services: I'm more than my label.* New York: The Haworth Press.

Smock, S. A. & Bavelas, J.B. (2013). Introduction to SFBT contributions to practice-oriented research. part I: Microanalysis of communication. *Journal of Systemic Therapies, 32*(3), 3–16.

Smock, S. A., Froerer, A. S., & Bavelas, J. B. (2013). Microanalysis of positive and negative content in SFBT and CBT expert sessions. *Journal of Systemic Therapy, 32*(3), 46–59.

Solution-Focused Brief Therapy Association (2013). Solution-focused therapy treatment manual for working with individuals, 2nd ed. Retrieved December 9, 2022 from https://irp-cdn.multiscreensite.com/f39d2222/files/uploaded/SFBT_Revised_Treatment_Manual_2013.pdf

Stams, G. J. J., Dekovic, K., Buist, K., & De Vries, L. (2006). Effectiviteit van oplossingsgerichte korte therapie: Een meta-analyse [Efficacy of solution-focused brief therapy: A meta-analysis]. *Gedragstherapie, 39,* 81–94.

Szapocznik, J., Kurtines, W. M., Foote, F., Perez-Vidal, A., & Hervis, O. (1986). Conjoint versus one-person family therapy: Further evidence for the effectiveness of conducting family therapy through one person with drug-abusing adolescents. *Journal of Consulting and Clinical Psychology, 54*(3), 395–397.

Taylor, L. (2005). A thumbnail map for solution-focused brief therapy. In T. Nelson (Ed.), *Journal of Family Psychotherapy,* 16(1), 27–33.

Taylor, L., & Fiske, H. (2005). Tapping into hope. In S. J. Cooper, & J. Duvall (Eds.), *Catching the winds of change: Inspiring healing conversations and hopeful stories with individuals, families, and communities* (pp. 82–87). Toronto: The Brief Therapy Network.

Taylor, L., & Simon, J. (2014). Opportunities: Organizing the solution-focused interview. *Journal of Systemic Therapies*, 33(4), 62–78.

Tomm, K. (2014). Introducing the IPscope: A systemic assessment tool for distinguishing interpersonal patterns. In K. Tomm, S. St George, D. Wulff, & T. Strong (Eds.), *Patterns in interpersonal interactions: Inviting relational understandings for therapeutic change* (pp. 13–35). New York: Routledge.

Tomm, K., St. George, S., Wolff, D., & Strong, T. (Eds.) (2014). *Patterns in interpersonal interactions: Inviting relational understandings for therapeutic change.* New York: Routledge.

Tomori, C., & Bavelas, J.B. (2007). Using microanalysis of communication to compare solution-focused and client centered therapies. *Journal of Family Psychotherapy,* 18(3), 25–43.

Waltzlawick, P., Beavin, J., & Jackson, D.D. (1967). *Pragmatics of human communication.* New York: W. W. Norton.

Waltzlawick, P., Weakland, J., & Fisch, R. (1974). *Change: Principles of problem formulation and problem resolution.* New York: W. W. Norton.

Weiner-Davis, M., de Shazer, S., & Gingerich, W.J. (1987). Building on pre-treatment change to construct the therapeutic solution: An exploratory study. *Journal of Marital and Family Therapy,* 13(4), 359–363.

Wittgenstein, L. (1958). *Philosophical investigations*, 3rd ed. New York: Macmillan.

Index